MORE PRAISE FOR

HOMELESSNESS: THE MAKING AND UNMAKING OF A CRISIS

"This book should be read by anyone who cares about making our cities better places to live and solving the problem of homelessness in Canada." — *Mel Lastman*

"In this readable, comprehensive history of homelessness in Canada, Jack Layton brings together an incomparable knowledge of the subject, an in-depth understanding of the politics underlying the issues, and a deep passion for social justice, in a lively style that brings it all to life. Compelling, disturbing, yet hopeful." — *Anne Golden, United Way of Greater Toronto president and author of* Taking Responsibility for Homelessness: An Action Plan for Toronto

"This important book will push the rational debate on homelessness and hopefully serve as a catalyst towards the creation of a national housing strategy." — *John Andras, Co-Founder, Project Warmth*

"Jack Layton's work on homelessness has helped create a national movement to protect and build affordable housing in Canada. This book helps us make the case for adequately housing all Canadians." — *Barbara Hall, Mayor of Toronto, 1994–1997*

"Layton shows that homelessness, unlike the great operatic tragedies, is avoidable. But like the great operas tell us, Layton shows that individuals and communities have the power to transform misery into joy and celebration." — *Jim Greene, British Columbia housing innovator, homelessness advocate, and one of Peter Gzowski's "greatest minds of our time"*

PENGUIN CANADA

HOMELESSNESS

Jack Layton is the leader of the New Democratic Party of Canada.

Jack served as a Toronto city councillor for 20 years, where he led the campaign to tackle homelessness. Jack served as president of the Federation of Canadian Municipalities in 2001–2002. His work at the FCM led to the development of a coalition of municipalities from across Canada that work together for a renewed federal housing policy. At City Hall, Jack co-chaired the Homeless Advisory Committee that provides a vital policy link to front-line workers and people who have experienced homelessness. Layton has taught urban studies at all of Toronto's universities and was an adjunct professor in the Geography Department and the Innis College Environmental Studies Program at the University of Toronto.

Understanding Canada

Thanks to the generosity of Charles and Andrea Bronfman and the matching commitment of McGill University, the McGill Institute for the Study of Canada opened in Montreal in the summer of 1994. The institute was committed to strengthening knowledge and understanding of Canada among students drawn from across the world as well as from McGill's own city and province. We inherited both a strong Canadian Studies department and a need for public education and involvement. We have responded with support for the university's departments and with a program of seminars, lectures and courses, and with national conferences on issues as varied as the expectations of aboriginal peoples and the consequences of Canada's ten-year experience with the Free Trade agreement.

Among the institute's programs is a series of books published in collaboration with a firm with a deep educational tradition, Penguin. Each is designed to help us understand some aspect of Canada, whether it is the complex expectations of the West or the painful conflict over the expectations and performance of public education. Homelessness is a tragic aspect of modern Canada and in 1999 we asked Jack Layton, a veteran

Toronto councillor, a professor at the University of Toronto and Canada's leading expert on homelessness, to help us understand why people are living and dying on our streets.

Homelessness is not new to Canada; its present form is.

Back in the 1960s, I worked in downtown Toronto, trying to do a hundred different things, among them organizing for the NDP in the city's downtown ridings. I walked a lot of streets, canvassed scores of apartment buildings, wrote pamphlets and speeches and did whatever was asked of me. Periodically, some visitor would be assigned to me for a Toronto tour. "Here is where the poor live," I would say, pointing to the still-glistening towers of Moss Park or a run-down block in South Riverdale. We could have gone closer, but is seemed impertinent. Sometimes we stopped as the Scott Mission to chat with guys waiting to check in. This was poverty and homelessness in the 1960s. It was brutal and sad, but largely invisible.

Then I married, changed careers and spent a quarter-century at the University of Toronto's campus in Mississauga. There was real poverty in the suburbs, though I remember how hard it was to convince good-hearted people that a food bank would have clients, lots of them. I saw little of Toronto.

In 1990, life took me back to Toronto. In December 1991, I took a friend's children to a Christmas concert at the old Massey Hall. It was dark and very cold when we emerged. I had promised a treat, and the chosen restaurant was a few blocks south on Yonge Street. You may know the scene, but I didn't then: dozens of fellow humans, huddled on grates, in doorways, under grubby sleeping bags, blankets, newspapers. Some were awake, lit by the faint glow of a cigarette. A young woman stuck her head out of a sleeping bag to ask the oldest child for spare change.

Canada's richest city was at the depth of the worst recession since the 1930s. How could such conditions exist with Bob Rae and the NDP in power? Didn't my neighbours complain that Rae was spending Ontario into ruin to coddle work-shy bums? What had happened to shelters? In a free society, a colleague suggested, maybe the homeless preferred fresh air to a stuffy dormitory and a prayer meeting. Not on a night that cold.

Now, a decade later, the recession is gone. UN statistics suggest that Canada is the best place in the world to live. Ottawa and the provinces collect more revenue than they spend. But in virtually every city and town across Canada, homelessness is worse than ever. The specifics vary. In some communities, even people with significant incomes cannot find a place they can afford. Here in Montreal, critics blame tenant-friendly legislation for shrinking the supply of rental housing; low incomes and high unemployment does the rest. Closing mental hospitals ended a brutal form of incarceration, but did we ever admit that humane alternatives cost more? Homelessness is not solely a result of poverty, but most Canadians are poorer than they were a generation ago, and the very poor are very much poorer.

Living on the streets in Canada's climate is an intolerable obscenity which any of us would like to end, but the problem is not straightforward. Simple solutions can be costly, brutal and wrong. That's why understanding should proceed action. Jack Layton brings experience, common sense, vision and passion to an issue that cries out for all these qualities. You will not read this book without enhancing your own share of these virtues. You may differ on any or all the points Jack Layton makes, but you will not emerge indifferent.

Let us know what you think and what other subjects we should try to understand. Get in touch with us at:

The McGill Institute for the Study of Canada
3463 Peel Street
Montreal, QC H3A 1W7
Fax: (514) 398-7336
www.arts.mcgill.ca/programs/misc

— Desmond Morton

homelessness

THE MAKING AND UNMAKING OF A CRISIS

Jack Layton

A Penguin/McGill Institute Book

PENGUIN CANADA

Published by the Penguin Group

Penguin Group (Canada), 90 Eglinton Avenue East, Suite 700, Toronto, Ontario, Canada M4P 2Y3 (a division of Pearson Penguin Canada Inc.)

Penguin Group (USA) Inc., 375 Hudson Street, New York, New York 10014, U.S.A.
Penguin Books Ltd, 80 Strand, London WC2R 0RL, England
Penguin Ireland, 25 St Stephen's Green, Dublin 2, Ireland (a division of Penguin Books Ltd)
Penguin Group (Australia), 250 Camberwell Road, Camberwell, Victoria 3124, Australia (a division of Pearson Australia Group Pty Ltd)
Penguin Books India Pvt Ltd, 11 Community Centre, Panchsheel Park, New Delhi – 110 017, India
Penguin Group (NZ), cnr Airborne and Rosedale Roads, Albany, Auckland 1310, New Zealand (a division of Pearson New Zealand Ltd)
Penguin Books (South Africa) (Pty) Ltd, 24 Sturdee Avenue, Rosebank, Johannesburg 2196, South Africa

Penguin Books Ltd, Registered Offices: 80 Strand, London WC2R 0RL, England

First published 2000

(TRS) 10 9 8 7 6

Manufactured in Canada

Photo credit: Nir Bareket Photography

NATIONAL LIBRARY OF CANADA CATALOGUING IN PUBLICATION

Layton, Jack, 1950–
Homelessness: the making and unmaking of a crisis

(Understanding Canada)
"A Penguin/McGill Institute book."
ISBN 0-14-028888-0

1. Homelessness — Canada. 2. Housing — Canada. 3. Housing Policy — Canada.
I. Title. II. Series: Understanding Canada (Toronto, Ont.).

HV4509.139 2000 363.5'0971 C00-932344-9

Visit the Penguin Group (Canada) website at **www.penguin.ca**

To
Eugene Upper

The author's net royalties will be donated to national non-profit groups working to achieve an affordable housing program for Canada.

Contents

Acknowledgements

I'm grateful to a large number of people for help, wisdom, inspiration and encouragement in the preparation of this work.

Many homeless men and women I have met who, with passion, dignity and tears, have impressed upon me the urgency of the crisis and the need for action.

The Toronto Disaster Relief Committee, Cathy Crowe, Beric German, Gaetan Heroux and the many hard-working front-line workers and activists across Canada who inspired the vision of a Canada that treats homelessness of its citizens as a disaster to be addressed accordingly.

Toronto's Advisory Committee on Homeless and Socially Isolated Persons and its co-chair Alison Kemper challenged myths and created focused solutions helping thousands.

Svend Robinson and Max Riveron for providing their wonderful refuge on Galiano Island to get away (almost) from the phone in order to think and write.

George Ehring for wise advice on the structure of the book.

Without the vision and capacity of municipal governments in Canada, the project of designing and mobilizing across the country to achieve a national housing policy could not have been realized. Now representing over 1,000 democratically elected municipal governments, the Federation of Canadian Municipalities (FCM), its board, executive and staff have been wonderful colleagues. As the project began, Robbin Tourangeau, former senior policy analyst, responsible for the Quality of Life Indicators Project and staff to the National Housing Policy Options Team, and her successor, John Burrett, have been instrumental in the project; James Knight, CEO of FCM, handled the tiller well, ensuring that cities stayed the course and reaching into the depths of the federal establishment with our message; the incomparable Louise Comeau, director of the Sustainable Communities Division of FCM, for her wisdom in structuring an appeal to the government of Canada; Past Presidents Bryon Wilfert, Claude Cantin, and Sam Synard for their continuous encouragement; FCM President Joanne Monahan and her entire executive for their combination of reality checks and enthusiasm; Calgary alderman Bob Hawkesworth, who co-chaired the National Housing Policy Options Team (NHPOT) and provided helpful counsel throughout.

The City of Toronto Council and its staff: Greg Suttor, of City of Toronto Housing Policy, who did a great deal of the research and writing of the FCM and NHPOT studies; Mel Lastman and his staff, who took up the challenge of homelessness and supported my efforts to create the NHPOT and who was the first mayor to devote cash and passion to the cause; my colleagues on city council who egged me on as my role at FCM grew; to Susan Shepherd, Shirley Hoy, Derek Ballentyne, Joanne Campbell, Barbara Emanuel and all the staff in the homeless and housing services at the city for their inspirational efforts.

The Canadian Housing Renewal Association for steady commitment and creative solutions.

Anne Golden, friend, visionary and intellectual and moral leader in the battle against homelessness and the injustice it represents.

Peter Zimmerman, who deserves special thanks for his limitless efforts working by my side as my housing policy expert and who is now actually building affordable housing for those in need as you read this.

Franz Hartmann, Monica Tang and Richard Barry, who together provide the most creative and reliable team of colleagues imaginable.

Linda LaPointe and Steve Pomeroy for their stunning work for FCM, much of which has found its way into these pages for more people to access. David Hulchanski for teaching me and all Canadians so much about housing over two decades.

Barbara Berson, Dennis Mills and the team at Penguin, who shepherded this first-time book writer through the initiation process with skills I couldn't imagine were in anyone's possession.

Mark Lehman and Jane Koster, who pitched in to help with last-minute details and corrections.

All my colleagues at the White Ribbon Campaign, who offered continuous support despite the way this work took me away from my duties there.

Olivia Chow, my life and work partner, whose wisdom, ideals, strategic brilliance and youthful enthusiasm combine to propel the work I do and to infuse joy into every moment I'm doing it. Michael and Sarah, offspring who make me proud and rarely let me get away with inappropriate exaggerations. Olivia's mom Ho Sze for care and feeding, Bob and Doris Layton, and my whole family for boundless love and advice about never missing opportunities to serve.

Despite all this help and advice, these writings on homelessness and how to solve the crisis through affordable housing will have missed key ideas and may well fall short of what is needed. These shortcomings are my responsibility alone.

Introduction

"So, what's your name?" I asked.

"John," he said, after he said he was OK, in response to my initial approach.

The first thing I, like many people, always say to homeless people is "Say, are you OK?" It's a rather stupid question, really. What homeless person is OK? Then again, you'd be surprised how many say they are. "Yeah, I'm OK!" In fact, it's by far the most frequent response on the streets. Next most common response is "Have you got some change? I could use some." John was no different.

"Your name, what's your name?" I pressed a bit. He was living a few feet from my house and we had some talking to do.

"John," his rough, tired voice told me. He didn't seem to mind my asking, at least not too much.

"I'm John too, but my parents always called me Jack," I said, "a nickname from my grandfather."

"I had a nickname once," John said. "My two kids called me Pop."

That encounter happened years ago, but the first story about homeless people I ever heard I was told as a child, much before I had even met any. It was about a time long ago, 1765—over 230 years ago. That's when my mother's ancestors landed on what we now call Canadian soil. Captain Monk and his small band of Protestant families were escaping religious persecution from pre-federated Germany on a tiny "tall ship." I can only imagine how they were tossed about by ferocious waves and terrified by the furies of the sea. Some did not make it.

They held out hope for a promised homestead in Pennsylvania. However, political storms hit with devastating force. On attempting to land, food supplies desperately depleted, with many ill on board, the refugees were turned away. The property they had been promised in America was a fraud.

Sailing north on a wing and a prayer, the passengers and crew almost starving, Captain Monk headed toward and then navigated the tricky current of the Petitcodiac River.

When my sea-worn, homeless ancestors clambered, exhausted, to shore, they were welcomed by the Mi'kmaq community to the raw New World coastline that we now call New Brunswick. These First Nation people reached out with affection and respect to the captain and the seventeen families in his charge. With winter rapidly approaching, lessons in survival were clearly needed and were quickly given, despite no common language.

Most of the immigrants made it through that winter, including the family of Joseph Steif, his wife and his eight sons—whose families eventually became known as the Steeves. Homes were built and a town was founded—Moncton, named after the captain. Hillsborough, a small settlement nearby, became the Steeves family headquarters. Lineage of the Steeves boys alone now numbers over 300,000 in North America. I'm one of them. My mother is Doris Steeves.

My ancestors would not have survived without the generosity and basic human dignity of spirit demonstrated by those Mi'kmaq people during that long, cold Canadian winter.

What a difference a quarter of a millennium can make. Homeless people today are left to die in our streets. They freeze under bridges or succumb to death by fire in substandard housing or in their own homemade shelters. Had those wandering homeless immigrants in 1765 received the welcome that the homeless receive today, in modern Canada, I would likely not be here, let alone writing this book.

Two hundred and thirty-five years after my ancestors arrived, homeless descendants of those generous Mi'kmaq huddle over exhausts of warmth in the middle of sidewalks and lanes, on the freezing cold streets of Toronto in the dead of winter. These pathetic vents wastefully discharge excess steam from overheated buildings.

Overheated buildings in an overheated economy. An economy that offers no warmth to the homeless native couple huddling over the grate. No place to call home, no succour, no thanks, no recognition and no justice for these, Canada's original peoples. Some cast-off blankets, some coins and more disdainful looks. Weeks pass, months. No one offers a home or help to find one.

As a member of Toronto's City Council, representing parts of the city with many homeless people, I was asked by the council and the mayor to head up a committee to respond to this crisis. As a table officer of the Federation of Canadian Municipalities—the national organization of local governments—I've been chairing our National Housing Policy Options Team, whose assignment it is to respond to the rapidly growing homelessness and affordable-housing problem in Canada. What have we to work with? Some sleeping bags. Some mats. A few empty warehouses that the city doesn't need anymore. An old armoury from the military. Church basements. Soup lines.

On Toronto streets, one homeless citizen dies every six days. The most recent as I write this was Jennifer Caldwell, a woman who had sought refuge in a ravine under a construction of boards, plastics and urban flotsam.[1] When the pile caught fire, she was trapped and died a horrible death. A visit to the city's morgue, on a typical day, can yield two or more unidentified bodies listed as John or Jane Doe with no fixed address. These days the desperate need for housing is met with little response from our longtime prime minister, Jean Chrétien, or from Ontario's re-elected premier, Mike Harris. They and many other political and business leaders are working on the more pressing problem of reducing the taxes of those with ample means to pay them.

Throughout urban Canada, too many communities turn their backs on those who are struggling. Some neighbourhoods even have zoning by-laws prohibiting emergency shelters. Not in My Back Yard, they say. And why should this be surprising? NIMBY neighbourhoods are just taking their lead from the federal and the majority of provincial governments. Some

Canadians seem to have adopted the attitude that they have no responsibility to house the homeless. "Let them freeze on the streets!" Sleeping bags dispensed by earnest volunteers—and those discharge vents—are Canada's official policy for dealing with homelessness, by default.

I am mindful of the limitations of my perspective: I have never been homeless. But as a social scientist, I recognize the importance of rigorous analysis, using the best evidence and studies available.

Thanks to the growing and widespread public concern about homelessness, significant new research has been completed, documenting the issue. One reason this book has been written is to allow the housing story, unfolding in the newest data, to be made available to more Canadians. Much of this new material is drawn from the unpublished studies commissioned by the National Housing Policy Options Team. Canada's Big City Mayors formed the team at their November 1998 meeting in Winnipeg, hosted by the newly elected mayor of that city, Glen Murray. For the first time in Canadian history, the mayors declared homelessness to be a national disaster. They formed a team (made up of mayors, councillors and housing experts) to document their case and present a plan to reverse the trends that they were seeing in their communities across the country.

As chair of the team, I have had the opportunity to work with some remarkable minds. Over fifty housing experts from across Canada prepared the material that formed the basis of the NHPOT reports, co-ordinated by the Federation of Canadian Municipalities. Now, a comprehensive description of this national embarrassment has been assembled. As well, the FCM team determined the scope of the solutions required: Over one million Canadians would receive housing assistance, effectively reducing Canada's homelessness and affordable-housing problems by 50 percent. The FCM report concludes with a comprehensive set of options to achieve these goals for housing Canadians. As support for a national housing policy grows in Canada, more and better ideas will, no doubt, come forward.

Drawing on this emerging collective wisdom and the experiences of other cities and countries, I hope to do justice to the many contributions of others. Still, I urge readers to explore ideas for themselves, using as a starting point some of the references mentioned in this book. I hope to answer questions about homelessness that may be on the minds of Canadians. I hope to offer some of the sometimes competing and sometimes complementary ideas about how we can solve this gnawing disgrace in our body politic.

But is homelessness connected to politics? Or do its causes lie in the lives and personal circumstances of those who find themselves on the street?

Perhaps it is inevitable that the political dimensions of homelessness come to the forefront in my experience, simply because this is the environment in which I live. Daily, at city halls across the country, those of us in municipal government try to tackle the effects of housing policy as constituents call up, in increasing numbers these days, with their housing crises. Councillors try to create policies and programs to help. We look at the actions of our own municipal governments and those of the provincial and federal elements of the Canadian state, and we call for policy changes. For several years, many governments' political priorities seem to have missed housing altogether.

However, homelessness has not grown just because politicians were not paying attention to housing. It was—and still is—a social construction, a result of our collective actions as a society, an artifact. Homelessness has not always existed in Canada. Neither has it been found at such pervasive levels before. As we will see in the pages that follow, governments at all levels became enamoured in the 1980s and '90s of a new wisdom. The thrust of this thinking (about government's role in society) was that the state should move out of the affordable-housing field (or the "housing business" as Ontario's Premier Harris called it).

The concept was simple: Government could not deliver what Canadians needed as well as the private sector could. Step by step, the state, at all levels, exited the policy stage. Pressed by housing-industry lobby groups, governments moved out of the housing-construction and support programs that had developed in the post-war era. As the political pendulum swung away from the interventionist state, housing programs, like many others, were left dangling by threads. One by one the threads were cut. First to go was the federal thread, as national support for new affordable housing was phased out. Then, in most provincial legislatures, the threads were sliced, too. Left alone, the threadbare municipal strand could no longer sustain the weight of the responsibility to house all Canadians. Housing production fell completely into the realm of private economic activity. Affordable-housing construction dropped off the radar screens of the statistical charts. Ideological propositions from the free-market side of the debate suggested that this abandonment of government intervention would, in fact, produce better, less expensive and more abundant housing for all, thanks to the endeavours of the private sector. These ideas have never materialized.

The political economy of housing rests on the fact that large economic forces have always come to bear on our communities in complex and powerful ways. Mockery is a charitable description of those simple slogans claiming that all can be made better by unleashing individual economic freedoms. Those forces have created shifts of wealth and a significant redistribution of the resources of our society. In the past decade, these shifts have transcended national boundaries. Multinational corporate strategies have created complex flows of wealth, which are leaving growing rates of poverty in their wake.

To understand the housing pressures (of which homelessness is only the tip of the iceberg) we need to keep a watchful eye on the interplay between economic restructuring and policy adaptation to that restructuring. We have to be conscious of the roots of unstable social circumstances in fundamental economic processes.

How did we manage to allow the growth of homelessness in Canada? Such social ills were not supposed to happen here. People begging in the streets was a phenomenon of big American cities. Surprisingly, many Canadians still do not believe that it has really happened here. Denial remains an easy out.

However, for a growing number of Canadians, our smugness in relation to American cities has been shattered. I was an enthusiastic part of that generation of Canadian urbanists who grew up believing in the ideas of Jane Jacobs, who became my neighbour in downtown Toronto, having moved here from New York City not long after she wrote *The Death and Life of Great American Cities*. A later edition included these words: "Whenever and wherever societies have flourished and prospered rather than stagnated and decayed, creative workable cities have been at the core of the phenomenon. . . . Decaying cities, declining economies, and mounting social troubles travel together. The combination is not coincidental."[2]

For years I had participated in the self-satisfied portrayal of Canadian cities as better, more liveable, safer and cleaner than those of our southern urban cousins. It's time to throw out this arrogance. The Americans are acting. So are Europeans. Canadians are sitting on their hands. Our cities and our people are paying the price.

Coming from a life in politics, I will probably focus too often on the political, policy-based origins of the problem and the program-based solutions. In the end, however, the evidence presented here should convince most sceptics that free-wheeling, private economic decision making left to its own devices, as it has been lately, will send more of our citizens out into the cold. Governments that allow housing, one of our basic needs, to swing in the wind without a significant response are directly contributing to the crisis. Politics and homelessness are enmeshed in the tight weave of Canadian public-policy debate. The weave's warp is pulled tight by the economic forces at play: real-estate and property developers and managers at one end, renters and homebuyers at the other.

Free-enterprise ideology teaches that citizens and their chosen governments can and should do nothing to intervene in the economic state of nature. This ideology denies that any negative consequences of non-intervention are rooted in this approach. Proof to the contrary comes first from those who suffer, then by the consciences of sympathetic citizens and by the activists who draw our attention to the shortcomings of public policies. Editorialists weigh in on one side or another as their biases dictate and, sometimes, as the facts require.

Some unreserved moral consternation occurs in the pages that follow. (How can safe shelter not be a moral issue?) However, I hope the facts will effectively make the case for political action to adjust the economic policies that ignore the housing needs of more than a million Canadians. Perhaps some of the consternation will strike readers as justified and help to increase the volume of the collective call for change.

homelessness

THE MAKING AND UNMAKING OF A CRISIS

1 Beginning the Debate

When John, the homeless person, told me he had two kids, I realized that we had three things in common: our first names, two kids and we shared this corner of Toronto. John's home was right beside mine. His digs were across the laneway. Not that our homes themselves had anything in common. His was a brick alcove lit by an incredibly bright halogen lamp that formed part of an Ontario Hydro transformer station. It's a towering five-storey building with the constant low buzz of electrical equipment and the eerie brightness of the security lighting. Piled up in the alcove were old blankets and sleeping bags, picked up from Project Warmth on one of John's foraging missions.

Right next door, with a recently repaved alleyway between, is our house. The lane, too, has bright lights—a place without shadows and absolutely no privacy for John, that's for sure. But then again, the powerful lights make his space safer than the dark corners where the homeless can find themselves rolled or rumbled. John was tucked away but clearly visible, night and day, to anyone passing by. The side windows of our family home look right out at his space.

I'd originally gone out to talk with John for two reasons. I really did want to know if he was OK; maybe he'd like a coffee. But my daughter was also concerned because John had the habit of standing in the lane near her basement bedroom window. She wondered if he was looking in. She was not in any kind of panic, but there was a distinct sense of discomfort. So I thought I'd get to know him and maybe establish some neighbour-to-neighbour ground rules about standing and looking in. Of course, we could always look at him, with his place being right out in the open like that. Still, despite this bizarre situation, John was totally onside once I told him about our concerns. He seemed to understand completely, and he never stood there anymore. A peaceful co-existence set in over the weeks that John was there.

So we shared the lane—our common street address. Except mine really was an address. His was borrowed space, to be his as long as no one pushed him out. Or beat him up. Or until his health failed and he had to go to the hospital, or maybe the morgue, like so many of his brothers and sisters of the street before him.

We shared the steady hum of the transformers in their vaults. I heard it from my third-floor deck, where I'd always go after a pre-bedtime shower to cool off in the summer. The evening breeze, the moon, even the occasional sarcastic star winking through the pollution: These were my magnets each night—a moment of cool calm before tucking safely into bed.

Homeless John shared only the lane and the hum. No shower, no cool breeze, no stars. Only cramped quarters, constant lights, musty sleeping bags and the fear of being kicked in the night by marauding punks with nothing better to do than roll a homeless guy.

Did I feel guilty about John? Sometimes I wondered about taking him in—or at least offering him a bed inside. Am I a hypocrite? At city council in Toronto I am speaking out about homelessness but doing little if anything to help the man sleeping in the shadows of our own home. It's nothing to be proud about. I rationalize, as a lot of people do. I say to myself, I'm doing my part by chairing committees. My comments in the media are helping to raise the issue with a wider audience. The mayor is taking some of my advice about homelessness and helping to put the issue on the national stage. So maybe I don't need to feel guilty, at least not for now: I've got more committee agendas to read.

Front pages of the daily papers can awaken even the most complacent Canadians eventually. Beginning in the mid-'90s and continuing for several years running, the faces of Canada's homeless appeared more and more often in the media. City by city, reports of homeless people who had died on streets were published and broadcast. Some people without homes were baring their souls to an increasingly curious media interested in preparing "profiles." Some homeless even began to cross the thresholds of Canadian city halls in angry, frustrated groups. Shouts for change, recognition, and, most of all, respect and housing resounded with growing passion and even fury. For half a century, Canadians' common understanding of homeless people had been limited to occasional wanderers, eccentrics, boozers or addicts. These stereotypes hid the personal stories and made the problem seem remote. Certainly, many decades had passed since the widespread impoverishment of the Depression, with its long soup-kitchen line-ups. But the late 1990s produced reminders of that past. Growing urban homelessness and the pathetic housing on First Nations reserves created a sense of shame.

As the twenty-first century begins, homelessness is a rapidly growing social problem in Canada.

Until recently, the world's experts in housing policy were giving Canada praise and prestigious awards for its progressive housing policies. Twenty-five years of refining and expanding mixed-income neighbourhood building had kept homelessness at bay. Computer searches of Canadian newspapers of the '60s, '70s or early '80s yields no mention of the word *homelessness*.

Then, in 1986, Drina Joubert died, a homeless woman, in winter, in Toronto. The news shocked the city, but it had a personal dimension for me and my family. On the night she died, she had sought refuge in the back of an abandoned pick-up truck one block from where I was living in a cozy co-op recently built on downtown Jarvis Street. When the news of her discovery the next day broke in the headlines, people were stunned. "How sad." "How could this unfortunate woman have descended so far that she was reduced to drifting alone in the city's back lanes?" "What a pity," sighed the city's sages.

Although many in the city took little notice of the death, a committed network of community workers and anti-poverty activists convinced a coroner's jury examining the circumstances of her passing that change was needed. They argued that Drina Joubert's death was not her fault. In depositions from street workers—at the time, the newest social-work profession—convincing evidence made crystal clear the difficulties facing a woman with mental-health challenges in finding affordable, stable and safe housing.

With an open ear to the case presented by the petitioners, the coroner's jury called for housing, especially housing with support for those escaping the demons of the type with which Drina Joubert had been struggling. Fortunately, these recommendations landed on the desks of municipal and provincial decision makers in the mid-'80s, before the 180-degree turn away from notions like social responsibility and intervention. There was actually a rapid and sympathetic response. Housing programs were expanded and customized to meet the needs of singles. More supportive housing projects were initiated. Ten years later, when deaths in the streets again came to the forefront of public attention, how different the reaction was to be.

Chairing Toronto's Board of Health in the mid-1980s, I was asked to head an inquiry into homelessness and health. Street workers who toiled in the emergency shelters were concerned about the early signs of overcrowding and the impact of these conditions on the well-being of the homeless. AIDS and hepatitis were flagged for attention. Early warning signals of TB were evident.

Front-line troops argued that a full inquiry was needed to show connections between poverty and homelessness—and to raise awareness. The investigation might help avoid more Drina Joubert tragedies. The Board of Health was convinced. Under its auspices, respected and credible citizens were pulled together to lead the inquiry. Among them were then lawyer and now judge Patrick Sheppard and the progressive mental-health specialist Dr. Ty Turner. As inquiries go, it was only a brief study, concentrated in one day, with both private- and public-hearing sessions in a downtown community-centre basement. That's when I first met street workers Cathy Crowe and Beric German. The name of their organization, Street Health, underlined in a shocking way the context of their work. Their personal stories—from their experiences serving homeless people in need of health care—were particularly influential. From that day on, these same people have often provided a window into the reality of homeless life. Not content to just hear from "experts," the panel also opened its doors to people experiencing homelessness on Toronto streets. This was a first, and everyone was nervous. People prefer to avoid telling their stories—the private circumstances that cost them their housing—in public. The deep feelings of guilt imposed by society, mixed with anger and fear, can create a paralyzing emotional communication blockade. Still, some courageous ones came forward. Their narratives set the stage.

Then came the public-health professionals and university professors, adding hard data. Their key message: There was an urban redevelopment trend resulting in the loss of affordable housing for singles. Downtown Toronto was becoming more popular as a place to live. Deliberate policies had been in place for several years to attract people back to the city, to avoid the pitfalls of the vacant central cities found in the U.S. as the middle class escaped to suburbia. Protecting threatened neighbourhoods was the mandate of City of Toronto Council in the '70s, under the leadership of such reformers as mayors David Crombie and John Sewell, as well as councillors such as Alan Sparrow and Michael Goldrick, who were urged on by the redoubtable intellect of alderman-turned-journalist Colin Vaughan and the wisdom of urbanist Jane Jacobs. However, saving quaint streets of old homes downtown made them attractive to new residents—professionals who could afford to buy these old structures and transform them into trendy quarters. Home to thousands of low-income singles and couples for years, these neighbourhoods used to provide affordable accommodation in rooming houses.[1] The process known as urban gentrification had begun to cost the city its affordable-housing stock.

Faced with compelling material, the Homelessness and Health panel then wrote a comprehensive strategy to house and serve the homeless, based both on stories from the street and recommendations from the activists and experts. The Board of Health and Toronto City Council fully endorsed the recommendations. Still, despite this support, only a few of the panel's suggestions about the need for new supportive housing and improved conditions in the hostels were eventually adopted. Momentum fizzled. Political will failed. The problems experienced by the homeless and socially isolated were not high on public-awareness meters. Homelessness, a problem affecting marginal people, was seen as a marginal issue. So homelessness found itself pushed to the edges of the public-policy discussion tables, soon to be forgotten.

Since then, however, the shame and the pain of homelessness in Canada have preoccupied a slowly growing number of people. In 1991, Paul Martin Jr. prepared a powerful analysis of the problem. It was powerful for several reasons: Martin was the millionaire ex-CEO of a major Canadian corporation and a policy leader in the then opposition Liberal Party; he was a prominent occupant of the front benches of Canada's Parliament, with full access to the corridors of corporate and government power. Two years later, he became finance minister. The words he wrote in 1991 would have weight, substance, credibility and effect. Or so you would think.

> . . . all Canadians have the right to decent housing, in decent surroundings, at affordable prices. . . . There is currently a vacuum in federal policy and direction. . . . Only the national government has the financial resources to address the full dimensions of the needs of this country.[2]

Just words.

Faced with the prevailing agenda and accelerating abandonment by governments of their historic role in addressing the basic needs of Canadians, Martin led his government into the most rapid dismantling of social infrastructure of any G7 country. Even as Canada received international awards for its housing policy, that very policy was being unceremoniously dumped.

From the mid-'90s, there has been virtually no housing policy in Canada. Only a few years before, several thousand units of new low-income housing had become available to needy families and individuals each and every year. With the termination of these programs, stanching of the wounds of poverty became a nearly hopeless task.

Searching for the causes of the current homelessness crisis is not such an impossibly complex task. In plumbing the depths of our social and economic processes to find answers—as many inquiries and studies have done—one common theme has emerged. Dr. Anne Golden and the team that worked with her to produce the Toronto Mayor's Homelessness Action Task Force Report (usually referred to as the Golden Report) summarized the essential causes of homelessness with a succinct list.

- Increased poverty: Both the incidence and depth of poverty have increased because of changes in the structure of the labour market and because of public policy changes such as restrictions on Employment Insurance eligibility and cuts to welfare.

- Lack of affordable housing: The dwindling supply of low-cost rental units and rooming housings, along with the withdrawal of support by both the federal and provincial governments for new social-housing programs, have made affordable housing much harder to find.
- Deinstitutionalisation and lack of discharge planning: Many people who suffer from mental illness and addictions are homeless partly as a result of deinstitutionalisation without adequate community support programs; in addition, their problems have been exacerbated by the inadequate discharge planning of hospitals and jails.
- Social factors: Domestic violence, physical and sexual abuse, and the alienation of individuals from family and friends have increased the incidence of homelessness. Homelessness is the ragged edge of the social fabric.[3]

There is no shortage of ideas about homelessness and what could be done about the crisis. In hearings at city councils and community meetings across Canada, especially wise ideas have come forward from the homeless themselves, and from those who work with them. Committed analysts from the social sciences have exposed truths, too. So have housing economists, mayors, columnists and preachers. Ideas about causes. Ideas about solutions. As a result, there is a growing flow of options from which to choose. As well, success stories from other countries are available. We'll read about some of them in this book.

In my city, homelessness hits close to home. Four years ago, a gut-wrenching incident forced me to address my own responsibility for the plight of the homeless.

On the cold and very snowy night of January 4, 1996, I was walking up Spadina Avenue with my spouse, City Councillor Olivia Chow. We were heading home, late as usual, from Metro Hall, in the shadow of SkyDome and the CN Tower. It was almost midnight. Along the way, we passed two homeless guys tucked into their sleeping bags in the cramped alcoves created by store doorways set back a couple of feet from Spadina's famous sidewalk. Snow was building up around them.

We checked on each man as we went by, not by disturbing them or waking them, but by looking briefly to see if there were any obvious signs that they were in difficulty. It's a habit. A lot of people in big cities do this all the time. It's not that you can really tell if the person you're studying is in trouble. All you usually see is just a fitful sleep—or maybe a deep motionless sleep. Seeing "motionless" can be a scary experience. Is he asleep? Has she passed out? There's no way to know unless you shake them by the shoulder and ask. But that seems so unfair, so intrusive, so wrong. The whole picture is wrong. I shouldn't be here asking these questions about this person who shouldn't be here either.

As we picked our way through the blizzard north towards College Street, under the garish signature neon calligraphy of Chinatown, Olivia and I talked about what anyone could do if they did see someone in trouble. What number should be called—911? The police? Somehow that didn't seem like the right answer. There's nothing about a homeless person sleeping in an alcove that is a police matter. How could you contact someone who was trained and who had a specific mandate to help—someone like the Anishnawbe Street Patrol?

Two city councillors—and we didn't even know how to reach proper help! A fine job we were doing. "Perhaps we should propose to council some sort of well-publicized hotline," one of us said.

As we reached Cecil Street, one block from home, we swung east around Grossman's Tavern, with its historic pale green paint and peeling posters advertising bands who had played there since time began. On our way home, we hadn't seen a man lying alone, across the wide swath of Spadina Avenue to the west. He had escaped the snow by stowing away in a Toronto Transit Commission bus shelter, but he had not escaped the descending cold. All night long, the southbound Spadina buses passed the prostrate figure every thirty minutes. But they didn't stop for him. Not that night. Not ever again.

The next morning, the ritual proceeded as usual for a Saturday: the obligatory indigestion-producing combination of news and coffee. Newspapers. Radio. Everything was normal until one radio news report stopped us mid-column. The announcer said that a man had frozen to death on Spadina overnight. We knew in an instant that we had been there, feet from his deathbed.

A shiver ran down my spine. Is there anything more awful for a Canadian to imagine than freezing to death? How could this have happened in Toronto? Were there no shelters? Were there no emergency services for the homeless? Wasn't this the richest city in the country? What the hell was going on?

Those questions were on the surface, but the deeper one was very personal. This was one of the homeless that we had passed by the previous night.

His name was Eugene Upper. Although he lay on the other side of the street, I should have seen him, I thought. Like so many citizens with homes, we had walked right by people on the street that night—and other nights—and maybe one of those people had died. Yet we hadn't called for help. We had assumed, somehow, that others would step in.

Also, my job on council required me to put plans and policies in place to prevent deaths on the street. I should have made sure that there were emergency phone numbers, more emergency beds, more emergency services, more housing. Guilt? You bet!

Front-page headlines proclaimed the tragedy.

Word also spread like brushfire through the streets. From emergency shelters to all-night doughnut shops, wherever the homeless were grasping for refuge from the cold, there were whispered words: "Did you hear?" The next night, faces of the homeless returning to their shelter beds were more anxious. All members of the street culture knew someone who would still be outside in the killer cold. Whose turn would it be?

Navigating their van through that night's snowy lanes, the Anishnawbe Street Patrol did its best to check the city's many nooks and crannies to find those who remained exposed. Some police and ambulance workers also spent extra time to find and offer help to the TTC shelter sleepers and the heating-grate denizens. Not that there was much anyone could do. The shelters were full that night, as they had been for several nights running. The city could no longer provide refuge to anyone in need.

Toronto was not alone. In Calgary, on the same night, three out of every ten people showing up for emergency shelter were turned away. Across Canada, "No room at the inn" was becoming commonplace.

Ever-defensive bureaucrats quickly rolled out statistics for the night Eugene Upper died, suggesting that there were a few beds in the 4,000-bed system that had not been taken. This posture allowed some commentators on talk shows to suggest that these deaths could not be prevented. After all, they argued, there were beds available and yet Eugene Upper had chosen to stay outside. He had made a conscious decision. Society had provided an alternative to death, but Eugene had chosen his own destiny. This victim had to be blamed.

The homelessness debate had begun!

Toronto is not generally identified by Canadians as the centre of moral goodness. Still, there is a largely unpublicized but widespread network of Torontonian good-deed-doers. As many as 5,000 people turn out, without fanfare, to volunteer at hundreds of Out of the Cold soup kitchens and church basement drop-ins that had been springing up in central neighbourhoods.

Small groups of health workers and community outreach staff at downtown agencies began to vent their frustration about the shortage of resources to help the homeless. Their numbers began to swell. The Ontario Coalition Against Poverty needed larger and larger halls for its weekly meetings. The combination of anger and passion overflowed into the committee rooms of city hall. Sessions to defend the rights of the homeless started to spring up. Letters to the editor about homelessness began to surpass other issues of the day.

On many fronts, the controversy about Eugene Upper's silent death appeared to break the silence about homelessness.

For Olivia and me, with such a preventable tragedy taking place one block from our home, we were galvanized into action. Acting almost on instinct, we planned an immediate press conference. We wanted to ensure that Eugene Upper's death was not for naught. We wanted to recommend a full plan of emergency action and response for presentation to city council in the following week. Our anger was directed at councillors, including ourselves, for not having done more, and anger at the federal and provincial governments, which had systematically cancelled virtually all the new affordable-housing construction programs. Our frustration grew as we thought about how a rich society like ours could let homeless people freeze to death.

For the previous few months, several community workers had tried to press council to create a special committee on homelessness. They could see that conditions in the shelters, drop-ins and on the streets were becoming dangerous. They called attention to the growing numbers of homeless. People were afraid to go inside some of the shelters, they said. The places were full and too dangerous.

Bureaucrats denied this, and politicians, as usual, tended to believe that the bureaucrats were right and that advocates were hysterical and "just being political." Well, if *political* means kicking politicians' asses until they wake up and act, yes—these folks were political. Most have stayed heavily involved for years, on the front lines of the battle against homelessness. Gaeten Heroux, the worker at the homeless drop-in; Cathy Crowe, the street nurse; Beric German, the street worker who visited shelters; and the two community centre directors, Alison Kemper of the 519 Church Street Community Centre and Ruth Mott of Central Neighbourhood House; they were all involved.

We all wanted city council to call for a coroner's inquest into the death of Eugene Upper. As well, we did not want council to wait for the results of the inquest to take some key emergency steps that were obviously needed. Here are the key elements of the plan that was put together in direct response to the Upper tragedy:

- Create an emergency phone line for homeless people to call, without requiring twenty-five cents, or for citizens to call if they saw a homeless person who might be in trouble
- Expand the street patrols on cold nights
- Create an emergency fund of $600,000 to open drop-ins on holidays and weekends and to make sure there were enough shelter beds
- Mandate the newly created Homeless Advisory Committee to work to prevent freezing deaths in the city

Late that same night, press releases flowed from our home fax machine, inviting the media to attend a press conference the next morning at the very site where Eugene Upper had died only twenty hours before. The idea was to call attention to this terrible situation and set out some plans for immediate action.

By Sunday morning at eleven o'clock, a full turnout of the city's press corps had positioned their cameras, tripods, notepads and tape recorders around the Plexiglas transit-shelter where Eugene Upper died. The clean cold snow was strangely beautiful in the bright, low, winter sun. In the background, the scene was passively observed by Toronto's architectural icons of affluence: the CN Tower, the Dome and the glistening bank towers of Bay Street.

As the working week began on Monday, prodded by media looking for "the other side," some councillors reacted negatively to our call for action.

They charged that ours was little more than an overemotional play for city funding, an attempt to guilt council into coughing up tax dollars for people who simply would not help themselves.

Some city bureaucrats went so far as to argue against a full public inquiry. They urged caution, offering arguments that if there was a coroner's inquest, the city would have to defend itself against any claims and accusations about the adequacy of the services to the homeless that were already being provided from city hall. Defending ourselves could cost money! We might be shown to be liable.

Prospects for a policy shift at city hall looked weak. Resistance was setting in. It seemed as though Eugene Upper's death would fade from the front pages, and other priorities would occupy the public's mind.

Then in the bright sunlight that rose over the morning rush-hour traffic, Mirsalah-Aldin Kompani was discovered frozen solid under the Gardiner Expressway. Kompani had apparently built his own version of a home—some construction waste piled up to protect him from snow and keep the heat in. That night, Toronto had had one of its coldest nights of the decade. His body couldn't be moved: It was frozen to the hard surface of the concrete and earth under the highway ramp. What a macabre spectacle: a whole city waiting and watching through videocam eyes as his lifeless body thawed. Hourly news reports captured the pathetic drama.

An exclamation point on the statement made by these homeless deaths followed soon after. Within a couple of days, a third homeless man, Irwin Anderson, was found dead in Toronto streets—tucked in a storefront vestibule, attempting to escape the cold like the others. The city was in an uproar. Public opinion began to rise from its complacent sleep, and local politicians found it more difficult to dismiss the crisis as a scare-mongering tactic. In the big city, one death could be dismissed—could have been bad luck, a tough break, something to be expected—terrible, of course, as it was. But three deaths?

A coalition of concerned citizens came together to support the inquest process. Their goal was to reveal what they considered to be the truth about homelessness in Toronto. A team of volunteers was created. They monitored the preparations for the inquest and played a prominent role in building community awareness through the subsequent hearings. Details of their work and a comprehensive account of the evolution of the inquest has been archived on the Internet at <www.communitygates.com/raisetheroof/current.htm>.

The impact was national. Even today, a surprising number of Canadians remember that there were freezing deaths in Toronto in 1996. It's a vague memory but it's lodged there.

In other communities, people remember other homeless deaths. In 1997 in Wood Buffalo, a northern Alberta resource town, a man had been found deposited by a garbage truck dead in his dumpster home. This left an indelible impact on Mayor Doug Faulkner, who became a major advocate of more affordable housing, and on the community, which had seen itself as a boomtown, immune from such urban terrors. An even deeper tragedy unfolded in the nation's capital: A pregnant First Nation teenager was discovered dead under a bridge in 1998. Two fatalities in one fragile girl's body.

Similar and sad stories emerged from other communities across the country. Like dark family secrets, they began to be talked about. Toronto streets were yielding more than one homeless death a week. A study by Dr. Richard Fung of the emergency ward at St. Michael's Hospital in downtown Toronto counted over 100 deaths of homeless men between 1996 and 1998. St. Mike's did not count the homeless women who died.

Homelessness has its small deaths—deaths by a thousand cuts. Most homeless people don't die suddenly. They endure, struggle and survive in whatever way they can. Pain and indignity must be endured daily by the 1,000 children and their mothers in Toronto's hostel system, for instance. "That kid is from the motels!" goes the schoolyard gossip. No money is available for school trips, and the only refuge is the small motel room with its TV, half-sized fridge, and two double beds for three kids and their mom.

Eugene Upper, the man frozen on Spadina Avenue opposite Grossman's Tavern, actually created something in the moment of his quiet, cold death. His passing created a snowball of public opinion and concern that was to grow slowly but with an inexorable momentum.

When it was agreed that an inquest should be held, would the highly publicized coroner's inquiry highlight collective responsibility? Would the coroner's jury call for action to end homelessness? Or would they focus on the discrete characteristics of each man who died? These are key questions surrounding the politics of homelessness in Canada today. Who is guilty? Does blame fall on the homeless and their immediate acquaintances? Or should it fall on the macro-economic considerations of public policy, on an economy and society that produced the conditions within which their lives and deaths occurred? Can we develop a better understanding of the arguments on either side of this debate? The following chapters will attempt to do so.

Homelessness is a political phenomenon—if we understand politics to be, among other things, the process that determines the allocation of our resources. Housing is one of these resources. Has our society determined that its resources will be distributed so that some community members have no housing?

In some respects, inquests are curious, even bizarre, affairs. Everyone knows that an inquest jury is not allowed to assign blame for a death, only to specify the time, place and circumstances of the fatality, including the cause. However, no large leap of logic is needed to extract from testimony and cross-examination the implications of guilt that lie in the evidence. Juries are entitled to make recommendations based on what they learn during the hearing. These juries and their findings are watched closely. People, especially the media, accept that because the jurors have no vested interest in the case or the circumstances of the case—and because jurors listen to a great deal of evidence from all sides and perspectives—their recommendations are often given considerable public credence.

However, history shows that coroner's juries are less well received by governments and corporations. Perhaps this is because jury recommendations invariably call for change, requiring big institutions to do things differently. Here's the issue: If an organization accepts the recommendations, the unmistakable implication is that things could have been done differently, and therefore that the organization is somehow "guilty."

So, the inquest into these three deaths was like a microcosm of the emerging national debate about homelessness. Did governments have responsibility here or not?

How widely can a jury cast its net?

This became a critical question in the hearing. Advocates for the homeless wanted the fact of homelessness to be addressed. They wanted the jury to recommend changes in government policies that would reduce or eliminate homelessness. At the very least, these front-line community workers wanted an acknowledgement by an agency of government that the homelessness of these men was a cause of their deaths, that not having a home could be fatal and that the state should take some responsibility to provide housing.

As the hearing opened, camped on one side of the room were community groups and advocates, a backdrop to their lawyer, Peter Rosenthal. The loose coalition had banded together to have a lawyer put forward the view that these deaths were the result of homelessness but also to bring forward evidence, witnesses, expert testimony and recommendations for the jury to consider. Leadership of this coalition came from Michael Shapcott and Cathy Crowe, supported by a network of dedicated hearing monitors, website updaters, newsletter producers and housing specialists. A number of group members had experienced homelessness first-hand.

Peter Rosenthal was an interesting choice. In his day job, Professor Rosenthal teaches mathematics at the University of Toronto, and in his spare time, he had picked up a law degree. He specializes in selected cases that he feels can serve an important social goal—cases that advance justice for those who have a difficult time finding it. He takes on many cases on a pro-bono basis, as in this inquest. Rosenthal is known for his gruff, tough style. Passion resonated in the gravelly deep voice as he pushed hard for the broader issues underlying the deaths of homeless people to be considered by the coroner. The lawyer and his supporting coalition were determined to have the affordable-housing crisis placed at the very centre of the inquest. They wanted recommendations that would call for new affordable housing in Canada. A straight line had to be drawn between the three fatalities on Toronto streets and the death of affordable-housing construction programs, if the case was to be effective. Faced with the mythology of homelessness and pervasive victim blaming, this was not going to be easy.

The politics of homelessness began with an attack on the politics of denial. Denial had set in deeply. In response to deaths of homeless people, Ontario Premier Mike Harris offered this question: "Isn't it sad that these people just seem to want to be homeless?" The subtext was clear: Homelessness is not political, it's individual choice and completely immune from government policy. The public was implicitly urged not to look at the cutbacks to the funding of Ontario social programs like affordable-housing construction.

Fortunately, many of these same players had previous experience with inquests into deaths related to the housing crisis. Some real successes had been achieved. Advocacy had become much more sophisticated since the days of our Board of Health one-day basement investigation of homelessness and health. Many of this inquest's participants had been involved in the 1989 inquest following a ferocious winter fire at a run-down flea-bag dump known as the Rupert Hotel, at Parliament and Queen in Toronto's east downtown. That fire took ten lives.[4] If you are ever in Toronto and passing near Parliament Street and Queen Street East, take a moment to pay your respects to those who died. The memorial is in the sidewalk, on the northwest corner.

The Rupert Coalition had pushed hard at the inquest for reforms in the ways that housing was provided to the lowest-income residents of Toronto. They wanted more supported housing for poor people, housing mixed in with the community at large, housing that was not a ghetto. They wanted the city's buildings department to take action to ensure that low-income housing was up to standard, particularly as far as fire safety was concerned.

At that time, there had been an attempt to claim that the residents of the Rupert were the authors of their own misfortune because of the way they lived. The jury was not convinced. Their recommendations amounted to a manifesto for action to improve the quality of housing for the poor. Their list became a "to do" list for governments, and the Rupert Coalition pressed every level of bureaucrat and politician to deliver the goods.

Armed with the 1986 experience of the Drina Joubert inquest, many of the coalition members who had formed around the 1989 Rupert inferno regrouped. They wanted to make sure that the voices of the homeless were heard, even more powerfully, by the Eugene Upper inquest jury.

Politics is not like sports. Sports presents two sides grappling for victory. Politics features many "sides," often grouped into what appear to be "teams." This inquest's hearing room was no exception. One group included the homeless and representatives of community groups. On another bank of benches sat the lawyer for Toronto's government, and other lawyers. The initially defensive and testy hostels management team kept a close eye on the process. Officials from the province were also on hand, wanting to be sure that provincial policies were not unduly implicated. Fortunately, city public-health officials were there, too. These nurses and doctors understood the causes of homelessness better than most.

One by one, the experts and advocates took their place in the witness box and described conditions on the streets of Toronto in graphic detail. For the first time in the 1990s, a thorough picture of the emerging homelessness crisis in Canada's richest city was permitted to be entered into the public record.

As the testimony unfolded, it seemed to become crystal-clear to the jury that the cause of death of these three men was rooted in the fundamental fact of their homelessness. Three life paths had brought them to a similar end, and there were differences in the physical processes that ultimately caused their hearts to stop beating. Still, each man's homelessness had played a key part in putting him at risk. In establishing the cause of death in each case, the jury emphatically named "homelessness." All three had died from homelessness!

For the first time in Ontario history (perhaps in Canadian history) the official cause of death was determined to be homelessness. Once the jury settled on this key conclusion, the five citizens who composed the jury accepted and adopted many of the community's recommendations for policy changes designed to prevent future deaths. Most important and fundamental of all of the recommendations was the call for a new affordable-housing policy to address the growing crisis. In rejecting the concept that homeless individuals were responsible for their own situation, the jury had moved the debate to a new plateau.

Here are some of the words of the jury:

> We the jury wish to express our condolences to the families of Eugene Upper, Irwin Anderson, and Mirsalah-Aldin Kompani. Cognizant of the plight of the three gentlemen who are the focus of this inquest and the many factors which may have contributed to their deaths such as addictions, mental illness, homelessness and cold harsh environment, we the jury have endeavoured to consider the aspects of the evidence presented to us. . . .
>
> We learned from the evidence that there is the growing problem of meeting the needs of a portion of our population who may have similar situations and circumstances as the three gentlemen aforementioned. . . .
>
> Our goal is to bring about a workable solution to prevent further similar deaths if the present situation is allowed to continue. . . .
>
> We urge all levels of government and society at large to make a concerted and serious effort to alleviate the burden of this group of people to allow them to live in dignity.

Dozens of recommendations followed. The jury suggested changes to the hostel system, called for more outreach programs and detoxification centres, better services from the health-care system for homeless people, including mobile health services. We took this latter recommendation to the Rotary Club of Toronto and the Wellesley Hospital (now St. Michael's) and they instituted a full-service health bus accompanied by a small fleet of vans to help people reach services. The jury also turned to the fundamental, long-term issues:

> The goal should be to identify successful models of affordable and supportive housing and community supports and develop a plan of action to ensure that the homeless, in particular those with substance abuse and/or mental illness, have access to appropriate housing and support services. Funding should be provided by the appropriate governmental ministries to carry out this plan.

In the end, Eugene Upper, Mirsalah-Aldin Kompani and Irwin Anderson left a powerful legacy. As the recommendations came back to governments for action, a certain credibility began to be established for the idea that the whole community had to take some responsibility for ensuring that there is enough adequate and affordable housing for those in need. While influential voices had been successfully preaching that less government is good government, and that governments should not be involved in the "housing business," the jury had challenged the prevailing wisdom. The jury said, quite simply, that reducing government intervention can actually create homelessness, and they certified that homelessness kills Canadians.

Perhaps the tide was about to turn. Three fatalities due to homelessness on Toronto streets had been investigated and judged by the jury to have resulted from inadequate social polices.

2 Defining Homelessness

Homelessness: A 1995 British Columbia publication gave Canadian urban voyeurs eight personal perspectives in a report called *Nowhere to Live*.

"If there were no hotels," said Mr. Sue, referring to the single-room occupancy (SRO) hotels that characterize Vancouver's Downtown Eastside, "I don't know, I'd find a shack, sleep on cardboard or in a sleeping bag. The only pain I have is existence every day."[1] To drive home the point, the cover of this report is made of corrugated cardboard, the same material that provides shelter to the dispossessed of Canada's cities. Another of the short biographies between these covers is Judy's story. She is 15 years old, aboriginal and pregnant. She is too young to qualify for welfare or other benefits. She lives in a motel room in Prince George with her boyfriend.

> It's actually $700 a month for this ditch pig of a place. Utilities are included. We have our own bedroom, bathroom and kitchen facilities. My boyfriend pays the rent out of his income assistance cheques. I don't get any money for myself. My old man gets welfare, but only

for himself. They won't give us money together because of my age. I have no monthly income.

I left Kamloops in 1992, because my situation at home wasn't very good. I came to Prince George because my sister lived here. I didn't know where else to go. I stayed with her for a while.

I don't live on the streets now because my baby is due any day. I have been on the streets, though, before, when my old man was in jail for a couple of months. I also stayed at the Association Advocating for Women and Children House for a while. I felt safer there. It was pretty good. I got food and shelter and had access to laundry facilities.[2]

So is Judy homeless or not?

By the late 1990s, in most Canadian cities, attention had been drawn to the fact that homeless people were literally "in the streets." In fact, street homelessness or "living in the rough" was not considered much of a problem in Canada until recently. In response to the activities of the 1987 United Nations International Year of Shelter for the Homeless, the Canadian Real Estate Association (CREA), in partnership with the Canada Mortgage and Housing Corporation (CMHC), commissioned a research document to review the national picture and to sketch the magnitude of homelessness in Canada. Testimony to the times was found in George Fallis and Alex Murray's introduction, wherein they felt they could set the parameters of their discussion of homelessness in Canada by saying that "if homelessness is narrowly defined as lacking a roof over one's head, the number of homeless in Canada is quite low. *Even the most stereotypical street person can usually find shelter at night if he or she chooses* [my emphasis]."[3]

A few community groups argued that the study understated the problem, but these critiques were modest and made little if any impact on public policy. Besides, in the mid-1980s, construction in Canada was in full swing, building affordable-housing projects, non-profits, seniors' homes and co-operatives by the thousands of units across the country every year. The International Year of Shelter for the Homeless discussions at the United Nations produced praise for Canada's visionary housing policies. Ironically, in the year that followed, Prime Minister Brian Mulroney and his Conservative government began to dismantle the affordable-housing construction programs. In the decade that followed, Canadian housing policies and associated spending were dismembered or downloaded to provincial and municipal levels, and then further dismembered.

Had the official definition of homelessness in the Canadian report been constructed differently, more appropriate policies might have been put in place to prevent the crisis levels of the subsequent decade. There are three fundamental problems with the "*stereotypical*" definition of homelessness outlined by Fallis and Murray.

First, consider the suggestion that there is a "stereotypical street person." Each person on the street or in a shelter has a unique story. To declare otherwise reveals ignorance or arrogance. The biographies of those who have become homeless are as varied as the snowflakes on which they sleep.

Fallis and Murray were also mistaken in suggesting that everyone who needed help could find shelter at night in the late 1980s. The authors simply had their facts wrong. In those days, as a city councillor, I had many conversations with people who were unable to find shelter. As early as 1986, a new volunteer position known as "street outreach worker" had come into being at the Anishnawbe Health Centre. With a working evening that began with sandwich-making at 10:00 P.M., they spent the night bringing hot coffee, sandwiches and a little basic human contact and care to the slowly growing population of dispossessed. It was 1988 when we found a van we were able to give to Anishnawbe's volunteer teams to use to reach the homeless.

Lastly—with the phrase "if he or she chooses"—Fallis and Murray leave the distinct impression that the homeless were making free and willing choices about whether they would stay outside or go indoors. One can't help wondering if those authors asked any street people that question.

Characterizations such as these are not limited to Canadian commentators. Consider Britain:

> Throughout the 1980s, discussions of homelessness frequently took place within the agenda set by the Conservative government, which was explicit in seeking to place the responsibility for the homeless directly on the homeless themselves. As Margaret Thatcher herself said in Parliament, in response to evidence of increasing homelessness in London: "There is a number of young people who choose voluntarily to leave home; I do not think that we can be expected, no matter how many there are, to provide units for them."[4]

Misleading and mistaken definitions can reverberate for years—in editorials, commentators' off-hand remarks and coffee-shop scuttlebutt. So, not surprisingly, ten years after Fallis and Murray's government study, the same mantra echoed from the highest levels of government. Perhaps the most outstanding example took place when Ontario Premier Mike Harris reacted to yet another homeless man's death in Toronto in 1997, claiming that homelessness is a lifestyle choice. Hearing the premier's claim, some of us tried to find proof that some people were choosing to be homeless. We invited any homeless people who actually wanted to be homeless to come forward. The media joined the search for the premier's voluntarily homeless. Despite considerable effort, no self-selected homeless people could be found. In fact, when told of the premier's claim, colourful language peppered the reactions of street people.

A decade earlier, by contrast, *Toronto Life's* David Olive observed:

> You think you know the homeless until you talk to them. It should happen more often, that simple act of putting real names to men and women who've fallen by the economic wayside. As their anonymity slips away, so do your assumptions. Because the common bond of destitution makes homeless people so apparently identifiable, we can't resist putting labels on them: this one is mentally disturbed, that one can't hold a job, another is chronically in trouble with the law. Yet in the case of each homeless man and woman, lack of shelter is the product of different circumstances. The middle-aged man at the hostel who has a drinking problem and hasn't had steady work for three years turns out to have left a wife and two kids behind in Timmins when the mine shut down, and never could summon the courage to go back to them when he failed to secure a job here that paid the same wages. The woman with no apparent grasp on reality, talking loudly to herself as she rocks back and forth in her lawn chair in front of the Laundromat, is a rape victim whose daughter is in the care of a distant relative. The teenage boy who has taken up more or less permanent residence in the Yonge Street pinball arcade left home after enduring one too many beatings.[5]

The word *homeless* so clearly expresses a human condition that it's hard to imagine anyone could have trouble understanding what it means. Yet the word *homelessness* is charged with powerful images, all bringing to mind moral mandates.

Just about everyone who has written or spoken about homelessness in Canada has used a different definition. These definitions become tools that justify action or inaction, depending upon who is doing the defining. Such differences matter because the way in which the problem is defined establishes the terrain of debate.

Anyone concerned about people dying homeless in the streets is going to be frustrated by any extended discussion of what homelessness actually is. "Don't they understand the problem?" The rhetorical question reverberates in meeting halls where panels of three levels of government point fingers of blame at one another. Putting aside such frustrations is important, because we need to accept that participants in the debate are often defining the problem differently. They usually get one of four things wrong—either out of inexperience, naïvety, or sheer bloody-mindedness: they minimize the problem; they structure the definition so the homeless are blamed; they define the problem so that it's someone else's problem; or they define the problem so that it is all-encompassing, absolutely huge.

Defining the problem so that it's small

In this approach, only rooflessness is "true" homelessness. After all, the roof keeps the rain out; what more do these homeless people want? Anything else is simply a matter of choices that people can and should make themselves.

At the Centre for Housing Management and Development at Cardiff University, Professor David Clapham calls this the "minimalist construction, with its emphasis on individual pathology and the division between those who are deserving of help and those who are not."[6] He argues that "social constructions of homelessness structure the way that public policy intervenes to deal with homelessness." In the 1990s in Britain, for example, the dominant minimalist definitions of homelessness structured the statutory homeless procedures with their emphasis on exclusion of the undeserving.

Defining the problem so it's theirs (not ours)

Have you ever heard these explanations for homelessness? "He's a drug addict." "She's a drunk." "She can't support her kids." "He really doesn't want to work at all." "They'd rather live on the dole." "Her parents kicked her out." "Most of them have a mental illness, you know." "That nasty business happened when she kept tantalizing her father. Of course he shouldn't have done it, mind you—well, she just couldn't stay under those circumstances, could she?"

From these statements, the victim is seen to be beset by personal problems brought on by personality flaws, individual pathologies or circumstances created by his or her own decisions.

Blaming the victim. This deceptively simple but brilliant turn of phrase coined by William Ryan[7], renowned American sociologist, captures the essential problem with definitions that slip into this causal mindset. Take this example from the literature: "There are many words for a homeless person, such as beggar, bum, derelict, drifter, floater, gypsy, rambler, vagabond, vagrant, wanderer, wino."[8] These days such an approach would add squeegee kid, street hooker and panhandler—the victim-blaming terminology receives constant updating.

When definitions and labels like this are accepted by society's decision makers, they easily lead to policy proposals that aim to make sure that the homeless are not "rewarded" for inappropriate behaviour. "After all, you wouldn't want to encourage them, now would you!" These are the origins of simple "solutions" such as the banning of the offensive behaviour. "We should ban panhandling—they only use the money to buy drugs or booze." "Let's not allow squeegeeing—it's just encouraging them not to get a real job." "Let's make it illegal for homeless people to loiter in parks—it hurts tourism and therefore gives the city less tax revenue to help the truly homeless people."

Sadly, many of these prescriptions have actually been adopted. Needless to say, homelessness has not disappeared as a result.

Defining the problem so that it's someone else's

Governments—politicians and bureaucrats—at all levels—federal, provincial, municipal—are all frequent users of this strategy. The definer pushes responsibility for the problem away from the institution that he or she represents. It rarely matters (to the speaker) who is supposed to solve the problem; shifting the obligation is all that matters.

Defining the problem so that it's colossal
Definitions that do this wrap themselves around so many types of homelessness, near-homelessness and housing problems in general that they lose any meaning, not to mention their listeners or readers. Mapping the scope of the problem in this way runs the danger of immobilizing people because of the immensity of the challenges.

All these tactics absolve governments (and the rest of us) from any responsibility. And where there's no responsibility, or at least not much, there's little need to act.

What a semantic mess!

Fortunately, in 1987, a useful perspective on the definition of homelessness was beginning to take shape—one that would influence writers in Canada a decade later. The official pronouncements of the International Year of Shelter for the Homeless, as defined and paraphrased from reports of the United Nations, International Year of Shelter for the Homeless, from various authors and reports, suggested two categories:

1. Absolute Homelessness or shelterlessness refers to individuals living in the streets with no physical shelter of their own, including those who spend their nights in emergency shelters.
2. Relative Homelessness refers to people living in spaces that do not meet basic health and safety standards, including

   - protection from the elements
   - access to safe water and sanitation
   - security of tenure and personal safety
   - affordability
   - accessibility to employment, education and health care
   - provision of minimum space to avoid overcrowding

More than a decade later, this broad approach towards understanding homelessness was convincingly advanced in the Toronto Mayor's Homelessness Action Task Force. Its final report, *Taking Responsibility for Homelessness: An Action Plan for Toronto*, was released in 1999 and captured national attention, partly because of the profile of its sponsor, Toronto's new mega-city mayor, Mel Lastman. At his request, Dr. Anne Golden, head of Toronto's United Way, chaired the task force. (The mayor asked me to be the city councillor who worked with her team.) The letter prefacing the task force's final report said: "We have included in our definition of homeless people those who are 'visible' on the streets or staying in hostels, the 'hidden' homeless who live in illegal or temporary accommodation, and those at imminent risk of becoming homeless."[9]

Toronto has stuck with this approach. The first annual *Toronto Report Card on Homelessness 2000* defined *homeless* to include people who

- live on the street;
- stay in emergency shelters; and
- spend more of their income on rent or live in overcrowded conditions, and are at serious risk of becoming homeless.[10]

In the international attempt to come to grips with the various versions of housing crises that exist worldwide, Kaye Stearman uses some new terminology. She divides the problem into these categories:

- rooflessness (people sleeping outdoors);
- houselessness (people in shelters, institutions or short-term accommodation);
- insecure housing (squatters or people in refugee camps);
- inadequate or inferior housing (people in houses without basic facilities).[11]

So what difference does it make how we define homelessness? Who cares?

Actually, we cannot do without a thorough definition. Governments have relied on the assistance they get from narrow and limited definitions of the homeless problem.

There are other agendas at work, too, in any public debate about social issues. Simplified or minimalist definitions of homelessness make for easy-to-manufacture slogans. A happy consequence for the purveyors of such rhetoric is how nicely this minimalism fits in with the prevailing ideology of global capitalism. It's a line of thought that claims there are too many government programs, too much public spending, too little personal responsibility and too many restrictions (translation: taxes) on the good people who simply want to get ahead.

An example of the rhetoric involved surfaced in Toronto's 1997 mega-city elections. "There are no homeless in North York!" Mel Lastman's flourish in the heat of debate with Toronto mayor and long-time homeless advocate Barbara Hall turned out to be a turning point, but not in the way he intended. Only one journalist, Adam Vaughan, then of Toronto's local CBC-TV news, aired the remark. Had he not, history might have taken a different turn.

Within two days, tragically, as though higher moral forces wanted to prove Lastman wrong, 48-year-old Linda Houston was found dead in a North York gas station's bathroom, where she had sought shelter. She had been living in a park, in a comfortable neighbourhood in the eastern part of North York, which Mel Lastman represented as mayor for decades. Residents objecting to her presence had succeeded in having her last remaining refuge, a simple park bench, removed. Lost and alone, she wandered and died. (Shortly after her death, a memorial fund was created to honour Linda. This memorial was established by Street Haven, an agency providing emergency services, and a drop-in centre for women.)[12]

Homelessness leaped again to the front pages, thirty months after the three men froze in Toronto's streets. The problem had not gone away. The homeless were, once again, speaking with their lives.

Before he was sworn in as the mayor of the new mega-city, Lastman told me that he was so deeply shaken by what happened that he was going to make homelessness his top priority—the first problem he would tackle as mayor. On streets he considered his, a woman had died—a woman whose very existence he had denied—and he was going to do something about it. I have never witnessed such a powerful epiphany in Canadian political history.

As his first act as mayor, Mel Lastman staged a press conference in a homeless shelter to launch the Mayor's Homelessness Action Task Force.

The Golden Report

In Canada, the Golden task force began to open the door to a more comprehensive view of homelessness. However, it was not the first to do so. We have already seen how work in British Columbia was leading the way. Similar perspectives had emerged from Montreal and Calgary. But Anne

Golden's group focused attention across the country because it was done under the nightly microscope of national media in Canada's biggest city. People noticed.

A typical response was that of Sam Synard, deputy mayor of the small town of Marystown, Newfoundland, who e-mailed a note to me. He had just viewed the coverage of the Golden Report on the news. As incoming president of the Federation of Canadian Municipalities, he felt that our organization had better make the issue of homelessness a national issue for all of our communities. (Until that time, the problem had only been seen as a big-city issue.) Sam said to me, "A homeless guy under a park bench in Toronto could have once been a member of a Marystown family. You're darn right it's a national crisis!"

Known as a frustratingly painstaking researcher, Anne Golden insisted that her study begin with the basics—the definitions of the problem. Ryerson professors Joe Springer and James Mars, with their research associate Melissa Dennison, were asked to define homelessness in the Toronto context and to set about the difficult task of counting the actual numbers of people who were experiencing this.

Along the way, these academics came up with two important new terms: "the literally homeless" and "those imminently at risk of becoming homeless." Their definitions were at once broad in scope and precise. They helped to point the way towards some of the resulting strategies and policies. Here, for example, are their categories:

- People who are at risk or vulnerable to homelessness in the near future, and who need short-term assistance to avoid being on the street
- Persons who can become quasi-independent but need housing as well as other supports such as literacy or employment training . . . to manage on their own
- People who have substantial and often multiple difficulties, but with help may be able to live autonomously in group homes
- People who need continuous residential care in an institutional setting[13]

While helpful in many ways, the four categories miss a fundamental fact: Hundreds of thousands of Canadian households face the long-term situation that they can't afford the housing available. Fortunately, other researchers working with Golden emphasized this key reality.

Golden's research team also introduced the idea of a "continuum" related to homelessness:

> The most useful conceptual definition of the population is one which offers a continuum of characteristics and conditions that is organised to acknowledge a hierarchy of need, and which recognises that individuals can, and will, occupy different positions along the continuum at different periods, and for varying lengths of time.[14]

> [T]he population estimated will include: all those men, women and children living together or on their own on the streets or in shelter, or temporarily or precariously housed, whether in a programme setting or another social or economic arrangement, including with friends or family, and without a permanent home. This definition also includes those living in commercial single room occupancy hotels . . . [15] [since] the similarities of personal conduct and illnesses between truly homeless individuals and those in marginal housing are striking . . . [16]

When applied to the task of counting the homeless, this broad definition gives a much different sense of the magnitude of the problem than the minimalist versions that define the problem so that it's small.

Over three times as many people are "imminently at risk of homelessness" than those who are "literally" homeless. As these authors put it, after consideration of the mountain of data in their study, "Simply stated, in any year in Toronto 25,000 people have some episode of literal homelessness, while 85,000 are at risk of that condition if *one additional* [my emphasis] life crisis occurs. This pattern has persisted and probably increased over the last ten years. The predominant need is for stable, affordable accommodation."[17]

In Toronto then, these 110,000 homeless or at-risk people represent one in twenty residents of the city, fully 5 percent of its population. This is enough to make a difference in an election. However, the homeless or near-homeless have so many obstacles to voting. Cynics say this "absence" steers policy-makers to more fertile turf. Homeless services and solutions are easy cost-cutting targets, because political fallout is low compared with that related to other cuts—like health or education, which touch so many more middle-class Canadians.

Still, the Golden task force pressed for acceptance of the larger view of homelessness. Dr. Golden herself emphasized that "a 'typical' homeless person is no longer a single, alcoholic, adult male. Youth and families with children are now the fastest-growing groups in the homeless and at-risk populations."[18] In the same document, in one of the most effective characterizations of the homelessness problem in Canada, Golden says, "Homelessness is the ragged edge of the social fabric." We are all part of the fabric and the ragged edge can fray until it touches all of us.

Other Canadian Reports

The Niagara Region adopted a restricted view of homelessness, defined as an "unstable living situation demonstrated by the use of emergency housing, health services or living on the street."[19] Four patterns of homelessness were suggested in the Niagara study:

- Chronic (living in shelters or on the streets most of the time)
- Episodic (moves often with periods of no housing)
- Situational (without housing due to a significant life event such as fire or domestic violence)
- Seasonal (finds housing during inclement weather)[20]

Meanwhile, other cities were joining Toronto in looking beyond the tip of the iceberg that "rooflessness" represents.

In the West, the authors of a report published in 1997 noted that "the changing nature and apparent increases in the size of the homeless population in Calgary (perhaps as high as 200 percent) have galvanized city agencies to take action."[21] They found from their survey of two overnight shelter users that

> the notion that homeless people are homeless because they want to be is no longer true, if it ever was. At least in Calgary, most homeless people want to work or find a better job, and virtually none are on the streets because they want to be. However, in the words of one

respondent, *"It's not easy to get into a job if you don't have a home. Wages here are too small; rent is too high."*[22]

The Calgary team, led by health officials, began its research a full two years before the Toronto initiative. It found that comparatively little research had been done on homeless populations and observed that

> who we define as being homeless is as much a statistical or technical statement as it is a political and value stance. A definition of homelessness is, ipso facto, a statement as to what should constitute the floor of housing adequacy below which no member of society should be permitted to fall.[23]

The Calgary team also found that

> experts are easy to agree on the extremes of a definition: total absence of shelter, sometimes called absolute or literal homelessness. But there are also many ambiguous cases. There are those who live in their cars or vans, those who temporarily "live" in jails, hospitals or other institutions, those who live in cheap hotels for two weeks of the month and on the street the rest of the time, those who live temporarily with "friends," those who live in abandoned buildings and those who consider emergency shelters their home.[24]

Calgary Alderman Bob Hawkesworth, who has provided leadership, with the support of the mayor, Al Duerr, calls for a comprehensive housing policy at the provincial and federal level in partnership with the city. Housing affordability is key in the definition of the problem in Hawkesworth's eyes.

The London Social Planning Council examined homelessness in this southwest Ontario city of over 300,000 residents.

> The 1998 survey found that perhaps realistically, individuals did not necessarily consider themselves to be homeless if they had some kind of place of their own at the time of the survey, regardless of whether it might meet general community standards. Perhaps because of the stigma of the label, "homeless," some agencies also do not perceive as

> homeless some of the clients whose accommodations may not be stable or adequate.[25]

Still, the London researchers tried to probe deeper into the experience of the people in the shelter and drop-in system on the night of March 23, 1998. They found that over one-third of women and 25 percent of men had stayed "at their home" at some point during the past three months, so the survey was missing those shelter users who were, in fact, at home on the night of the survey. Instability at home—through violence, abuse, incompatibility and other problems—put these people in the ranks of the literally homeless on an occasional basis. Sometimes they just revolved through a cycle—home to friend's home, to the street, to the shelter, then back home for a while. Other times, they could not afford rents for a full month, so the cycle began with a rented short-term room or motel, then proceeded to a shelter, then to the street, then, perhaps, when social assistance came their way, back into the motel for a few more days.

In a stroke of understatement, the London survey found the deeply rooted common feature of the homeless: "Most people don't appear to have enough money to get or keep accommodation."[26] Poverty emerged as a key common element for the London homeless.

People who develop social policy need to use a comprehensive definition of the problem. It allows us to understand its full magnitude and its broader causes, giving us at least a fighting chance to do something about it.

In their report on Canada's progress during the 1987 International Year of Shelter for the Homeless, Peter Oberlander and Arthur Fallick take us towards the broader issues, noting that

> homelessness involves more than simply the presence or absence of shelter. The search for the nature and scale of homelessness in Canada rests on the definitional problems. Is homelessness an issue of poverty? or employment? . . . Is it an issue of discrimination? or of location? of education? Or is it primarily an issue of measurement? Varied evidence increasingly points to the answer: It is all of these factors and more; no single causal factor can be used to define homelessness exclusively or successfully.[27]

An acute version of this same sentiment comes from the Alternative Housing Subcommittee for the City of Toronto, as far back as 1985: "Homelessness is not simply the lack of stable shelters; it is a life in disarray. The homeless person's existence is a public existence—there is no privacy."[28]

Is Homelessness the Opposite of "Homefulness"?

Building on this idea in his report for the UN's year of the homeless, Canadian housing researcher Alex Murray turns the table on the definitions of homelessness when he asks us to think about *homefulness*. It's a word that reminds us of other warm sounding ideas like "gratefulness," or "fulfilment," or "warmth and safety."[29]

Think about how these features of home life are completely absent in the day-to-day existence of someone who is homeless—or on the edge of losing a secure home.

Home life means:

- *Centrality, rootedness and place attachments:* Home is the physical centre of human existence. It would be hard to think of a place around which our lives revolve more completely and fundamentally.
- *Continuity, unity and order:* Home is where we create and nurture the next generation, as we were raised by the previous one, in our parents' home. Murray reminds us that there is an almost sacred quality to the notion of the home. Imagine the richness and meaning of the simple words "I'm going home."
- *Privacy, refuge, security and ownership:* Where can you feel more comfortable, safe, private and free? Imagine never having a private place. Somewhere to undress and tuck into bed. A place that's yours. Imagine not having somewhere to call "my home."
- *Self-identity:* Home is a place where you can create your identity—for the most part, you can feel in control. There are downsides to this image: Some become homeless because they were controlled or abused by others.
- *Social and family relations:* It's hard to think of a place where there is more family intimacy than home.
- *Community:* Our homes and those in the neighbourhood which surround us define our place in our community.[30]

So much for academics and task forces. What do the homeless themselves have to say? Here are just a few talking about the condition of their daily homeless lives:

> "I try to manage. I can't do it. Every month I think it will be better, but I run out of money. They're kids; they want stuff—a candy bar or a Popsicle. You can't always say no even when you know what will happen" (mother, Toronto, 1999).
>
> A 31-year-old man has difficulty in keeping a home due to clothing, food and related expenses not covered by social assistance (London, 1998).
>
> "I believe that people don't understand the homeless people at all. About their problems. . . . They don't want to listen to us. . . . We come out with our concerns, and people just say 'you're no good—you're trash.' We're all human beings and we want to be treated equally, with opportunities like other people have—and work" (a man in Calgary, 1999).
>
> "We are sons, daughters, mothers, fathers, grandmothers, grandfathers. The look of hatred is very hard to take" (woman, Calgary, 1999).

3 Counting the Homeless

One man was living in a makeshift lean-to in a Toronto ravine. There was a shallow grave nearby. This is where he had buried his wife, Mary Louise Sharrow, who had died beside him as they struggled to fight off illness "in the rough."

When firefighters showed up to put out a brush fire in a ravine, they pulled at the sticks, plastic, and haphazard sheets of wood only to find what they thought was a mattress. Using hooks, they tried to pull it out. Instead of a mattress, they pulled out the smouldering body of Jennifer Caldwell, who had been living in the pile of rubble. Jennifer had tried to live in the rough and ended up dying there. "She was 20 years old, and she had lived there for months," according to Cathy Crowe, community health nurse and founding member of the Toronto Disaster Relief Committee.[1]

A heating grate had provided warmth to a homeless man, with his sleeping bags, for several months. The corner was a busy one, exposed to traffic twenty-four hours a day. One day, a car crash sent one of the cars careening over the sidewalk, killing Brent Simmons, who was sleeping in the rough.

These are just three sad incidents. How many unrecorded homeless deaths have there been? How many people are homeless in Canada? No one knows for sure. Official, confirmed, accurate data are simply not available.

But it is important to know. Having an accurate estimate of the severity and magnitude of the homeless problem is essential to develop viable social policy. The question is comparable to the medical importance of knowing the vital signs of a patient. Data, the more accurate the better, will help accomplish the diagnosis and the cure. Also important would be an assessment of the number of people imminently at risk of becoming homeless.

In a society obsessed with data, governments might be expected to have a variety of statistics about the homeless. After all, the Canadian government spends considerable amounts of money in gathering data. A whole department, Statistics Canada, does little else.

So can the Canadian government tell its people how many people are homeless?

The simple answer is no!

On March 12, 2000, I searched the Statistics Canada web page to find an answer. "Sorry, your search for '*homeless*' retrieved 0 results." A similar try on the general Government of Canada website, with a query for "homeless" produced "Didn't find anything."

Why is there no estimate of the number of homeless people in Canada? Could documenting a problem imply an obligation to address it? Without concrete numbers, estimates or well-informed ranges, planning and policy-making stand little chance of succeeding.

No matter what the community, counting our homeless co-habitants is not an easy thing to do. The challenge is to carefully find these people, accurately identify individuals, keep track of their migrations and do all this in a way that respects personal dignity and individuality.

In Canada, sadly, most estimates of homelessness have had to rely on anecdotal evidence from a few cities. National estimates can then be attempted, through extrapolation, with final adjustments made according to the wisdom, guesswork, tea leaves and ideological predispositions of the estimators. When it comes to knowing how big a homelessness problem we have, Canadians are stuck in the statistical snowbank from which American researchers were digging themselves out fifteen years ago.

With our national government taking little responsibility for assessing the extent of the homelessness and affordable-housing situation, cities have had to step in.

The first effort was Calgary's, in 1997, where Alderman Bob Hawkesworth combined with a member of the provincial legislature, Bonnie Laing, to lead a Homelessness Initiative Ad Hoc Steering Committee. Their best estimate concluded that "for approximately 3,800 Calgarians, homelessness is a reality. For an estimated 10,000 near-homeless, it can be just a pay cheque or a life crisis away. For 130,000 working-poor Calgarians, it is something we hope they never have to face."[2]

Perhaps the largest undertaking was Toronto's Golden task force which asked Professors Springer and Mars to see if we could catch up to the Americans. As it turned out, this was possible in Toronto because a database had been kept of every "admission" to the hostel system over a nine-year period. But no one had ever organized and tallied the numbers in this huge database. However, thanks to the dutiful data-entry staff, social workers and computer specialists at Metro Hall, it became possible to conduct accurate studies.

To document the extent of homelessness, Springer and Mars used two statistical techniques. First was the snapshot approach (a method they called Point Prevalence analysis). This involved counting the number of people who were homeless at a particular moment in time. The second technique was an extended-play strategy (which they called the Period Prevalence approach) monitoring a number of people experiencing homelessness over a longer period of time. Both, they argued, are helpful in allowing us to understand homeless experiences. As it turned out, both approaches give real insights. Each can inform the design of solutions.

Where possible, it's best to use the Point and Period Prevalence approaches together. Combining the two makes sure the count includes those homeless people who do not regularly use shelters because they stay outside or occasionally crash with friends. It is likely that they will have visited a facility at least once during a year. Still, the combined estimates, while more accurate, are likely missing some homeless people who never use the available social services at all. I've met some of these people—usually living in very rough conditions in situations carved, with their own hands, out of the wilderness, tucked away in river valleys, hidden completely from the dense urban society nearby.

However, looking at homelessness data from both Point and Period Prevalence gives us a parallax effect to improve our understanding. As one of the pioneers in the approach to research has suggested, "Homelessness is neither a short-term crisis nor a long-term situation for most homeless people. It is part of an experience of residential instability that involves a patchwork of various housing strategies stitched together by people in dire housing situations."[3]

Here is what the City of Toronto Action Task Force reported:

- Almost 26,000 different individuals used hostels in Toronto in 1996. Between 3,100 and 3,200 used the system on any given night (this number is much higher on winter nights). Over the nine years from 1988 to 1996, about 170,000 different individuals used hostels.
- Seventy-one percent of hostel users are male; 29 percent are female.
- Families represented 46 percent of the people using hostels in Toronto in 1996. The fastest-growing users of hostels are youth under 18 and families with children.
- In 1988, 24 percent of households in the hostel system were headed by women; by 1996, 37 percent were headed by women.
- Nineteen percent of the homeless population, or 5,300 homeless people, were children!
- Only 25 percent of shelter users use shelters for emergencies only, that is, they stay for only one or two nights. The other 75 percent use them as transitional housing or are chronic hostel users.
- About 4,400 people (17 percent of those who use the shelter system) are chronic users who stay in the hostel system for one year or longer. As a consequence, this 17 percent uses about 46 percent of the beds and services.
- At least 47 percent of hostel users come from outside of Toronto.[4]

Unfortunately, in most Canadian cities or communities, such data do not exist at all, are only partly tabulated in others and are complete in only a few.

So when we review the dimension of homelessness in Canada, we mostly stand on sand. Every study, estimate, projection and count seems to be based on different assumptions, employs incompatible statistical techniques and uses differing definitions. Compiling these numbers into a full, totally accurate and agreed-on picture may not be possible at this time in Canadian social-science development. It's a rather sad commentary.

With comprehensive data from across Canada, we would know how large a problem we face, and we could design a response appropriate to what people are experiencing. But we cannot. We can only stitch together the scraps of available data and try to view the problem from many angles, even if parts are a little out of focus.

Descriptions of the homeless may include some unfamiliar phrases. These terms amount to a hierarchy of homeless experiences. Collectively, these images and terms constitute a sad catalogue of the variety of homeless circumstances confronted by thousands of people in Canada today.

Sleeping Rough

Sleeping rough is a street term. For the uninitiated, it sounds like wilderness camping. Almost romantic.

For the homeless resorting to this last-ditch effort to survive, there is nothing romantic about it. Sleeping rough is rough—there are no two ways about it. Some simply do not survive. You read about three people who did not survive this at the beginning of this chapter.

Where do people sleeping actually sleep?

Park benches

How often do the media show that prostrate fellow with his brown bag, sprawled on a bench? However, these benches have become less safe in recent years. You can get easily rolled and have your stuff stolen—that last photo of your kids, your medicare card, your only remaining photo ID. You can also be badly beaten up in the process. In the late spring of 2000, a man sleeping on a bench in front of City Hall had his fingers chopped off as he slept. Homeless people have even been murdered on or near park benches. Some old-timers have found safe benches, under lights and visible, especially in the summer. But inevitably the park-bench solution finds you miserable and wet in the rain, cold in winter and totally exposed all the time.

Bushes in parks sometimes provide privacy. However, many bushes have been cut to improve safety, panoramic views or to protect the innocent from the horrors of witnessing a couple necking or having semi-public sex. So much for that option.

"Homes" are also found in park washrooms—in those few places where they still exist. A wonderful European tradition—and social-justice facility—has become an extraneous "cost centre" in most Canadian municipal budgets. We complain that street people relieve themselves on other people's property, but we've left them no alternative. A visit to a nearby restaurant washroom is usually met with a prohibition or with disdain. Little wonder that many homeless people have mastered the art of drinking one cup of coffee, for hours, in the corner shop. At least this buys access to a toilet and a place to clean up a bit. The coffee costs some coin, one of the motivations for panhandling. But imagine panhandling by telling the truth: "Can you spare a loonie for a coffee—and so I can empty my painfully full bladder?"

Diverse nooks and crannies

I once counted fifty people sleeping rough on the campus of the University of Toronto. That school's officials had no idea there were so many stairwells, alcoves and bush clusters that provided hidden havens. Their solution? Trim the bushes. To their credit, they also opened a food bank that provides some nourishment to the non-tuition-paying campus residents.

Store doorways sometimes provide safety and protection from the most severe elements. Although many homeless people have been found dead in these horribly inadequate niches, the advantages are obvious. The doorway alcove is a little protection and the store's closed. No one is likely to bother you, especially if you get up and move on before opening time.

In the past decade, bank machines, in their heated little rooms, have provided security—and what's more secure than a bank? Usually, an after-hours customer will let you in, perhaps feeling guilty that he's taking out money while you have none. Occasionally, a compassionate bank manager will tolerate this situation come morning. Eventually, though, customers complain or the rate of night-time transactions falls, and the police or private security are asked to move these people along. Sleeping rough inevitably faces the legendary ruthlessness of economics.

Bus shelters

Eugene Upper died in a transit shelter—another "popular" spot to sleep rough. A Bay Street bus shelter in downtown Toronto was also the final resting place of 50-year-old Adrian Vernon Filmore in the summer of

2000. Having left New Brunswick six years before, he had struggled with his housing crisis for some time. In the middle of the night, his throat was slit as he slept in what he believed might be a safe haven, in the moon's shadow of a nondescript Ontario government building, which at one time housed the Ministry of Housing.

Most people don't mind seeing someone sleeping in their local bus shelter; there's often a sense of relief that the poor soul has somewhere to be at all. However, such sentimentality hasn't stopped some communities from removing the benches in the most-used transit shelters, making it less appealing to the street residents. Protests from local businesses have even resulted in the total dismantling of bus shelters in some places.

Eugene Upper's Spadina Avenue bus shelter disappeared within a week after he froze to death in it.

Sidewalk grates

Where does the heat that the roofless attempt to capture with their pieces of cardboard, or their charity-given sleeping bags or their blankets, come from? Cities with old energy systems have exhaust pipes that release unused steam through steel grates in the sidewalk. Where energy is wasted, usually through some sort of vent, the wintertime homeless will naturally be attracted like heat-seeking missiles. We are all attracted to the warmth of the fire on a cold day. Steam may be as close as it gets for someone living on the street. For the homeless, these hot grates can be precious, but they're also among the most dangerous of refuges—dangerous, because steam can scald. Asleep, even unconscious, a person exposed to the pressurized hot vapours can be injured and sent to the health clinic or, worse, to the emergency ward. But sleeping on a heating or exhaust grate does not guarantee survival on Toronto streets. In the spring of 1999, a man named Al died on a grate just under the Queen's Park office window of the premier of Ontario. (His family requested that Al's last name not be released.)

However, the most rapidly growing form of housing for low-income Canadians today is the sleeping bag. These donated survival suits are left on the street and picked up by volunteers and city workers, to be cleaned and redistributed. In a poignantly pragmatic gesture, one formerly homeless man, now an artist, has created laminated plastic corrugated fold-up mini-tent-like covers for homeless people. These are designed to protect sleeping bags from being soaking wet by morning. Ontario College of Art and Design students held an exhibition of various designs for street and sidewalk accommodation. The show was held at the tony Design Exchange at King and Bay Streets, chosen, I suppose, because of its proximity to the practical applications.

Under bridges, in tunnels

Toronto's most affluent census tract, Rosedale, has a concentration of under-bridge fabrications, sometimes for whole families. Some things don't change, though: The rusty oil-barrel heater of the '30s still makes its appearance on cold nights, charged with the cast-off wood of a comfortable city. Passersby don't call the fire department—or any other department—as they drive past, late at night. It's just part of the scenery. Elaborate "homes" of discarded construction materials can be found under railway and highway bridges. They make a common refuge, despite the noise above or the dinginess below.

If the pattern of some U.S. cities is repeated in our metropolises, trackside accommodation in the subways may become a reality one of these days. Subterranean maze towns are part of New York's venerable network. Michele Landsberg, writing while she lived in the Big Apple for a few years in the 1980s, recounted her experiences in *This Is New York, Honey!*

> Worst of all, of course, is the deepening chasm between the incalculably rich and the destitute homeless. Though Mayor Koch advised people who complained on behalf of the homeless to "see your priest if you feel guilty," most New Yorkers I met care passionately. Few Canadians would believe the horrific sights that are shrugged off here as routine. One evening last week, I carelessly clattered down the stairs of Grand Central Station to a lower concourse and abruptly stepped into a scene from Dante's *Inferno*. In a vast, dim hall, mine were the only echoing footsteps. All around the floor, misshapen figures crouched silently by the walls. Nothing moved but a few heads, lifted to stare at my intrusion. About three hundred people live in the station all winter. Many of them are too immobilised to make it outside to the food lines and shelters. "Severely swollen legs are the results of being on your feet all the time and sleeping while sitting up," a young worker from the Coalition for the Homeless told me. "Eventually, the condition can be fatal." Every night at ten o'clock,

coalition volunteers hand out sandwiches, apples and cartons of milk to those who cannot walk as far as the doors.[5]

Landsberg tells us that there were 40,000 homeless in New York in 1989. In 1997, Toronto reported 26,000 different people using its shelter system, and 5,000 emergency beds (hostel bed or mat) full every night—the street people who were not inside weren't counted. Given the population of the two cities, the relative proportion of homeless in Toronto is alarming.

Squats

With squats, expect the unexpected. Even the rooftops of factories or stores have been tried. Who checks the tops of buildings? So have the lowest of the lower floors, tucked away under ramps, in parking garages—where security staff rarely venture. Obscure emergency-exit trenches and stairwells usually turn out to be temporary accommodation. Then the squatters' emergency becomes rooflessness—without an exit.

In street parlance, a makeshift home in a building left to rot is called a *squat*. The word used to mean "to crouch" or "to hide." In Europe, squatting became a major human-rights issue and social-justice controversy. In Amsterdam in the early '80s, squatters insisted on their housing rights and won important new legislation. In Canadian cities, squats are fiercely defended and surrounded by secrecy, to avoid police or building-inspector hassles. Only trusted outreach workers are privileged to know the precise location of entrances. Surprisingly caring social networks can form within a squat community. On the flip side, frustrations can also flare up in these often dangerous spaces.

Abandoned buildings provide the most used and obvious escape from the elements. However, empty structures hold their own dangers: Fires are the most frequent killers in the night.

In December 1997, just after the new mega-city was born, I visited the Rooster Squat, which had been set up in the dark interior of the soon-to-be-demolished Victory Soya Mills factory, at the east end of Toronto's largely silenced harbour. Built in the early part of the twentieth century, these massive industrial structures had long been abandoned. Few people I knew had ever ventured onto these properties, which had recently been taken over by the city for tax arrears. Despite holding the position of city councillor for this area, I had not known anyone was living in this derelict industrial backwater. I was not prepared for what I saw. As we made our way through the gigantic and terrifying property, the massive processing hoppers seemed to reach out in the gloom, ready to suck anyone without a sure footing into their forty-foot depths.

Street workers had alerted me and Olivia (the councillor who represented the city ward just across the street) to a plan to evict the young squatters—mostly squeegee kids. The decision was apparently made by the city's real-estate lawyers.

It was Christmastime. The deed would happen within days. The squatters (over a dozen, led by the strangely charismatic "Moose," the father/mother figure of the group, along with his very young wife, who was five months' pregnant) were joined by homeless advocates. These included the Ontario Coalition Against Poverty (OCAP) and other street workers like Beric German and Cathy Crowe, who ministered to health needs as best she could while quietly raging against a system that could have runaway teens living in such Dickensian conditions.

Granted admission by both city staff, who looked the other way, and the squatters, we made our way up dark staircases, through a huge grain-processing hall, between monstrous columns that held up the ceiling sixty feet above. Only thin slits at the roofline provided light that showed deep concrete pits lining the central corridor. Once through this horror movie set, we climbed more metal stairs to reach some rooms, five storeys up. Here, a fire pit was smouldering—the only source of warmth on this minus-ten-degree day. Even though it was noon, flashlights had to work the spaces, like a classic *X-Files* scene. Under mounds of old sleeping bags and blankets, a few of the street kids were still awakening. Others, Moose said, had already headed for their spots under the Gardiner Expressway, where they were picking up a little cash for food, washing windshields where they could.

I'd seen squats before, but this was the worst. The fumes from the burning wood were clearly dangerous. These kids' lungs were being poisoned, and they could easily freeze if temperatures dropped. And no emergency-care workers could negotiate the labyrinth, even if they tried.

In response to an appeal for an outdoor tent to relocate the kids, a Quebec leasing company shipped three large collapsible ones down Highway 401 by bus. There was a big celebration—especially as it was Quebeckers who had come to the rescue of the homeless in rich downtown

Toronto! Full media attention fell on the motley crew of homeless frontliners who had refused to go quietly. Public support began to build. Normally jaded journalists were moved. They even brought coffee and doughnuts. Reporters got to know some of the kids by name. Perhaps it was the Christmastime morality play–like scene or maybe it was that homelessness could no longer be ignored, the kids couldn't be blamed anymore. Whatever it was, this squat was shifting public opinion. Suburban strangers brought food to the windswept dock. Whole turkey dinners appeared from nowhere. Was this *The Miracle on Cherry Street*? The city hired a security company to watch over things and make sure the kids were OK. The security company, Intelligard, had once been targeted by OCAP, who alleged nasty treatment of street people. Now the guards were protecting the kids.

Still, these defiant kids said, "We won't go!" But the building was dangerous and clearly hurting them physically—never mind the other pains they lived with, the ones that brought them there. When Moose's wife was taken to hospital with terrible lung problems, everyone agreed that something had to change.

No hostel spaces existed so that this community could keep their extended family together.

Faced with this, a team of us got together to figure out how we could have a "new" squat built right next door—on vacant land that was in legal limbo. Two huge used transport trailers were hauled to the site. No longer roadworthy, they were lent to us by a philanthropic organization for a couple of months. Green City Construction, a small local contractor, joined with Local 27 of the Carpenters' Union to install doors and windows to meet the fire chief's specifications. They involved some of the teenagers in their work. Public health ordered portable toilets. A generator, to give a little heat and light, came from donated funds through OCAP. The kids moved in. Demolition of the old squat began. As spring arrived, the kids relocated, mostly because the trailers were promised to far-off lands, filled with the beneficence of Canadians wanting to help developing countries.

Each squat has its own narrative, and the politics of this one were determined because homelessness had become a defining issue in the city's recent election. No one wanted the council to evict homeless kids, but no one wanted the kids to continue to get sick in their terrifying digs. Caught without a housing policy for the homeless, the city had to resort to absurd lengths. All this helped pave the way for a call for a renewed federal involvement in affordable-housing construction.

The vast majority of those confined to the street are not as fortunate as those with refuge in empty buildings. Most street people live lives of constant migration, moving like nomads to reach the services they need to survive. These services, inevitably disconnected, keep the homeless on the move. Damaged and diseased feet are the most common ailment at the clinics.

Parking garages

Huge, multi-level parking structures, especially the extreme lower or higher levels, have become housing for some. Typically, camp will be set up as far away from the ticket taker as possible. Under ramps and stairs is best. Weekends downtown give people a chance to drift into the garage, when there's no commuter parking demand. When Cathy Crowe and I were called to a five-storey, above-ground parking structure, we knew from the tone of the voice what was in store. Another death. Three frozen, piled-up sleeping bags, remnants of coffees and doughnuts bought with panhandled cash, a few cigarette butts, a candle in a can were all that was left of this man's life. He had died in the bitter cold.

Cars

Many of Canada's homeless start out by living in their cars. As rents and other expenses overtake the monthly budget, the car becomes a last-ditch attempt to stay sheltered. For others, abandoned cars, even furloughed railway cars, make campsites. But it can be a cat-and-mouse game that includes property owners and parking-lot managers. In Calgary, a policy allows individuals with cars to sleep in them in heated parking facilities.[6]

Tents

Far from their "proper" place on groomed campgrounds, makeshift tent accommodations are signs of desperation. Usually hidden from the view of passing motorists, they are difficult to find. Most locales are overgrown industrial sites that owners and insurance companies have abandoned owing to the costs of toxic soil clean-up. But it's easy to be beaten up when there's no one around. The violence is senseless: There's nothing much to steal. Perhaps the tent. Urban hikers stumble on remains and have to report the casualties.

Makeshift homes are also springing up in ravines—lean-tos, stick constructed tepees, dugout caves or underground tunnels. Construction materials hauled great distances can make the structures more elaborate. These places can know tragedy: Witness the man who buried his wife, Mary Louise Sharrow, in a shallow grave in the woods along Don River Valley, near the spot where they'd made camp for months. She couldn't withstand the cold, and she died of a massive heart attack. He wouldn't leave her side.

Emergency shelters for the homeless

Emergency shelters, the institutional response to homelessness, are what Canadians know best. Most larger communities now have shelters, although some places still resist—believing that such an initiative would be the beginning of a slippery slope.

Shelters come in every shape and size imaginable. Some come close to providing respectable accommodation—Victoria's Cool Aid Society's Street Link hostel is a standout in this regard. Others barely qualify to be called helpful, because of crowded conditions and inadequate provisions to meet the basic needs of those they serve.

In 1987, according to the Canadian Council on Social Development, there were 472 shelters in Canada, with a nightly capacity of 13,797. Average occupancy at that time was 77 percent. (Ontario occupancy was 101 percent.[7]) Overall, this would suggest that about 10,000 homeless people were bedded down in Canadian shelters on a typical night in 1987. As we turn the century, Canada does not have a complete or current count of emergency facilities. Are new ones opening their doors too quickly to keep up?

Since that report was completed, housing activists suggest that about two to three new shelters opened every month in Canada during 1998 and 1999. With an average occupancy of fifty to seventy-five people, this would have added 2,500 to 5,000 new beds in that two-year period alone.

The Canadian Council on Social Development study of shelter use in 1986 found that 260,000 people spent at least one night in a shelter. The average stay was 19.4 days. The study estimated that, taking into account people who stayed in more than one shelter during the year, about 130,000 people had used the 283 shelters that reported data.[8]

Funded by combinations of provincial governments, city governments, community organizations, non-profit charities, churches and benevolent philanthropists, shelters struggle along on budgets that are always tight. When all operating costs are taken into account, the daily cost for a hostel or shelter bed runs between $20 and $60 a night, depending upon the city and the specific nature of the facility. Quick mathematics shows that this cost amounts to $7,300 to $22,000 a year per bed. Many reports have documented that building and maintaining permanent affordable-housing units would be significantly less expensive while, at the same time, being a more healthy and supportive environment for the people involved.[9]

Canada's largest hostel, and one of the oldest, is Toronto's Seaton House, which has been used as a shelter since 1957. Over 600 men can sleep on sheetless double bunks, boots and shoes tied tightly together around ankles to avoid thefts. Many staff are on shift—managers, intake workers. Procedures, regulations and security issues are ever present. Many rooms, each of which is approximately the size of an elementary school classroom, have twenty to forty men each. In row after row of double-stacked cots in the dark night, the mentally ill, terrified, are packed inches away from the addicted and the panicked, bewildered and recently homeless. It's a hellish existence. The facility has been nicknamed Satan House and the big concrete sign at the front seems consciously designed to look like a tombstone. What a welcome! Still, the city's social workers and hostel staff do their best to provide as safe and respectful an environment as they can. Despite these best efforts, there can be flare-ups. Violence in such conditions is hard to avoid, although various inquests and public hearings have produced changes in security practices and other management approaches. After years of pressure for change from advocates for the homeless, city council instructed Seaton House to abandon their practice of turfing all 400 of the nightly residents (of the emergency hostel section) onto the downtown streets at 7:00 A.M. to fend for themselves until re-admission time at 4:00 P.M. Bag lunches are provided for those heading out to find work.

Hostel manager Boris Rosolak has been working in the heart of the debate between homeless advocates and downtown bureaucracies to restructure the place. A committee headed by then local Councillor Olivia Chow had called for a downsizing and humanizing of the huge hostel. The mega-city council is now putting millions into the remaking of Seaton House, even abandoning the old name with its bad memories.

Four separate, more specialized programs and facilities will replace the monolith. It remains to be seen if the complex "new vision" of emergency services for the homeless can emerge—with tailored approaches and services for those with addictions, people dealing with mental-health challenges, short-term emergency housing and longer-term transitional homes.

Most communities have smaller hostels. Even big cities have many little facilities, with only dozens of beds instead of hundreds. Council approvals for modest facilities are easier, because neighbourhood opposition is less likely to be an insurmountable problem. I'm choosing my words carefully because hell hath no fury like a neighbourhood faced with a proposed hostel, no matter what the size. My most recent experience was being energetically and enthusiastically chewed out by a crowd of over 100 residents of my ward: They were opposing a shelter for thirty homeless women to be housed in an old and empty police station. Frankly, while I understood the crowd's fears—reduced property values and safety concerns—I honestly believed they would not materialize. With my support, in the end the hostel was accepted by Council. In a very positive development, a neighbourhood support group came together to organize a welcome barbecue, fundraising events and social outings. Eventually, the emergency hostel was transformed to a sixteen-bed, longer-term transition housing project. Fortunately, properties for sale in the immediate neighbourhood, including one right next door, continued to sell above asking prices.

The Cool Aid Society's Street Link hostel in Victoria is one of Canada's newest multi-purpose emergency shelters. Manager Bill Wong took me through a few months after it opened, in the spring of 1999. Dignity is clearly the watchword for staff and volunteers. Here, there is a secure section for men and for women alike, with common rooms and cafeteria for casual getting together. Imagine my reaction, after the Seaton House experience, to a facility with two to a room maximum, with no double bunk beds. Sheets and pillows! Windows! It's not luxury. But it gives both soul and body a chance to recover.

In the late 1980s it became clear that there were not enough beds in the shelter systems of most cities, and their councils were not geared up or motivated to expand. Morally concerned citizens stepped in—especially the churches. While they quietly prayed for justice for the homeless, some congregations decided to put their bricks and mortar and their volunteer time and energy into providing rudimentary shelter—mats for the church-hall floor, coffee and home baking served from the synagogue, church or mosque kitchen. They began to open their doors on weeknights to give shelter to strangers.

Again, with sad predictability, some neighbours objected. What would the nighttime refuges do to property values? Don't we pay taxes to make sure that the homeless are cared for—elsewhere? Fortunately, do-gooders normally prevail in these backyard battles, and the programs proceed.

The food banks of the early 1980s, the first founded in Edmonton, were the initial warnings of the building wave of income transfer from poor to rich in Canada. The church-basement emergency refuges were the next. Like the food banks, they were supposed to be temporary—just until prayers were answered and governments faced their responsibilities. Now, food-bank use includes a huge proportion of the low-income populations of Canadian cities. As much as one-tenth of the population in some metropolitan areas now relies on the cast-off food products and charity of others for basic monthly nutrition. For a growing number of Canadians, it's *Pay the Rent or Feed the Kids*, as publisher and author Mel Hurtig titles his recent book.[10]

But now, two decades after food-bank philanthropy began, even free food cannot stave off homelessness for a growing number of Canadians. Hundreds of thousands are paying more than 50 percent of their income in housing costs. The slightest personal crisis, illness or other financial misfortune drives them into rental arrears and inexorably into homelessness. Today, the church basements are no longer large enough. Shelters are having to expand into the sanctuaries, with the dispossessed stretching out on hard pews. For the homeless in these circumstances, it's back out on the street first thing in the morning.

Motels and Hotels for the Homeless

"Hey, Mom, are we going to a motel? That's cool!"

After exhausting the options for permanent housing, social workers are increasingly turning to temporary emergency motel accommodation for the families at their office doorstep. Please understand that these are not the luxury motels of TV promotions. The facilities of choice are barely able to keep their accounts current, struggling for customers on barren throughways, because their former trucker clientele has moved to the superhighways.

Typically, the motel room is small. The walls are thin. The washroom is tiny. If there is a pint-sized fridge to keep some food fresh, that's considered lucky. Desks, tables, chairs and lamps are all scarce. The extra bed stuffed in to allow a maximum of two per mattress leaves little space for walking. In some urban areas, nearly every vacant, low-rent motel room is now contracted by the municipal government. (Toronto now contracts with motels as far away as Niagara Falls to find space.)

Homelessness is a boon to the fleabag motel industry. Somehow, the mothers (there are a few families with fathers, too) manage in these strained circumstances. Showing up at a new school in the neighbourhood can be tough for a "kid from the motels." The Scarborough motel strip, east of Toronto, is infamous for the concentration of hostel facilities. An infusion of kids in the past few years has put pressure on the local elementary schools, now stuffed to the rafters with the extra unplanned population. Tensions have run high in the area because the motel crowd seems to be putting the education of the "regular neighbourhood kids" at risk. Matters are not made easier by the inevitable racial mix of the newcomers from the motels. Established communities now feel that the pace of change has accelerated beyond the acceptable.

The waiting time for rent-geared-to-income social housing is desperate. It ranges from six months or a year in provinces like British Columbia, Quebec or Saskatchewan to Ontario's astounding *eighteen years for a family of four*. (By the time your family's name comes up for assisted housing, your kids are too old to be called kids and you no longer qualify for the home you have waited so long to secure.)

Some cities, like Vancouver, have hotels rather than motels. Historically, the hotels have been a mixed blessing. Remnants of a former resource economy, the hotels of the Downtown Eastside became infamous. They usually featured bars where fellows fresh from six months in the bush could spread their enthusiasm. Rooms were not meant for long-term housing. High-spending flings were the norm. As the resource world settled down and migrant work transformed into permanent inland communities and economies, Vancouver's hotels had to "take what we could get" and saw the opportunity to rent rooms to permanent residents with low incomes. Hotels became a substitute for affordable housing. The poor maintenance and appalling conditions in some of these hotels became legendary. Hundreds of these hotel rooms shifted towards a clientele that embraced those most in need. Addictions of residents had a magnetic affect on preying dealers. Health conditions deteriorated for residents and the community alike.

Eventually, this led to an uprising by community activists like Libby Davies, a founder of the Downtown Eastside Residents' Association (DERA). Davies is now member of Parliament for the area and author of a 1999 national study on homelessness.[11] She is probably the leading advocate on homeless issues in Parliament. With no "living rooms," the hotel district forced people into the streets to escape the oppressive conditions of their confined spaces. DERA created a public "living room" through the transformation of a magnificent old public building now called the Carnegie Centre. Low-cost meals, a library facility, education and health programs are all combined with a non-judgmental atmosphere in which the homeless can feel at home. With this momentum, efforts to bring some of the slum hotel landlords into a zone of appropriate behaviour were pressed forward by city councillors and some brilliant community activists like Jim Greene.

Even more positive were the investments by the provincial government in facilitating the purchase of some of the hotels by community groups, with involvement from the city. Anyone interested in transformative social policy should visit the community-run hotels, right beside the slumlord establishments. What a contrast! It's amazing how the same type of physical facility can be made to work in such different ways vis-à-vis the lives of the residents. As one man who had lived through the transformation of his hotel told me, "You can get your life back together and make a contribution, once you have a decent roof over your head." This wisdom from the street still eludes national policy-makers.

The "Proto-Homeless"—On the Knife-Edge

Proto-homeless is a term invented by sociologists to describe people who are on the edge of housing security. It's one step shy of walking out of your home forever—or being kicked out. The proto-homeless live on the knife-edge of fear. Their circumstances are as varied at month-end as one can imagine. One person is staying on a family member's couch—"just till I get myself together." "Couch-surfing" is the new bittersweet term used by people shifting from friends' homes to families' family rooms and back. Another person is moving back home with the folks. Another is a young couple, recently married, living at home, much less likely to have their own place than was the case ten or twenty years ago. They tried to afford life on their own, but with one in school and the other holding down that minimum-wage retail job, there's not enough for rent in the overheated markets of many Canadian cities. Yet another is borrowing from friends and family to cover rent arrears.

The proto-homeless double up with siblings' families—two sets of parents and children living in an apartment designed for one family. Such overcrowding is commonplace is some urban high-rises. Because such places have fewer square feet per person than the standards set by the international codes for the treatment of prisoners of war, it's not surprising that doubling-up (and even tripling-up) produces strained relationships.

Are these people housed? Not in the way they have a reason to expect, given the contribution they are making to the social and economic well-being of their communities. They should be making their own homes as their parents were able to do. The fact that so many fewer are able to do so today is testimony to the shifts in resources taking place in the Canadian economy. Low-income part-time work has grown quickly, while long-term full-time substantial wage work has declined, except for a spike in the employment curve involving the high-tech sector. Absurd lottery-winning-like salaries in the computer world are more than matched by the growth in low-paid work. The old days when minimum wages were periodically increased at the rate of inflation are long gone. Now, government policies keep minimum wages constant for a decade while rents increase 10 to 30 percent in the same period.

Do standards in Canada match the criteria set by the United Nations for stable housing, considered a right by the Universal Charter of Human Rights? No.

The "At-Risk of Homelessness"

Any family with a falling income relative to the rising costs, or even stable costs, of necessity faces homelessness at an accelerating pace. For years, Statistics Canada regarded any household that spent more than 30 percent of its income on housing as poor. This was the official definition of poverty.[12] Now, over a million Canadians belong to households paying more than 50 percent of their income in rents. Researchers are especially interested in those who rent as opposed to those buying homes. This is because those who are purchasing housing may be paying a high percentage of income on mortgage payments, but they are building equity and security at the same time. Experts working in housing policy have begun to look closely at the number of people who spend more than 50 percent of their income on housing costs and they are redefining the poverty line.

Tenants paying more than 50 percent of their income in rent are locked into a revenue/expense structure that can lead to the risk of losing their housing. Falling a few days behind in rent becomes more likely and more frequent as competing demands challenge even the most careful home-budget manager. Evictions for a day's late payment of rent are rising in some provinces, partly due to changed legislation, partly due to low vacancy rates. Both have provided incentives for landlords to evict tenants and raise rents. The Ontario government recently made this practice easier and more lucrative for landlords because there is now no rent control on vacated units. An empty unit can fetch a 20 to 100 percent rent increase in the tight market. Pushing out a tenant on a technicality can reap huge rewards.

Only a few provinces provide this hard data on evictions. From the few studies available, I estimate that 5,000–7,000 Canadian households are subjected to eviction proceedings every month: 60,000–84,000 households a year. This does not include those who leave voluntarily before any eviction procedure begins.

The Poorly, Dangerously or Inadequately Housed

A final aspect of Canada's growing housing problem needs to be highlighted. The disturbing decline in the quality of low-income rental housing stock is another manifestation of the crisis. In some municipalities, this is the dominant face of the housing problem. There may be few homeless in the street but there are growing numbers of houses, flats and apartments with slum-like standards.

Fires are the most terrifying and lethal consequences of substandard housing. Deaths by fire in poor-quality housing have risen to alarming levels in cities such as Winnipeg, prompting Mayor Glen Murray to join the effort for a national housing strategy—not because street homelessness was a big problem in his city, but to stem the tide of fires in the homes of the poor. The issue surfaced at the 1998 meeting of the Big City Mayors held in his windy city. Mayor Murray reported to his fellow mayors that twenty-six people had died in house fires in the previous two years.

Winnipeg is not alone. Regina and Saskatoon reported that substandard housing conditions created the housing problem in their communities.

Aboriginal housing conditions have continued to be a national embarrassment. Not even the United Nations has been able to ignore the disproportionate numbers of homeless First Nations citizens on the streets of Canadian cities. Much of the housing in the aboriginal communities and reserves does not even come close to basic standards.

Are They Really Homeless?

In an attempt to portray the "reality" of homeless life in a big city, *Globe and Mail* reporter John Stackhouse spent a week on the streets of Toronto in December 1999. Armed with a $5 bill and little else, he wrote a multipart series about his experiences in the world of the homeless. The series provoked widespread discussion, and the paper printed many responses, including one that I contributed. Here are some of Stackhouse's observations. (Readers will note that Stackhouse's "My life without a home" is only one week without a home.)

My Life without a Home

Saturday, December 18, 1999

After eight years of covering the Third World, an award-winning Globe and Mail *journalist returns to confront a mystery: Canada obviously is prospering and yet it now has legions of people adrift on the street. Who are they? Do they have to live this way? There is only one way to find out.*

By John Stackhouse

Toronto—I did not appreciate the true meaning of homelessness until a white stretch limousine stopped beside me in Toronto's downtown theatre district, blowing its exhaust in my face for five, then 10, then 15 minutes as I slouched against a fire hydrant, panhandling for dinner.

It was the humiliation more than the pollution that grated me as I repeatedly asked the driver to pull forward or back up, explaining that I was breathing fumes and my business had collapsed since his limo had stopped there, obscuring my slight presence.

I could have moved as easily as he could. I knew that. But this was my spot. The limo was on my turf, and when you're on the street with so little else, turf means everything.

"Well," the driver said smugly, "I guess the car is allowed to be here."

"This is a fire hydrant," I replied, growing angrier.

That was when the driver started laughing. "Do what you have to do, fella. Why don't you call the police?"

When his passenger emerged from La Fenice, a popular upscale restaurant that the driver kept calling La Finesse, he, too, laughed at my request to move the car.

Another man, dressed in a golf sweater and cords despite the cold, stopped to listen to our dispute. "Call the cops if you're so bothered," he told me.

I rose from the sidewalk and said: "Excuse me, sir, I am a human being. I have a right to be here."

Just then, a young man in a stylish overcoat intervened. "Actually, there is a bylaw that says a car can stand next to the curb and idle for only three minutes," he explained to the man in the golf sweater. "Really, the limousine should move."

"You're going to listen to this guy?" Mr. Golf Sweater said, seeming to be genuinely astonished that someone would do so. "He's just a street person."

"I'm a human being," I repeated.

"You're a loser," he snapped back.

I felt like punching him flat across the restaurant's patio fence, but the smartly dressed young man spoke up again.

"Sir," he said to Mr. Golf Sweater. "He lives on the street. He doesn't need to be degraded any more by you."

"He's a loser," the man said, now laughing. "Look at him!"

"He's a human being," the young man said.

A larger crowd was now around us, prompting a nervous restaurateur to push his way through to my side, where he encouraged the onlookers to move along.

"You don't even know my name and you're judging me," I said to the man in the golf sweater.

"Oh yeah. I'm sure you have a name, and a mother and father and all that crap," he replied, and then took his wife by the arm and walked away.

In a few moments, the rest of the crowd was gone too, some laughing, a few shaking their heads, a couple cursing the homeless, and I was back on the pavement, feeling an invisible chill slice through the concrete and my blanket, and then up my spine.

It was numbingly cold, damp and now dark. The theatre crowd was gone, and I was alone again, sitting next to the limousine's exhaust as it continued to idle, 20 minutes after its arrival.

"Aren't you going to move?" I asked the limousine customer, who was waiting for the rest of his party to emerge on the sidewalk, wine glass in hand.

"We'll be another minute," he said, not looking at me.

Ten minutes later, the car pulled away.

During seven days and six nights on the street, without money, ID, a surname or history, I never sank as low, at least psychologically, as that night on King Street West.

The driver and his customer, like the man in the golf sweater, knew a homeless person like me would never call the cops, not for a case of John Doe v. The Big White Limo. They knew they could carry on as though I did not exist. They knew I amounted to nothing in our society, and I knew it too.

When I moved back to Canada recently, after eight years in India, I was surprised by the level of public debate about homelessness, but more by how few voices were coming from the street.

It was obvious there were more people living on the streets—begging, sleeping and, it seemed, just trying to get by—than I had remembered growing up in Toronto.

Yet most of the people I saw on the street did not look desperate, however bedraggled their appearance. And why not? The city was more prosperous than ever, with more jobs than people in the booming Southern Ontario economy, so many that anyone not physically or mentally disabled would be challenged to stay unemployed.

Out of confusion as much as concern, I moved to the street to gain a different point of view, with only a change of clothes, sleeping bag and $5. A week later, returning home with $350 and a few extra pounds from starchy shelter food, I was convinced the "crisis" that the federal government spoke of yesterday when it announced more money for the "homeless" often bears little resemblance to life on the street.

For instance:

Scarce public resources are abused by crack dealers, chronic alcoholics and drug abusers, professional drifters and other criminals.

Beggars earn professional wages, tax-free, that easily run over $200 a day at this time of year, and rarely dip below $10 an hour in slow times.

Many publicly funded shelters are grossly mismanaged, and have become havens for contraband traffickers.

There is more free food available than all the homeless can eat. But because it is free in most shelters, it is doled out to those who do not need it as well as to those who do.

There is a deep well of public concern and charity, but much of it is misspent while those with the deepest needs, physical and mental, are overshadowed by panhandlers and others who crowd the public view.

Most of the panhandlers I got to know are serious crack addicts and alcoholics and spend almost all their begging money on their addictions.

After his first day on the streets, Stackhouse recounts his first experience spending a night in a shelter:

Glancing at my wrist in frustration, I fear only that I'm late for the Good Shepherd's shelter opening at 5:30.

When I get there, 10 minutes late, a man explains to a dozen of us that the shelter is full, as are most others in Toronto. He suggests that we try Council Fire, across the street from the Regent Park housing project, where the Salvation Army runs a shelter for native people.

Somehow, alcoholism seems as rampant among natives on Toronto streets as it was two decades ago, and far greater than in any other community on the street.

The shelter, which takes in non-native people as well, does not open until 9:30 P.M. Located in one of the city's roughest neighbourhoods, it is a well-known crack centre and a last resort for the drunk, wasted and working homeless who can't get to the other shelters that follow earlier curfews.

Before the Good Shepherd man turns around and locks the door in front of us, Tim, a big guy who looks like a Junior A hockey player, asks for hot chocolate for his girlfriend, who is passed out on the floor of the shelter entrance.

Another reject, James, laughs at the sign above us warning that anyone caught with drugs or alcohol will be barred from the shelter for 30 days. He has been barred from more hostels than he can count, but there's always one that will take him in, he says. Especially when it's cold outside.

There is still no sign of hot chocolate, so I head back to Yonge Street to panhandle with the few winos who are still on their feet.

Frankie, an old pro, is one of them. "Bad night," he says. He has positioned himself just north of Dundas, outside a big Gap store that is dominated by a two-storey billboard projecting beautiful people for blocks.

"How much you got?" I ask Frankie.

"Three bucks in three hours," he says.

Frankie is so drunk he can barely stand, but he continues panhandling, leaning against a doorway as he holds out a cup to the evening shoppers.

"I don't like this place," he continues. "I'm gonna get off the street. Really, I am." He laughs, showing only a few remaining teeth, and they look ready to fall out. His stringy hair, dangling from his tuque, is also dry and falling, and he reeks of booze.

I figure he must be 50.

"I can't do it like I used to," Frankie continues. "I'm 38, you know. When I wake up in the morning, my bones hurt. I've applied for a place. Really, I'm gonna leave the street. I used to live in the Valley—Rosedale-Bayview. You know it. I was one of the original bush people. You can check. They came and interviewed me.

"But now they're getting tough with the squeegees. It's no good now. You can't do anything. I used to just stand with my sign. I didn't bother anyone. It was good money. I made 500, 600 a day."

I look shocked.

"I'm not shittin' you! Five hundred a day. At least! I swear on my mother's grave and my father's grave. These people didn't bother with coins. Everyone gave me fives and tens. These were the richest people in the country comin' outta there. They used to stand up for me."

When I get to Council Fire, a big man has just thrown an empty booze bottle across Parliament Street, where it shatters across the middle lanes. The throw saps his last ounce of energy, and he falls to the pavement, immobilized.

I step through the dark entrance, over more broken glass, and down the stairs, past a dazed man smoking a cigarette. At the bottom, a beefy volunteer, who looks more like a bar bouncer, frisks me for bottles, scans me with a metal detector for weapons and tells me to check in at the desk. I can give any name I want, he says.

With a lit Christmas tree in one corner and big-screen TV against the far wall, the shelter would look like a suburban rec room decked out for the holiday season if it were not for the bodies lying across the floor and the crowd of people around a table of coffee and crackers.

The people on the floor mats, the ones under their own sleeping bags with alarm clocks set next to their heads, are the working homeless, I figure.

They are the ones without enough money for first and last month's rent, or without a bank account to please a landlord. Or they're just plain poor, earning too little to get by in a city where $400 a month—about half the minimum wage—will get you only a room with wafer-thin walls and a shared kitchen and toilet.

Most of the rest of us are freeloaders, happy to enjoy a piece of warm floor and a hot meal at night after a day chasing other pursuits.

Before lying down, with an extra Council Fire sleeping bag that stinks of urine, I count close to 100 people on the floor, covering almost every available patch.

The only vacant spot I can find is next to Jim the wino, the one with a beard down to his stomach and a cloud of booze around a parka that he seems never to take off. He is well beyond motor skills at this hour, and one of the staff, wearing surgical gloves, has to bend over beside me and unzip the sleeping bag doled out for the night. The next moment, Jim is fast asleep, snoring loudly with the rest of the room.

Day 2

I wake up when Jim the wino rolls on to my mat, his bearded chin resting heavily on my shoulder as he continues to snore. It feels like a locomotive, one hauling thousands of crates of whisky, rumbling through my head.

It's approaching 5:30 A.M. and I can't sleep anyway. The staff, as if to get a few kicks, has cranked up the kitchen radio, blaring the Rolling Stones' "You Can't Always Get What You Want."

Slowly, most of the bodies on the floor start to stir, except for Jim, who sleeps peacefully until the guys in surgical gloves roll him over to retrieve his mat and shake him awake.

"Breakfast at Bart's," someone shouts.

St. Bartholomew's Church, on Dundas Street, serves a hot breakfast of lumpy scrambled eggs, pancakes, greasy sausage, a bucket of cereal, orange juice and coffee, which the others say is better than the early morning fare of stale strudel and coffee we've left behind at Council Fire.

The next day, Stackhouse experiments for a night outside, at the large square in front of Toronto's City Hall:

The temperature rises a little more and then holds steady through the afternoon, making it warm enough to be almost comfortable for sleeping out at night. Which is good because the downtown shelters are full again tonight, and I don't feel like trekking uptown. I don't want to eat dinner again with a bunch of drunks, so just before 9 P.M., I walk across Nathan Phillips Square to a row of wooden benches where people are already bedding down for the night.

I count 16 bodies: old bag ladies with their shopping carts parked next to the benches, young men with 10-speed bicycles at their side and inebriated men under blankets, as well as a few squeegees snuggled under mounds of sleeping bags and boxes.

Next to the bag ladies, I lay out my sleeping bag on an open piece of lawn, pulling my tattered blanket over my head. There is no snoring in the still night, no stench of stale alcohol rolling across the square, just a gentle warm breeze, the twinkle of Christmas lights around City Hall and soon a light rainfall.

Strangely, for the first time this week, I feel a sense of place. I feel like I know the faces on each street corner, and can sense the rhythms of the street.

For all its discomfort and alienation, homelessness also has its allure that gets little mention when we talk about the "problem." The freedom from personal commitments, social mores, rules and taxes cannot be undervalued, or easily replaced. The sense of complete charge over one's daily destiny—hardly the oppression that activists speak of—cannot be denied.[13]

The impression left by a cursory reading of his account was that many homeless people were in fact misusing the system. In Stackhouse's account many of those with whom he spent his time were filled with bravado about the ways that they took advantage of the offerings of the emergency social service network. Much was made of the $275 that he collected on one day at a particular subway stop as he panhandled his way towards a better understanding of the plight of those without homes. Other readers reacted differently. *The Globe and Mail* published my response on Wednesday, December 22, 1999.

Don't Blame the Victims

By Jack Layton

It couldn't have been worse timed.

Just when we thought we had broken through the Canadian consciousness and begun to forge a national consensus on the problem of homelessness, along came Globe and Mail *reporter John Stackhouse and his pretense of life on the street.*

The day after Claudette Bradshaw, the federal co-ordinator for homelessness, announced in Toronto that the government would contribute $753 million to build housing and shelters, Mr. Stackhouse, ignoring years of research in favour of a week outdoors, told us that public resources are used by crack dealers, that beggars earn professional wages and that "there is more free food than the homeless can eat."

Most people I know have been reading and talking about the series ever since, but for many of the wrong reasons: I could hear the cynical "I told you so" reverberating over morning coffee.

Mr. Stackhouse's seven-day masquerade among the thousands of legitimately homeless on Toronto's streets has done a great disservice to these people.

This is not to say that there was nothing valuable in the three-part series. Reading all the diaries allowed us to reach the conclusions where Mr. Stackhouse offers wisdom. He suggests that simply expanding emergency services month after month will not solve the problems that the homeless face. More government money, he says, will solve the problem only if it gets to the root of the high cost of urban housing and addresses crack and alcohol abuse. In these solid conclusions, the author is repeating fragments of the comprehensive plans developed by those who devoted years to the study of the issue.

The problem is that in getting to these conclusions, he fans the flames of the "blame the victim" psychology that motivates those who deny any social responsibility for the homeless crisis.

Now, anyone who spent eight years reporting on the affairs of countries with average per capita incomes measured in hundreds of dollars would have a unique perspective on homelessness in Toronto. To someone who watched as meagre amounts of rice were distributed to outstretched hands in war-torn refugee camps, a church basement breakfast served up by volunteers complete with eggs, fruit and hot coffee would seem luxurious.

But does that warrant calling people who go to these breakfasts "freeloaders"?

In a way, still, the series had the surreal feel of a report from the front lines by a journalist dropped into a foreign land by parachute. This journalist was, fortunately, secure in knowing he'd be brought back to home base after the seven-day assignment. His security made his situation fundamentally different from that of the people he was trying to mimic.

And therein lies the problem. Pretending not to have a home can never be the same as not having one at all.

Knowing you have a home means you are not without hope. Many on the street are, literally, without hope or home. The bravado we saw some homeless people express to the newcomer on the streets is only one expression of that hopelessness—carving out an identity, masking the reality with display.

When the entrepreneurship that beggars illustrated as they ganged up to protect their turf forced small fry such as Mr. Stackhouse out of the subway station, the actions were implicitly criticized. Yet the same entrepreneurship exercised upstairs in the bank towers is celebrated. The more takeovers, mergers and market share, the better! Panhandlers were merely replicating the actions of titans of business.

The reportage was best in its accounts of how ordinary Torontonians reacted to the homeless: "I've seen women give money and kind words ten times more often than men."

Mr. Stackhouse's successful days of panhandling suggest that Torontonians are generous people and do not blame others for the conditions in which they find themselves.

Let's suppose that the series about seven days in the lives of a city's homeless had been written by people who had been homeless themselves but had found a way out. How would it have been different?

The daily struggles to find housing would have played a more prominent part in the narrative. Thousands of people calling the homelessness hotline trying desperately to find a place. Those who have escaped from the cycle of homelessness invariably focus on the importance of having their own safe and affordable place. A home has often been the starting point for recovery.

In Toronto, a homeless addict finishing a treatment program is tossed back out into the street and emergency environment. There's no home in which to carry out a long-term recovery. A person struggling with a mental-health challenge, complete with a medication regime, is left on the streets with no secure place to be well. A convict is released from prison, again to the streets, only to be recycled through the system once again. Emergency wards and hospitals discharge people to the streets and hostels when what they really need is a healthy house and some personal support so they can recuperate.

The diary of the truly homeless would also see the simple desire to be treated with respect rising powerfully to the surface. Whatever the pathway to homelessness might have been, support and respect have to characterize the way out.

Success stories can be found among the emergency programs. These are the ones that have been founded on these three key principles: The housing must be secure so you do not have to line up night after night in the cold for a mat or cot; respect, encouragement and careful support for the wounds and personal challenges faced by each homeless individual must be present; and, in the best programs, homeless people themselves actually have some say about what happens to them.

Emergency shelters alone are not the answer, that's for sure. The old slogan "homes not hostels" still applies. Besides, shelters are terribly expensive compared to permanent housing. At $25,000 to $40,000 a shelter bed a year, we could *house five people in long-term housing for the same price. The taxpayer would win and so would those facing homelessness. Do we really want more hostels when we could have positive supportive programs such as* Homes First*, an operation in the city centre?* Homes First *focuses on providing permanent housing while addressing the individual needs of each resident. It's all done in a climate of respect.*

Mr. Stackhouse acknowledges the effects of the loss of respect he felt as a homeless person on our streets. Even though his homelessness was temporary, he knew in his gut what could happen to his humanity, stripped of an identity, of his own place in our city. Re-establishing his place, and the place of all those facing the looming housing crisis, requires housing, respect and support, all of which will take dollars. But they will be well spent.

4 A Cross-Canada Survey

A growing homelessness and affordable-housing problem is in evidence almost everywhere in Canada. This chapter lays out some aspects of that problem in each region of the country. The national picture follows. Much of the information presented here would not have been available were it not for the actions of the mayors of Canada's largest cities and the Federation of Canadian Municipalities, who put together a wonderfully committed team to gather the evidence. In the late 1990s, there was little national or provincial activity and there were few programs to address the issues. Communities were, in a very real sense, left alone with the growing problem on their collective lap.

This whirlwind tour of our country shows what the researchers, community organizations and city staffs have documented. Watch for different conditions, including the effects of the migration of people in search of jobs, combined with varying regional economic and labour/market conditions. These waves of movement create very different housing challenges. Watch, too, for common trends, like the reduction in support systems and the cutbacks in social assistance, which have caused meagre incomes to fall significantly behind inflation just about everywhere in Canada.

My once homeless family started out "Down East" 235 years ago, so let's start the cross-country check-up on the housing crisis where the sun rises first.

The Atlantic Provinces

St. John's, Newfoundland

When we first met, the deputy mayor of St. John's was not happy. Marie White was speaking to the National Symposium on Homelessness and Housing in March 1999. She was emphasizing the housing crisis faced by disabled people who are homeless or near-homeless. As a person dealing with mobility disabilities herself, she has a passion, based in experience, that is palpable. And, as though to drive home her message, she pointed out that the facilities provided for the symposium were not accessible to people in wheelchairs. Her message hit with a powerful wallop: We all recognized that, once again, the disabled had not been fully included.

She outlined how housing that should facilitate mobility and enhance quality of life for disabled residents was not available in her community—and funds to convert were scarce. She argued that even in the background papers for the National Symposium, these issues did not seem to be a priority. The housing crisis for a disabled person can be hard for a community to see—with people suffering virtually locked away and hidden.

Street homelessness in St. John's is rare and not visible in the way it often is in big cities. However, the "hidden homeless" are a major problem. Considerably more people live in substandard and inadequate boarding and lodging homes than are roofless. Poorly housed as a result of deinstitutionalization, many of these people have mental-health problems.[1]

In the past ten years, there's been an explosion in the number of empty apartments in St. John's. Many cities in Canada would envy such a high vacancy rate. From a low of 1.8 percent in October 1990, vacancies climbed to a high of 16.6 percent in 1997, just seven years. Most people say it's the departure of so many young people to find work elsewhere in the Canada that's to blame for the empty apartments.

Private-enterprise economics says that when supply increases, prices drop. St. John's seemed ready to prove the economists wrong. Rents did not begin to fall until the past two years, despite the steady growth in the number of empty and available units. More recently, rents began to return to the rent levels of the late 1980s. Job growth in 2000 began to tighten the market and push upward on rent levels.

True, modest inflation during the '90s would mean that rents had dropped, in real terms, a little—but nothing like a freely operating marketplace would suggest they should. Besides, incomes of renters, especially those with low incomes, had lost ground to inflation during that same decade—meaning that for them, rents had risen as a percentage of their total income.

As we'll see in community after community, the costs of housing for low-income tenants across Canada have been rising, leaving less for other essentials, let alone the occasional luxury.

Lately in St. John's, some landlords have been adopting a new strategy: reducing vacancies by turning rental units into condominiums. Since 1997, about 300 apartments have been lost from the rental market this way. Low-income tenants can rarely afford the down payments; condominium conversions simply reduce vacancy rates. Eventually, this will drive up rents again. Although the number of units involved represents only 1 percent of the 38,000 homes in St. John's, the trend could be disturbing.

Despite these high rental-housing vacancy rates, perhaps the highest in the country, St. John's still has a substantial waiting list for social housing. According to FCM data, 293 households registered for affordable housing in 1998. Families, 116 of them, with 288 children, represented 40 percent of those on waiting lists.[2]

Consider these statements (from 1999 FCM data) on the growing numbers at risk of homelessness in St. John's:

- The proportion of tenants paying 30 percent or more of their income on rent grew from 36 percent in 1990 to 45 percent in 1995—close to half of all tenants.
- In 1995, one in four tenants paid 50 percent or more of their income on rent, representing 3,665 tenant households.
- In 1995, tenants were five times more likely than owners to have a housing affordability problem.[3]

There are more people living in substandard and inadequate boarding and lodging homes.[4]

St. John's is fortunate to have an active social-service-agency network, and some city councillors push hard for recognition of the underhoused and precariously accommodated. The newest data shows that for the first time in many years, there was a net in-migration to Newfoundland in 1999, so new pressures on rents can be expected. As often occurs in cities experiencing economic growth, the economic success of some residents often drives the more vulnerable into the streets. We will see this pattern in many other Canadian cities as we move across the country, especially where there are few new affordable-housing projects coming onstream to meet the demand.

Still in Newfoundland, Sam Synard is the deputy mayor of Marystown, about an hour's drive along the coast from the capital. As president of the FCM for the year 1999–2000, he found himself thrust into the discussions of homelessness. His small town, just over 3,000 people, does not have any homelessness on its streets. But Sam has watched the young people leaving for other parts of Canada, looking for jobs. He has listened as his colleagues from bigger cities spoke more and more often about the growth of homelessness in their communities. When Anne Golden's report hit the national news, shortly after the Big City Mayors had declared homelessness a national disaster, Sam e-mailed me. "These homeless people on the streets of big cities—they're our children, our people, they're from our communities. Of course homelessness is our problem—even if we have no homeless people sleeping on our streets. Our homeless people are sleeping on other cities' streets."[5]

The government of Newfoundland and Labrador does maintain funding for 13,500 existing assisted-housing units, but new construction of this kind of low-income housing has been dramatically curtailed as federal programs have been eliminated. Rental supplements are available to a number of households through the Newfoundland and Labrador Housing Corporation. However, as in many provinces, funding levels have not kept pace with the need for assistance.

Moncton, New Brunswick

It was June 1999 when Moncton mayor Brian Murphy stood in front of 1,500 councillors and mayors in Halifax. The theme of the opening session of the FCM Convention in Halifax was homelessness and the housing crisis in Canada. Toronto's firebrand mayor, Mel Lastman, had already delivered a barnburner, accusing the federal government of delivering nothing. Mel put it in his unique way with the words: "el toro poopoo"—a phrase destined for headlines across the country. Anne Golden followed Lastman's attention grabber and calmly laid out the findings of her task force in Toronto, leaving everybody shaken by the magnitude of her numbers.

"Wasn't this just a Toronto problem?" mused a sceptical press gallery. "Were the heavy hitters from Canada's largest city simply trying to entice the FCM to join its homelessness crusade?"

Mayor Murphy's message shattered any preconceptions: Moncton was having to build its first full-sized shelter for the homeless, with capacity for 100 additional beds.

Murphy's staff noted that "our municipality does not maintain statistics on social assistance and low-income housing, as housing and social assistance are within the federal and provincial government jurisdictions. . . . The Provincial Department of Human Resources Development does not collect statistics on homelessness."[6] In New Brunswick, the buck is passed and dropped. Other provinces do likewise: no data, no problem.

In Moncton, the main indicator of homelessness is a local temporary shelter called the House of Nazareth, which served 1,165 persons a year, with average stays of five or more days. The House reports that a growing number of young people, between ages 15 and 19, are seeking shelter. "Most are troubled and are unable to live at home for one reason or another." Other studies have shown that abuse, incest and neglect are often at the root of the family situations that drive out young people. Reports from the House of Nazareth say that the number of their clients who should be receiving special care in homes is growing—they are increasingly, "mentally handicapped or have psychiatric problems that make them incapable of looking after themselves properly (medication, hygiene, nourishment, etc.). Organizations providing support such as the St. Vincent de Paul Society report that many patrons live in rooming houses which are poorly maintained, however, their options are limited because they are on social assistance."[7]

The provincial government has several programs to help people who are in danger of becoming homeless. It has policies to assist with the production of new low-income housing; however, the public accounts for these provincial programs show declining spending through the 1990s.

Signs of change in New Brunswick emerged as the Minister of Housing, Percy Mockler, co-chaired the first meeting of housing ministers in Canada since 1994. I was invited to meet with ministers in Fredericton to outline

FCM's plea and proposals for a national housing policy. As community groups gathered and called for urgent action outside the meeting room, the combination of reluctant and enthusiastic housing ministers debated inside. The September 19, 2000, meeting could prove to be a watershed.

Halifax, Nova Scotia

In this city, estimates of the number of homeless differ widely. Halifax's social-service staff member Barbara Nehiley said, "Those in the know calculate that there are about 300 to 500 people without a permanent address. It's a guess, but there may be fewer than ten people who really live 'outside.'"[8]

Halifax is not alone in struggling for data. In Nova Scotia, the "uploading" of housing issues to the provincial government has left city council and its bureaucracy reluctant to wade very far into homelessness issues. Feeling shortchanged by the provincial government in many areas, the majority of city councillors rejected the idea of taking a stand on housing issues. After a forceful debate, a clear vote by council indicated that the city wanted no part of the FCM resolutions calling for the declaration of homelessness as a national disaster. Little surprise that in Halifax few resources are directed at homeless issues by city council.

Community members, however, have been active for many years in Halifax. The wonderfully named Hope Cottage soup kitchen, situated in a church facility, has ladled out the good stuff since 1971. It also provides support of other kinds to the homeless and socially isolated people of this old port city. Up the hill, the North Halifax Health Centre, with its pragmatic activist executive director, Carol Anne Wright, has been a beehive of community action, providing better and more affordable housing. Wright, a black single mother who ran for mayor of Toronto in 1988, returned to her roots in Halifax and has helped build an impressive and creative team. Although her organization is a health centre, it has affordable housing at the top of its agenda, evidenced by the full-time housing worker, Paul O'Hara, who toils steadily on these issues. The Metro Non-Profit Housing Association managed to build a few affordable-housing units in the past few years. Dogged determination by Carol Charlebois worked miracles in making this project happen.

Still, the need continues to grow. Marilyn Berry, of Adsum House, the Maritimes' only short-term emergency shelter for homeless women and their children, reports that "every day a woman becomes homeless in the Halifax Regional Municipality." Adsum House itself has opened its doors to close to 7,000 women and their children since 1983. In the experience of these shelter operators, "Women on limited incomes are often forced to compromise their safety, their recovery from addictions, their struggle to be independent and their general health for substandard housing."[9]

It's not easy managing emergency facilities in Halifax. Take the saga of Metro Turning Point—the shelter that will "take almost anybody"—as related by Barbara Nehiley:

> The shelter had a capacity for 100 beds, but for the last several years growing health problems for staff and guests caused portions to be closed. The Municipality finally undertook testing and found that there were toxic moulds and fungi throughout the facility. The costs and lack of a guarantee for success meant repair was not feasible. The Municipality was no longer in the business of social housing or social services [these had been passed up to the province]. The Municipal Grant Program gave a $100,00 grant to help with relocation costs. Many sites were investigated. But no neighbourhood wanted a shelter for homeless men located within its boundary. Property owners would not sell empty buildings to the agency. After two public hearings failed to come up with permit approval, it was clear that a new, purpose-designed facility was the remaining best option. For years, such agencies had been put up in left-over buildings that were nearing the end of their lives and in poor repair. Municipal officials asked the agency if they were willing to go for a new shelter. The agency needed to make a commitment to fund-raise big time. They agreed. Six months after the municipality agreed to sell the land for a dollar after an emotionally charged public hearing, where neighbours opposed selling land just across the street from the existing site, the Province received support from the federal government and Metro Turning Point had the go-ahead to build.[10]

Nestled into the side of the hill on Barrington Street, the shelter has the look of a very residential building with its clapboard siding and hip roof. The site has been known over the years as "the jungle," where many homeless people not only lived in the rough but responded to their addictions with needles and Lysol. Homeless people have died in the jungle. Now, the emergency shelter stands in defiance of such misery. Doors opened at the new Metro Turning Point Shelter in February 2000 with enough room for fifty men.

Despite council's lack of support, other hopeful efforts are underway. One of these is the innovative Creighton-Gerrish Development Association's collaborative project for an affordable-housing complex under the stewardship of Harbour City Homes. With a budget of $7 million, this initiative hopes to move solutions in Halifax beyond stopgap shelter measures and towards longer-term sustainable housing.

In Halifax, just like other communities across Canada—despite the barren soil of negligible government support, involvement or even acknowledgement—community groups are struggling to create hope and housing with whatever resources they can scrape together.

Quebec

Homelessness has a long history in Quebec's bigger communities. Whether the city be Quebec City, Montreal, Sherbrooke, Drummondville or Trois-Rivières, these communities have weathered the periodic collapse of their local economies, the Depression and the recessions in each of the 1970s, 1980s and 1990s.

My initiation into the world of homelessness was in 1964 on Rue St-Laurent, "the Main." The occasion was the Thanksgiving Sunday excursion taken by the United Church Bible Class from the little town of Hudson, forty miles outside Montreal. From the advance description, we assumed the experience was designed to embody some of the ideas we'd studied in our Sunday evening Bible study sessions, helping others less fortunate than ourselves by offering some service to those in need. Of course, when your father doubles as Bible class leader, you have little choice but to follow along. By midday, we found ourselves serving food to the 200 homeless and poor on the Main, in the church-basement soup kitchen.

To this day, I can recall the images. The faces belonged to men more old than young, eerily weather-beaten, with brows furrowed in apparent anger, fear or sadness. These temporary inmates sat at long tables and waited patiently for the food they could smell in the otherwise musty air. Young, scrubbed-faced "anglo" kids smiled as we brought plates of turkey. Judging by the focused attention that the food received, it was obvious these guys were really hungry. Today, thirty-five years later, the same scenes are duplicated in hundreds of church basements across Canada. *The Gazette* (Montreal), September 16, 2000, featured an advertisement calling for volunteers to serve Thanksgiving dinner at the same church where I had been initiated to the realities of homelessness thirty-six years before! The faces are different now: There are many women and lots of children.

Quebec is one of the very few provinces that maintains a new affordable-housing construction and rehabilitation program. Accès Logi—a Quebec program—has produced 1,200 units per year. Fully half of this funding has gone to the Montreal area. Still, the effort falls short of affordable housing that will stem the tide of growing homelessness and the increasing tenant crunch.

In fact, there has been a huge reduction in the new affordable-housing construction and renovation activity in the province since the federal program funding was slashed. For example, former Montreal housing director Bob Cohen ran a program for the city that renovated as many as 5,000 rooming houses. According to Bob, there are still 40,000 to 50,000 rooms that need major renovations. A new provincial initiative is allowing many of these rooming houses to be bought and added to a non-profit housing network. Money for this comes from Accès Logi, funded to the tune of $43 million annually. This will certainly assist in maintaining some affordability in the housing stock that otherwise could have been lost. Renewed federal funding of the Residential Rehabilitation Assistance Program (RRAP) is also allowing some reinvestment into such housing stock, to ameliorate the living conditions. In the Accès Logi program, there are components for families and seniors, and support is provided for street-involved people who otherwise would have difficulty integrating into ordinary accommodation. The funding is often directed through credible organizations and networks such as PROUD/FRAPRU (see below).

Still, with vacancy rates in private rental stock falling in both Montreal and Quebec City, upward pressure on rents is increasing. Quebec City's rental vacancy rate fell from a high of 6.9 percent in 1994 to 3.3 percent in 1999. Montreal's experience was similar, with a fall from a 1993 high of 7.7 percent to 3.0 percent in 1999.[11]

City councils in both communities have since stepped up their pressure for increased federal funding of housing programs. Quebec City deputy mayor Claude Cantin, himself a past president of the FCM, has pushed hard in his city, as have several members of Montreal's administration such as executive committee member Jerry Weiner, pressed on by opposition critics like the Montreal Citizens' Movement leader, Councillor Michel Prescott.

Montreal

In Quebec's largest city, urban policy-makers and community groups alike have understood, for years, that poverty and homelessness are strongly linked aspects of city life. A pattern seen in American cities in the '70s has emerged in Montreal, with central-city household incomes falling behind incomes in the outer regions. Average earnings in some communities like Parc-Extension and Point St-Charles stood at $25,000 in 1995. Living under the official "low-income cut-offs" that define poverty is the experience of 41 percent of the population of the city of Montreal itself. Meanwhile, average income in the outer regions is $44,593.[12] With industrial employment falling to only one job in six, the traditional incomes of working-class tenant neighbourhoods have been trashed. Approximately 75,000 people have been on social assistance for more than two years. Meanwhile, throughout the 1990s, new immigrants found themselves arriving in a city with an economy in recession. This especially affected refugees—according to the Immigration Board of Canada 46 percent of all Canadian refugee claimants are living in the Montreal area.

At the same time, many people coping with serious problems are living in Montreal's downtown neighbourhoods, such as young runaways, individuals suffering from mental-health problems and those affected by situations that require care and services, e.g., multiple-drug users, former inmates undergoing social reintegration. These vulnerable populations, whose social and economic integration is difficult, are at high risk of homelessness. Their growing numbers in Montreal's neighbourhoods and streets also reflect (although it is hard to pinpoint their numbers) the process of deinstitutionalization in health and social service institutions over the past decade.[13]

Estimates of the homeless population in Montreal are hard to come by. People's Rights Over Urban Development (PROUD, FRAPRU in French),[14] a popular activist group in Montreal, estimated in 1993 that "nearly 20,000 people can be considered homeless."[15] Current official documents indicate:

> In Quebec, homelessness is unquestionably prevalent mainly in Montreal. According to one survey conducted in 1996, there were an estimated 12,660 homeless people in Montreal. Some 15,000 other individuals rely on other facilities, day centres and soup kitchens intended for the homeless. However, it is important to note that the figure 12,660 may not tell the whole story. It reflects only the number of people who were homeless during the year of the survey (1996–1997) and who have been counted in shelters and day centres in recent years.[16]

Front-line organizations in the shelter network "are unanimous in noting a marked increase in cases since 1996. Most centres have reached the saturation level and often turn away people."[17]

Breaking down these raw numbers to give a sense of who is coping with homelessness,

> the Regional Health and Social Services Department estimates that the number of homeless people between 18 and 30 years of age in Montreal ranges from 2,000 to 4,000. Moreover, in Montreal, 395 of the users of shelters and nearly 315 of the users of soup kitchens and day centres are under 30 years of age. Intervenors note that young people between the ages of 14 and 18 are becoming increasingly numerous in such facilities. They also note a significant increase in the number of homeless women.[18]

Numbers of homeless had risen to 28,000 according to data provided by the social-policy experts at Montreal's City Hall.

Trends in Quebec as a whole indicate a worsening situation, driving even more people into high risk of homelessness. For instance, the number of households paying more than 50 percent of their income in rent rose rapidly from 194,220 (16.9 percent of tenants) in 1990 to 273,825 (22.5 percent of tenants) by 1995.[19]

Montreal itself represents a major proportion of this problem. While in 1990, 114,735 tenant households were paying more than 50 percent of their already low incomes in rent (17.7 percent of tenants), these figures had risen to 163,415 households, almost one in four tenants (23.7 percent of tenants)—almost 50,000 more. These grim statistics gave Montreal the distinction of being the needy tenant capital of Canada as of 1996.

Although new census data is not yet available, Toronto may have surpassed Montreal by now.

Added to this problem, the quality of rental housing in Montreal gave many poor tenants almost slum-like conditions in which to live. Fully 52,580 apartments (7.9 percent of the units in multiple-unit dwellings) needed major repair as of 1995.[20]

Who is poorly housed in Montreal? Women, the young, the pre-retirement singles and seniors seem to stand out. More women are tenants rather than owners. "The 1991 census showed that when a woman is the principal financial support of the household, there are two chances out of three that she was a tenant. The proportions were reversed in the case of men! Even among tenant households, the ones most poorly housed are those whose principal financial support is a woman."[21]

"Age also plays a major role: The categories most poorly housed are young people from 15 to 24, pre-retired people from 55 to 64, and seniors over the age of 65, even though the situation of this last group has improved significantly over the past two decades."[22]

With over 350 agencies providing food assistance in the city, it is clear that the double punch of hunger and housing crises is striking thousands of Montrealers.

Virtually every neighbourhood has problems with affordable housing. From the Notre Dame de Grâce Community Council, to the housing committee of St-Henri–Petite Bourgogne (Little Burgundy, below the tracks), to Justice and Faith collectives, there is wide consensus on the need for an agenda of more housing and services. Non-profit housing co-operatives, like the legendary 1,800-unit Milton Park Co-op, provide some of the basic infrastructure for the networks and coalitions of organizations in the city. Substantial leadership on the issue has come from PROUD/FRAPRU for many years.

When it was reported that a homeless man had lain dead for many hours on a sidewalk in downtown Montreal as people walked by, the debate intensified. PROUD/FRAPRU staged numerous demonstrations. Community groups expanded their efforts to prevent these deaths, despite limited resources. On the initiative of the mayor, Pierre Bourque, the city instituted a major program to revitalize eight sensitive zones. Particularly stricken with poverty, substandard housing and community facilities and, in some cases, homelessness, these communities were to receive intense, focused effort by governments and agencies, in co-operation with local groups. Over $50 million was pledged in city and provincial funds.[23] The concept appears bold because it attempts to integrate many urban issues and problems in a combined strategy. The communities themselves seem to be withholding their assessment of the move until concrete results are clear.

A distinctive feature of the Montreal situation is the relatively high vacancy rate of rental housing. As a result, rents have been relatively stable, increasing at roughly the rate of inflation in the last half of the 1990s. With 21,650 vacant rental units in the Montreal region in the spring of 1999,[24] there would seem to be less need for new affordable-housing construction until the vacancy rate drops somewhat. The economic conditions of the city will largely determine when this becomes the case.

"Between 1993 and 1998, there were 335 requests to convert rental units to condominiums, representing 1,277 dwellings. The City generally favours conversion as a way of encouraging accessibility to affordable ownership housing. However, the city froze conversions in the central zone because the vacancy rate in that area fell below 3 percent."[25]

Citizen activism around housing issues continues to rise in Montreal. The network of sixty-six community groups that make up FRAPRU most recently launched a campaign of letter writing to the federal and provincial governments. Women living in poverty have composed detailed accounts of their attempts to raise their families while trying to avoid slipping into homelessness themselves. As the letters accumulate, a powerful case for anti-poverty policies and affordable housing is building through these community initiatives. When FRAPRU activists built a homemade house in the prime minister's Shawinigan constituency in September 2000, their protest captured national attention for the issue.

Quebec City

A capital city with historic grandeur, Quebec City and its environs is also the second-largest urban region in the province. Although it is not as deeply mired in the poverty trap as Montreal, significant and growing percentages of the city's population are facing housing crises. The following data illustrate the problem: In 1990, 18,680 tenant households devoted 50 percent or more of their income to rent (16.0 percent of all tenants); by 1995, the number had risen to 26,975 (21.7 percent). This increase of over 30 percent in five short years underlines the pace of change and the rapid growth of poverty in Quebec City. In 1995, substandard housing comprised 6,715 units.[26]

Ontario

In Ontario, the two longest waiting lists are of those qualified and waiting for affordable housing (as I noted, the wait is many years, eighteen for a family with four children) and buyers of luxury import cars (where the wait can be as long as nine months).

Some commentators still launch into a repeat of the accusation that homelessness is really only Toronto's problem. In March 2000, the sharply opinionated journals *Alberta Report* and *B.C. Report* both derided the federal government—which had just announced $750 million over three years for homelessness—for succumbing to the hysteria created by Toronto.

Whenever Toronto calls for more funds for just about anything, objections by the West are understandable.[27] But the *Alberta* and *B.C. Reports* dramatically miss the mark in their claim.

The facts tell the story. Stark numbers show the reality in a report called *Where's Home?*, released in the spring of 1999. Based on a study of the rapidly changing circumstances of low- and moderate-income families in eight Ontario communities, the bombshell report confirmed in severe statistics what many families were experiencing: escalating poverty, increasing need to use food banks, and swelling ranks of the homeless turning to shelters and the street.

"Homelessness and the lack of affordable housing are Ontario-wide problems, and not confined to Toronto. The plight of renters, as measured by the twin indicators of affordability and availability, is getting worse. The private rental market is not addressing these problems."[28] Key trends identified in housing affordability are:

- Vacancy rates are declining: Extremely low vacancy rates such as Barrie with 1 percent, Peel Region at 0.6 percent and Toronto at 1 percent are forcing up rents.
- Contrary to free-market theories, even communities with higher vacancy rates are experiencing rent increases (we saw this same problem in St. John's, Newfoundland).

- Rents are increasing significantly faster than inflation: Even in Ottawa-Carleton, with the mid-1990s civil service downsizing and consequent higher vacancy rates, rents rise faster than inflation.
- Tenant incomes have declined during the past decade as rents have increased. In some cities, the lowest 10 percent of the population, almost entirely tenants, experienced collapsing incomes between 1991 and 1996 to the extent of –30 percent in York Region, –23.6 percent in Toronto, –29 percent in Peel Region, and –21 percent in Ottawa.[29]
- In 1995, average incomes for Ontario home-owners is now twice that of Ontario's tenant households and trends suggest that this gap is widening rapidly.
- Almost 25 percent of tenants are at risk of homelessness, because they are paying more than 50 percent of their meagre pre-tax household incomes in rents. Prolonged exposure to this financial drain produces increased likelihood of eviction.
- Between the 1991 and 1996 census, the proportion of tenant households paying more than one-half their total income on rental costs leaped dramatically, by 47 percent [from 194,920 households]. This amounted to 300,645 Ontario tenant households in 1996 and this number is certain to have increased significantly since the last census.[30]

Various policy changes to liberate the private rental housing market from the bonds of rent controls and other "red-tape" restrictions were introduced by Al Leach, the minister of housing in the Conservative government elected in 1995. The post–Common Sense Revolution period was to feature an explosion of private-sector rental housing construction. The plan didn't work. The Ontario Non-Profit Housing Association study found that rental apartment construction had collapsed:

- Rental housing production has virtually disappeared in Ontario in the past decade, from 27 percent of all new housing in the 1989–1993 period to only 2 percent of new housing built in 1998.
- Non-profit and co-operative housing made up 17 percent of new housing between 1989 and 1993. There was none built in 1998.

- Had the provincial government not cancelled assisted housing construction, over 54,000 new units would have been developed for needy households by 2001.[31]

Fifty-four thousand homes in affordable price ranges would provide a lot of beds—over 130,000 of them—many of them for kids currently crashing in cribs in crowded emergency shelters.

It's hard to find a community in Ontario not affected by the new reality of people without homes. One million overnight stays in emergency shelters were logged in Ontario communities in 1998. This is only part of the dismal count. Add the growth of homelessness since then and the uncounted overnight refuges provided by church-basement programs and temporary shelters. Then add the communities that could not provide data or were not a part of the eight-city study. In Toronto this further increase has been approximately 20 percent, bringing the year 2000 total to 1.2 million nights of homelessness. This means that roughly one person-night of every 2,500 person-nights in Ontario is a homeless person-night.[32] So if homelessness were spread with absolute equality across all citizens of the province, at this rate each and every resident should expect to spend eight or nine nights homeless in his or her lifetime. If this were announced as official government policy, as though it were some sort of "accepted" or "naturally occurring rate of homelessness," the likelihood of this government's re-election would be rather severely compromised. Relatively few people in Ontario believe that they will ever have to endure such an experience. Shaking any complacency is Anne Golden's finding that 170,000 different individuals spent time in Toronto's shelters during the nine years from 1988 to 1996.[33]

Barrie, the most rapidly growing community in Ontario, has a vacancy rate of only 1 percent, a higher rate of tenant affordability problems than Toronto and "has had a ten-fold increase in people seeking shelter over the last five years." Even Peterborough records "almost a 100 percent increase in the same five-year period for their men's and family shelters." Peel Region, the sprawling network of middle-class communities west of Toronto, including Canada's fourth-largest city, Mississauga, has had a 41 percent increase in shelter use between 1994 to 1998.[34] Peel Region uses the Rosetown Inn for housing homeless families, because the Salvation Army facilities are working full-time. The number of bed-days (or homeless nights) for families accommodated in the Rosetown tripled in one year—from 595 nights in 1998 to 1,670 in 1999.

Food banks served 293,105 (123,104 children) people across Ontario during the month of March 1998, an increase of 31 percent since 1995. In addition, 37,000 people had some of their nutrition needs met from meal programs.[35] Kitchener-Waterloo had perhaps the most rapid expansion in food-bank and meal-service programs, with an increase of 136 percent over the past four years.

As one of its first acts, the Harris government cancelled 17,000 units of non-profit and co-operative housing that had already reached final design, approval and funding stages. This brought new affordable-housing construction to a standstill. Not only were these new homes cancelled, but the annual allocation of funds for affordable housing was terminated. Clamping down on new construction allowed the government to help the private rental sector create an artificial shortage and a lower-than-healthy vacancy rate. The government then removed the rental caps on any unit that became vacant. Glee pervaded the private rental sector. A free-for-all of huge rent increases resulted, jumping 20 to 30 percent immediately in the "apartments to rent" section of classified ads. Some landlords doubled rents on vacant units. The ironically named Tenant Protection Act accomplished precisely the opposite result for tenants—exposing them to increased pressure by making evictions more profitable and easier to accomplish.

My calculations show that landlords in Ontario were scoring an additional $80 million in cash flow from tenant households in Toronto alone after only one year under the new laws. Curving upward, these rent revenues transformed the stock price and underlying wealth of the landlords of Ontario rather handsomely. No wonder so many landlords took their companies to the public stock exchange in the few months following the new legislation. The prospectuses on file at the Ontario Stock Exchange ironically tout the cash flow and profitability virtues of the Tenant Protection Act for publicly traded landlord corporations.

Eviction Court is one of the most depressing places imaginable. Here, unabated greed meets struggling families and individuals face to face. A recent Homeless Advisory Committee report shows that even before the new tenant laws, the sheriff was processing over 3,000 evictions a month. This would produce at least 36,000 vacant units a year prime for the picking. One lawyer, fresh from over a dozen evictions, easily accomplished under the said Tenant Protection Act, confided, "This is embarrassing!"

Embarrassing perhaps, but also lucrative. Here's how empty apartments have actually become more valuable to landlords than apartments with dependable long-standing, rent-paying tenants in Ontario:

The average rent for one-bedroom, rent-controlled apartments in the centre of Toronto is about $700 a month. Vacant apartments are now going for an average of $1,000 a month. This amounts to a 40 percent increase.

If 10 percent of Toronto's housing stock turned over within the first year of the legislation (47,500 units)[36] and if we assume that 75 percent of these were in the "affordable" range, then 35,625 units of affordable housing ceased being available to people with low incomes. That's about 100 affordable units a day in the first year of the Act.

The Ontario government simultaneously cancelled rent registration systems, which used to give accurate records on an apartment-by-apartment basis. Such data could have replaced my estimates with indisputable facts.

Based upon our conservative estimate of total annual turnover of apartment stock, let's see what the cash-flow benefit to landlords is after 10 percent of the stock has changed hands in the first year of the vacancy decontrol legislation. We'll use the City of Toronto rental situation for this analysis.

We will use the "low-ball" figure for reported rent increases, a 20 percent increase or $140 a month on an average apartment of $700 a month. The result is an increased rent of $1,680 a year for each vacated apartment. If we add these average increases for all 47,500 vacated units, the resulting transfer from tenants to landlords amounts to $79.8 million a year. A normal investor would calculate the "present value" of that increased cash flow and would value this increment at $798 million! And this total is just for Toronto properties. Smaller but real impacts were also felt in other Ontario communities. And they continue to be.

The polarization process is clear when this increased cash flow and capital value is placed beside tenant household incomes, which have fallen significantly in Toronto and across the province. The fall has been even more rapid for lower-income families. Add an alarming reduction in full-time employment and growth in part-time jobs. Consider global economic trends that make full-time well-paid employment prospects weak. Finally, don't forget the cutbacks to mental-health and addiction services that continue to leave people helpless in the streets.

Against all this stand the rising incomes of the most affluent as a result from tax reductions. The ratio between the highest and lowest income households is rising to an extent that spreads the extremes of wealth and poverty further and further apart.

None of this was enough to satisfy the government that an opportunity had been provided to the private sector to build affordable housing on its own. Convinced that more had to be done to liberate the constraints on the market that had been imposed by governments over the years, Premier Harris added some enticements—all of which hurt tenants and increased homelessness as a result. Laws protecting tenants from having their rental homes converted into condominiums were stricken from the books. Few tenants can afford to buy their own apartment because of the requirement for a large down payment, which is almost always beyond the means of the tenant family. Within weeks, applications to convert long-standing apartment complexes housing thousands of tenants were received. Court challenges by tenants and municipalities attempting to protect this affordable-housing stock were rebuffed.

Permission to demolish apartment buildings for redevelopment was also provided, eliminating the requirement that an equivalent number of affordable-housing units had to be constructed to replace those lost. A field day of speculative investment followed. A wonderful thirty-year-old apartment complex in North York (the first apartment I lived in once getting a job) received permission to be torn down and replaced by condominium towers. Thankfully, Toronto City Hall insisted on some affordable housing and some financial relocation help for tenants as a condition of the rezoning. This assistance only muted the blow.

Looking still further to open up the market, Harris and his minister of housing discovered that several thousand very low-income tenants were receiving some assistance with their rents as they lived in private rental buildings. This was a program called "rent supplements" that was once advocated by landlords to help them fill up buildings that they had constructed principally for full-rent-paying tenants, while at the same time housing those of modest means. Landlords entered into contracts to provide a certain number of units to families and singles qualifying for low-income help. But in the late 1990s, the vacancy rates were so low that many landlords were just as happy to see the low-income folks go so that they could be replaced with higher-income tenants, and so that they could ramp up the rents to a level higher than the government's rent supplement program would have permitted. Three thousand such subsidized units were phased out in one announcement, but an insidious process of phasing out contracts actually reduced the number of tenants helped by an even greater number. Cities all across the province saw the number of rent supplement units fall significantly, even though the waiting lists for those in need were growing faster than ever. In Peel Region, the drop in apartments receiving this kind of help was over 1,000 units from 1993 to 1999. Peterborough lost 40 percent of such assisted housing. Durham Region's supply of rent-supplemented housing fell by 40 percent.[37] Later, announcements that some of this funding would be restored were made, but as of this writing, it has not been.

More avenues for cutting low-income housing were found by the enthusiastic Harris ministers and their staff at Queen's Park. Policies were implemented having the effect of reducing the number of low-income units in the non-profit and co-operative buildings that had already been built. Most social housing built since 1970 has featured a mix of market-rental units and subsidized units. The ratios differed by project and program, but roughly 50 percent of the units tended to be rented at prices similar to the private market and the other 50 percent were subsidized by provincial or federal funds. As the need for affordable housing increased, many non-profits and co-ops had received permission to add more subsidized units over the years. Seeing an opportunity to cut provincial costs, the provincial housing ministry not only ended this practice but forced the housing providers to reduce their quota of low-income units. No government has kept records of how many units have been lost as a result of this bureaucratic sleight of hand. Some communities report a 10 percent reduction in low-income units in their projects. If such a trend were able to be confirmed across the province, the loss would amount to thousands of units.

Finally, incomes of tenants are falling in Ontario's communities. Globalization's restructuring of the labour market has certainly been part of the problem for tenants with jobs in affected industries. Service-sector and part-time jobs have taken the place of steady better paid jobs. The provincial government made sure that tenants on social assistance did not see their incomes stay steady while other tenants' incomes were falling. A major cut to welfare payments of 21.6 percent in 1995 left many tenants reeling and finding they no longer had enough to cover rent and food costs. With falling incomes, rising rents and reduced availability of affordable housing, the crunch has been inevitable.

Perhaps all this could have been excused had the essential premise of the policy package turned out to be true: "the private sector will build affordable housing for all as long as government gets out of the way!" After all, said the Common Sense Revolution, "Government should not be in the housing business!" This rhetorical wave of the hand was well constructed. Boiled down, it suggests what appears to be a truism: "Government should not be in . . . business." Who could disagree? The deception involves the unstated assumption that the provision of housing in a society like ours is only a business matter. Imagine this statement: "Every child has a right to safe, adequate housing for herself and her family." Again, here's a statement few would disagree with.

Still, the test of all this rhetoric should be seen in the results of the policies constructed on its basis. Virtually no rental buildings at all have been constructed in Ontario since the entire framework of Ontario housing policy was erased from the law and program books. Freedom for the private-sector rental builders, the likes of which they could never have imagined, was provided, as requested. Yet the sector has not stepped up to the affordable rental housing plate. The result has been more homelessness.

Extensive studies have shown why this could have been predicted. Low-income tenants are living on such modest means that they can never produce rental payments sufficient to cover the construction, mortgage and maintenance costs of newly built housing.[38] Affordable-housing construction and supply will always have to receive some form of financial help from the government if the lowest-income tenants are to be able to be embraced in its mandate.

With essentially all financial support and protection having been removed from tenants in Ontario, the experiences of poor households has become increasingly dismal. The following accounts provide some indication of the accelerating problems across the province.

Kitchener-Waterloo

If we were searching for a barometer of homelessness for Canada, the Kitchener-Waterloo area would be about as unbiased a view as you could find. Stolid and staid, the straightforward middle- and working-class neighbourhoods knit together farming, industrial and community traditions. In the '90s, homelessness introduced some ripples into the region's otherwise calm social structure.

The following data were reported to the Community Action Forum on Homelessness in February 2000: "In the [Waterloo] region, each year, it is estimated that 1,500–2,000 people stay in emergency shelters and 150 people sleep on the streets at some time or another."[39]

Successful economic growth lately helps explain why the area had the second-lowest vacancy rate for housing among the ten Census Metropolitan Areas (CMA) in Ontario and the fourth-lowest of the 26 CMAs in all of Canada.[40] Only one out of every 666 apartments could be found vacant at any moment in time during 1998. Rents reached $768 a month for three-bedroom homes in that year, a 22 percent increase over the decade. One-bedroom suites were hit harder, with rents rising 32 percent since 1988. Tenant income was essentially stagnant during this time, registering a 1.1 percent increase for tenants in family units and a 0.2 percent loss in income for non-family tenants (singles, seniors and students) measured from the 1991 and 1996 census. Single-family homeowners fared better, posting a 9.6 percent income boost for the same period. The number of tenants shelling out more than 50 percent of their income in rent rose from 10,065 in 1991 to 15,470 in 1996. Always on the knife-edge of meeting the monthly rent, these are precisely the types of people who find themselves newly exposed to homelessness in Kitchener-Waterloo.[41]

Despite the preponderance of neat lawns and spacious suburban properties, panhandling, sleeping rough and crashing in abandoned squats is the new lifestyle in some neighbourhoods. While the sheer numbers and rates of change have been more modest than in other Ontario cities, social-service agencies have noticed significant increases in need, particularly for children, youth and people with mental disabilities.

As usual, the voluntary sector has stepped into the breach first. Out of the Cold programs have opened in local church halls on selected nights, complete with food hampers and floor mats. The YWCA and Salvation Army both operate centres as well. The count of homeless shelter bed-nights increased from 1994 by over 3,000 to reach 28,105 by 1998—an 8 percent jump.

Social-planning councils in the region are getting together to prepare a background report on homelessness. The regional government is joining in with staff assistance and a grant of $5,000 towards the study. Another

$5,000 was given to each Out of the Cold program. A modest start, to be sure. Kitchener is also looking at ways to build affordable housing, by waiving municipal fees, giving tax holidays, using city land, and so on. The preliminary research seems to be indicating that capital financial assistance is crucial to make new projects viable.[42] So far, these have yet to yield actual projects. Four thousand people on waiting lists for assistance with housing will have to continue to try to hang on.

London

In 1997, increasing poverty in London was flagged by the Anti-Poverty Action Group. Their report found that the city had a higher percentage of low-income private households (15 percent) than in Ontario as a whole (13 percent) and a higher percentage of children aged 0–14 in low-income families (18 percent) than Ontario as a whole (13 percent).[43]

Concern about homelessness seemed to start shortly afterwards, when the London Social Planning Council Research Committee turned their attention to the quietly growing phenomenon evidenced by shelter beds. Believing that numbers could be important, that data and words from the experiences of the homeless themselves could inform the development of better responses, the committee put together the London Homelessness Survey. A questionnaire was delivered to those staying in shelters and hostels, with the help of experts in social science research. Volunteers and front-line shelter workers all helped out, as did the homeless themselves. Enlightening fragments of their stories appeared in the final document.

The report was dedicated to those homeless men and women who had "generously agreed to complete the individual questionnaire, sharing their experience and thoughts on homelessness." And to "Michael Gligor, a member of the London Social Planning Council Research Committee who, for many years was a broadcast news journalist in London; whose psychiatric issues led him to briefly experience homelessness and led him to jump to his death on May 4, 1998."[44]

Forty-six females and eighty-seven males without homes filled out the questionnaire. One reason for asking questions of these people was to figure out why homelessness was occurring in London. There may be a precipitating reason or combination of reasons for someone's homelessness: Poverty, family discord, abuse and breakdown, addictions and psychiatric issues may all play a part. The most frequently given reason for women (52 percent) was "unsafe at home." For men (57 percent), the most frequent reason was "no money." Three times as many men (25 percent) as women (9 percent) gave psychiatric issues as a reason for homelessness.

The survey snapshot also included a three-month retrospective video of the housing histories of the people who had shared their lives with the surveyors. About 30 percent of men thought they had been without adequate housing for more than a year.[45]

The conclusions of the study motivated some civic leaders to respond. Here is a portion of the closing remarks of the researchers:

> Most people surveyed don't appear to have enough money to get or keep accommodation. A recent *Globe and Mail* article discussed the fact that, between 1973 and 1996, the ratio of income disparities between the poorest 10 percent of Canadian parents of children under 18 and the richest 10 percent has increased from 8.5 to 10.2.[46]
>
> Some of London's families are part of that statistic. An October *London Free Press* story refers to some 1996 Census data which indicates that "the percentage of children living in low-income homes is 24.3 percent in London compared to the provincial average of 22.1 percent."[47]
>
> And the London homelessness survey shows an increased number of sheltered children.[48]

Numbers of financially troubled families and singles were growing rapidly. Households facing rent bills in excess of 50 percent of income each month increased from 9,650 in 1990 to 14,115 by 1995. Fortunately, London has had relatively higher vacancy rates (in the 4 percent range), which has had a moderating effect on rents. After a jump in the early 1990s, they did not increase by much in the last half of the decade.[49]

With strong women's leadership on City Council provided by a United Church minister, Susan Eagle, and supported by Mayor Diane Haskett, an initiative to turn some city resources towards affordable housing began to come together. In February 1999, a task force was created with Eagle and Controller Russ Monteith at the helm. Their work exploded more myths about housing in London. They reported, for example, that when three separate waiting lists for assisted housing in the area were amalgamated, there was a significant increase in the numbers of households that qualified for and needed affordable housing. "It was a popular but incorrect assumption that the three channels for housing applications were previously receiving applications from the same families and that when the process was co-ordinated the numbers would go down. Currently our waiting list stands at approximately 2,500 families."[50]

But what if a federal housing construction initiative had been announced?

When the FCM Annual Convention met in London, June 2000, over 30 mayors joined community groups in wielding hammers as they built a house in a park in just one day, showing that solutions were not rocket science.

The City of London had to report that if federal funds were to be released for housing, "at this point in time, we have no official housing staff or office to respond to such federal programs that address gaps or housing need in the municipality."[51] As a result, the task force set out to explore ways of creating some affordable housing in London. Preliminary plans emerged in a summer 2000 report outlining modest first steps.

The 905 Area

"We live in 905," goes the common phrase. Like a moat around Toronto, suburban housing sprawls in concentric rings and cul-de-sacs. The moniker "the 905" refers to its telephone area code.

Of the four regions—Durham, Halton, Peel and York—Peel is the most populous. It reaches from the heavyweight lakeside Mississauga past Pearson International Airport and farther north to Brampton and the rolling hills and small-town environment of Caledon ("We're Canada's fourth-largest city, you know," the diminutive, near-octogenarian mayor, Hazel McCallion, always reminds us).

Living in the 905 used to define your comfortable housing circumstances—a cozy home. Not so now.

In 1999, Peel Region had to provide 28,403 nights of emergency accommodation in four shelters, up 41 percent from five years earlier. Overflow families who could not fit into the shelters were put up in motels, and that number nearly doubled from 351 in 1997 to 689 in 1998. In addition to the 905ers sheltered in hostels, other people tuck into nooks and crannies at Pearson, squeeze into cold and wet spaces under bridges and lodge in suburban ravines and parks.

The chief housing official of Peel Region, Keith Ward, estimates conservatively that there were twenty-five people living on the streets of Mississauga and Brampton, and that 4,712 individuals (in 2,993 family units) used the emergency shelter system in 1999. In responding to my query about those as risk, or the "hidden homeless," Ward suggested that this would be difficult to ascertain, "but from all indicators the numbers are far greater than currently estimated."[52]

Although the majority of 905ers elected and re-elected the Harris government, homeless advocates are doing battle for the soul of their communities. As early as 1996, the Peel Coalition for Shelter brought together community agencies and municipal staff. The first overnight drop-in in Peel for single men resulted. In 1998, 300 men sought refuge in this renovated former Public Works garage in Brampton.[53] Survey research by the coalition showed that long-term and comprehensive solutions would be needed, so the Peel Regional Council, with strong support from McCallion, kicked off a Task Force on Homelessness in 1998.

In 1999 alone, Peel region opened a new forty-bed facility for males in the Brampton area. February 2000 saw another Mississauga shelter open, with capacity for twenty men and twenty women. More plans remain for expansions and new facilities throughout the region.

Once again, poverty surfaced as the core cause of homelessness in the region. "Between 1990 and 1995, the number of Mississauga's poor people increased by 5.5 percent (10.9 to 16.4 percent) and Brampton's percentage of poor increased 5.2 percent (8.5 to 13.7 percent)."[54] Child poverty shoved more stark statistics onto the table: 21.3 percent of kids up to 14 years old were living in poverty in Mississauga; Brampton was a little lower at 17.4 percent. Youth poverty was 17.4 and 14.9 percent respectively in these two cities. Retired and comfortable in suburbia? Not for all. In 1995, the incidence of poverty among seniors was 18.8 percent in Mississauga and even higher, at 19.1 percent, in supposedly comfortable Brampton.[55]

Figure 4.1 shows the production of rental housing plunging, like the descent from Mount Everest. In 1992, over 1,800 units of new assisted rental housing was produced—a veritable anti-poverty boom. This fell to 0 units by 1998.[56]

Piled on top of this problem is the provincial government's cancellation of 17 percent of the units for which it was providing rent supplements for low-income people. At the same time, rents in the private sector were stepping up the pressure on households, rising from $681 a month in 1989 to $894 a month in 1998. Vacancy rates dropped from a comfortable 3.1 percent in 1992 to 0.7 percent—seven empty units per thousand at any one moment. This vacancy rate essentially captures the brief time between one tenant's move out and another's move in, hours later.[57] All this happened as tenant incomes fell in the region by 5.3 percent between 1990 and 1995. Homeowners' incomes, by the way, increased by 4.1 percent during the same period.[58] Gaps have been growing, even in the suburbs.

Figure 4.1: Peel Region: Rental Completions, 1989 to 1998

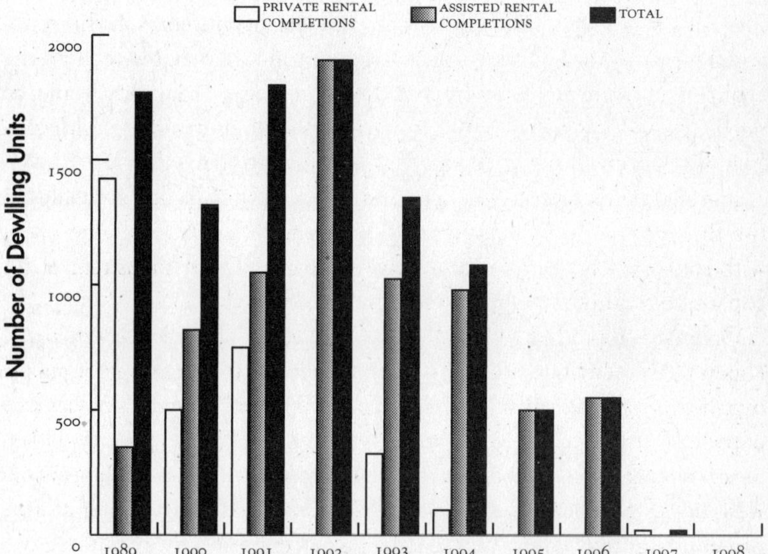

There was a 100% decrease between the average rental unit production from 1989 to 1993 (1,625 per year) and the 1998 production total (0)

Source: Ontario Non-Profit Housing Association and Co-operative Housing Federation of Canada, *Where's Home? A Picture of Housing Needs in Ontario* (Toronto: Ontario Non-Profit Housing Association, 1999).

Never one to shrink from a fight, Mayor McCallion has launched offensive measures on three fronts. She delivered blistering and very public criticisms of the federal government's abandonment of its affordable-housing mandate; she worked with her communities to establish emergency shelters; and she dispatched Peel Region housing agency head Keith Ward to help create the National Housing Policy Options Strategy of the FCM. A McCallion unleashed is a force that few voluntarily contend with. After all, as *Toronto Life* put it, "Her Town, Her Rules."[59]

Not that an explosion of affordable housing has begun in Peel Region. A summer 2000 policy and planning document put together for Peel Regional Council sets aside some modest funds for small affordable housing projects and supportive initiatives for the homeless, but, as so many other communities, Peel is waiting for Ottawa.

East of Toronto lies the massive Durham Region, its locus the prosperous centre of auto manufacturing in Canada, Oshawa. With a population of over 400,000, Durham covers almost 1,000 square miles and includes towns and villages as well as mushrooming bedroom communities. Here, too, homelessness has become evident. Many service workers and volunteers who are doing their best to cope with the housing problems pressed their council to act. As many had done before them, the regional government created a Homelessness Advisory Committee, and two co-ordinators helped pull together a picture of the patchwork of services for homeless people scattered across the huge area.

Never appearing on the nightly news, poorly heated, often collapsing trailers and cottage-like homes are sprinkled throughout rural Ontario. The tough employment situation, the absence of community supports because of the remote locations, the isolation of the families struggling to get by and the seclusion of the poverty have made life tough on the fringe of suburbia for those ignored by the recent economic boom. Rarely owning their often-dilapidated homes, these families find that the costs of providing basic necessities often exceed their reach.

Durham's homelessness workers saw that the rent pressures were driving families into their hostel system. These workers convinced Durham Council that spending $35 a night, or more, to keep people in temporary shelters made no sense when a loan of $100 to $500 could help them pay the rent. A "rent bank" was set up. People on the edge of homelessness were able to borrow from this special bank and avoid eviction. The scheme was copied from American systems, also duplicated in Toronto. A similar community trust approach was established to help deal with utility bills when poor households fell behind, helping to keep people in their homes. A bit of optimism in the gloom.

Beyond the 905s, smaller cities showed shocking statistics. Peterborough, a two-hour drive northeast from Toronto, was historically home to many manufacturing plants. Free trade cut away the economic foundations. Plants closed, only to relocate in the American South or Mexico. Still, summertime tourism, a university and a few determined industries stayed. Some commuters whose jobs lay in the Greater Toronto Area prefer small-city life (Peterborough has a population of 60,000).

Long considered immune from the imagined evils of urban living, this community watched food-bank use climb by 233 percent from 1990 to 1999. Waiting lists of households qualifying for affordable housing jumped by 199 percent between 1992 and 1996. Some apartments were available, with a vacancy rate of 4.9 percent, but those in need couldn't afford them. Brock Mission, operating shelters from two locations, struggled as the overnight stays climbed from 1,902 in 1994 to over 3,700 in 1998. One cannot assume that just because there is a high vacancy rate in a municipality that the rental market does not have any problems. While Peterborough appears to have sufficient rental housing, the incomes of tenants are too low to afford what is available and so they are spending too much of their income on rent. "The City of Peterborough has a serious housing affordability problem that needs to be addressed."[60]

Windsor

Despite the magnetic economic impact of the casino, not to mention Windsor's strong auto-manufacturing link with Detroit, there were still 150 shelter beds provided for customers on a typical night in 1998. Over 900 individuals received emergency accommodation in the Salvation Army shelter in 1999. When the city set up its Homelessness Advisory Committee, priorities emerged quickly: There were virtually no facilities for homeless women, so a small, three-bed program was started. Windsor is one of the few municipalities in Ontario to fund "domicilary hostels" or rest homes as accommodations for the vulnerable who require twenty-four-hour care in a supervised setting. In 1999, the city funded an average of 412 persons in rest homes each month, and about 80 percent of that number have a serious mental illness that precludes their maintaining independent living. That means that by placing people who may be at risk of homelessness in rest homes, Windsor does not have the visible homeless problem evidenced in other cities.[61]

North Bay

North Bay, home of Premier Harris, has a bleak outlook for homeless services. Hard hit by the recession in the metals industry, the city has a population that actually dropped in the late 1990s. That did not stop emergency-shelter use from rising by 21 percent from the winters of 1995–96 to 1998–99. Even though almost 6 percent of rental homes were vacant, falling tenant incomes forced upwards of 23 percent of tenants to pay more than 50 percent of their income in rent. Even though there was a high vacancy rate, "Rents for most units increased approximately 1.5 times the rate of inflation (except for one-bedroom units where rent increases have been below the rate of inflation)."[62] It's not as though new supply was on its way: Only four rental units were built between 1994 and 1998, fewer than one unit a year.[63]

Ottawa-Carleton

Governments are well housed in Canada's capital city, but not the homeless. They lie in the shadows of the flapping flags of state, and they die under bridges, as a pregnant young aboriginal woman did one recent winter. Complacency was shaken, but not enough to produce real solutions.

The multimillion-dollar tunnel between the East Block and Centre Block ensures the prime minister temperate passage from one office to another. Not so for Ottawa's homeless on the sidewalk between the Château Laurier and the Parliament Buildings. The wind blows cold through the underpasses along the Rideau Canal and swirls around its locks. An old chair, some blankets and a rusty woodstove are part of the daily evidence of someone's home.

Indicators incite enthusiasm about Ottawa's economy: growing employment, rental housing being converted to condominiums, budget surpluses. But other data delineate declining conditions for Ottawa's desperate and dispossessed. Indeed, the positive produces the negative. Job growth creates competition for scarce accommodation, driving rents beyond the means of many. As a result, there has been a major increase in the number of households on the waiting list for assisted housing in the Region of Ottawa-Carleton over the past five years. In 1993 there were 8,575 households on the waiting list for City Living [Ottawa's Non-Profit Housing Corporation] and the local Housing Authority. By the end of 1998, there were 15,000. In 1998 alone, 5,500 new applications for assisted housing were received. New applicants on the waiting list can expect a wait of 5 to 7 years.[64]

Why? Because many more Ottawa region tenants pay a greatly increased percentage of their falling incomes on rent. Ottawa's least affluent 10 percent experienced a drop of 21 percent in their incomes between 1992 and 1996. And half of all wage earners experienced income losses, capturing just about all tenants.[65] These data do not include further income drops for households who rely on social-assistance programs, which were significantly chopped by the Harris government in 1995. Later, changes to the national Employment Insurance program pushed incomes even lower for those in seasonal jobs.

Simultaneous to collapsing tenant revenues were increasing rents, which on average were up 24 percent in the ten years from 1988 to 1998.[66] The squeeze was on. Simple math produced simple stress on Ottawa's renters. The vise tightened in 1999 and 2000, as the twin effects of lowering vacancy rates combined with landlords charging what the market would bear under their new-found freedom. "The proportion of tenants paying 30 percent or more of their income on rent grew from 30 percent in 1990 to 41 percent in 1995.[67] Severe housing affordability crises, defined by rents greater than 50 percent of income, became the experience of 24,020 tenant households in Ottawa region by 1995, up from 16,290 households in 1990.[68]

New housing was madly manufactured in Ottawa to meet the boom; too bad for tenants that it was 99 percent ownership housing and only 1 percent rental.[69]

Faced with all this grim news, an Alliance to End Homelessness formed itself into a non-profit group in the region. It has a mandate to work collaboratively to eliminate homelessness through a better understanding of homelessness, with specific goals to

- Increase public awareness of homelessness and the will to end it
- Include people who are homeless in the initiative
- Increase understanding of the changing nature and causes of homelessness
- Create intervention and prevention strategies to end homelessness
- Advocate for the implementation of the strategies developed by the Alliance

When homeless advocates and some elected representatives like Councillor Alex Munter threw down the gauntlet at the Ottawa-Carleton

Regional Council and challenged colleagues to call for national and local action, the council of the cautious community of Ottawa endorsed the call, joining the FCM's campaign for a Canadian affordable-housing strategy.

Locally, a number of projects involving city and regional initiatives are now underway. They range from health and ID card replacement blitzes (to help homeless people whose identification has been stolen or lost) to small new-housing projects developed with local groups, like the energetic Centretown Citizens Ottawa Corporation. However, with the gulf widening between low-income tenants' falling incomes and their rising housing costs, the available resources for solutions are falling far short of what's needed.

Niagara

When the District Health Council issued its Report on Homelessness in Niagara in 1997, the tourist haven saw its pristine image tarnished by the findings. Volunteers from the Out of the Cold programs, which had been quietly serving singles and youth for several years, told of an acceleration of the need. Families were the newcomers to their suppers and beds. Despite the injection of mindless but lucrative casino operations, the entertainment economy was not making it possible for the low-income earners to have secure housing.

Toronto

Like a bright light drawing moths, Toronto glows. It attracts impoverished immigrants from around the world, tantalizing them with glittering images of riches and freedom. And it pulls the dispossessed from the North with its warmth, colour and the sense that somehow life will be sweeter and kinder. For too many, it's not.[70] At least 47 percent of hostel users in the city over the past ten years have come from outside Toronto.

"A meeting place" is the original meaning of the word *Toronto*—drawn from the First Nations societies that had assembled in the bay between the Don River and the Humber for hundreds of years. Today, there's a drop-in centre for the dispossessed called the Meeting Place. Ironic. Imagine if the homeless drop-in were actually called Toronto!

"I've lived on the streets in Toronto for one year," says one man inerviewed for the Golden Report. "I've stayed in squats, hostels and mostly slept outside. I can't say that it's been easy but you learn to get by. I come from Nova Scotia. I came to Toronto because there is supposed to be more opportunity here."[71]

One example of the challenge of counting, much less housing, Toronto's homeless is the Home Depot site on the waterfront. Retail development giants who speculate on the possibility of rezoning purchased a vacant property at the northeastern corner of Toronto's port. The owner is the Home Deport chain, which has visions of a huge waterside big-box outlet at this prime location. In an effort to preserve public access to the waterfront and to provide some protection to the small "mom and pop" stores nearby, city council opposed the huge complex.

While the debate raged, a little community of homeless families, couples and singles in shanty homes sprang up. No friendly Home Depot construction advice or building materials here. No bureaucrat or expert counts the people who are living here. Brush grows chaotically on this site as nature attempts to reclaim the land that a metal manufactory abandoned years ago, leaving behind its toxic excrement.

These makeshift shanties are sitting on the key piece of land in Toronto's waterfront Olympic plans. Right now, on land that will someday host hundreds of millions of dollars of development, panhandling is the prime source of income for the occupants. One couple has minimum-wage part-time work in the service sector, but they can't find an affordable apartment in the city. They calculate they would need to work 140 hours a month just to cover the rent of a one-bedroom apartment. Food, clothing and hydro would be extra. They park the car near the tent and hope that Home Depot won't repair the gate to the fenced property. When that gate is fixed, they'll be stuck, because the shelter system has no space for couples. Home Depot's big-box plans were quashed by City Council to make way for bigger dreams. So, for the moment, it's rent-free refuge for uncounted castaways.

Rosedale Valley Road is a secluded, woodsy passage through and away from the exclusive Rosedale residential enclave. Until bridges and access points were built, the valley served to ensure social segregation between those living in the area and everyone else. North Rosedale has the highest average household income of any census tract in the city ($160,000 in 1996). Downscale South Rosedale ranks second with $140,000 as the average household income.

But Statistics Canada forgot the homeless. Tucked, hidden, tented, in the nooks and crannies of the Rosedale Valley are dozens of homeless people. It's the same in the Don Valley, which forms the eastern perimeter of Rosedale.

Sometimes these encampments light up the night as their occupants burn to death. On March 7, 2000, beneath a footbridge, firefighters arrived at what they thought was a brushfire. Poking their pikes into the debris, they discovered soft resistance, which suggested a mattress could be lying under the incinerating belongings of someone, uncounted by Statistics Canada, who might have sought refuge there. When the pulling and tugging was over, the shaken firefighters found the body of Jennifer Caldwell, of Vancouver, B.C., who had apparently been drawn to Toronto's lights but could find no refuge, except for the dangerous outdoors.

For the past decade, a new breed of caregivers has cruised Toronto's nights in vans, providing relief, especially to the "hard to find" homeless. The first time I heard about the project I was simultaneously relieved and shocked. (Now, nothing would surprise me.)

It was 1988. The Anishnawbe Health Centre called me to say that they had volunteers who would take sandwiches, hot coffee and concern to the small (at that time we thought it was small) number of people who couldn't come in from the cold. Could I find a way to get a van, any old van, so that they could carry their supplies? Council had recently appointed me chair of the Board of Health, so I raised the idea with Toronto's medical officer of health, Dr. Sandy MacPherson. His staff soon found a van that was scheduled to be auctioned at the bi-annual sale of municipal flotsam. The Board of Health invested a few bucks in decent shocks and basic engine repair, and it became the first official Anishnawbe Street Patrol van. More than ten years, countless sandwiches and cargo loads of coffee later, this once tiny team now serves, face-to-respectful-face, 33,800 people in the streets every year.

The first time I took the opportunity to join one of their late-night van excursions, I was shown people and places I never knew about: hidden stairwells, the unplumbed depths of parking garages, thorny hedges and public parks harbouring sleepers. That voyage humbled me, city councillor for downtown Toronto, supposed to be able to solve urban problems.

Toronto's Homelessness Action Task Force, taking into account the inadequacies of our measurement systems, gives estimates of the size of the problem. Here are some key findings:

- Almost 26,000 used hostels in Toronto in 1996.
- The fastest-growing groups of hostel users are youth under 18 and families with children. Families accounted for 46 percent of the people using hostels in Toronto in 1996.
- Fifty-three hundred children were homeless in 1996.
- Between 30 and 35 percent of homeless people suffer from mental illness. The estimates are higher for some population groups; for example, 75 percent of homeless single women suffer from mental illness (based on data up to 1996).
- More than 100,000 people are on the waiting list for social housing in Toronto. At the current rate of placement, as we've noted, families would have to wait eighteen years to obtain housing.
- Poverty is getting worse among the applicants for social housing; more than one-third of the people on the waiting list have incomes of less than $800 a month. (Few apartments are now available in Toronto at less than $800 a month.)[72]

When Toronto's Homelessness Advisory Committee called for more shelters to be opened, bureaucrats responsible for emergency shelters reacted: "We have enough space; in fact, there were empty beds on the night that man died" was often the refrain.

On several late-night excursions, I set out to find out what was going on. With Peter Zimmerman, at the time my executive assistant who specialized in housing issues, the trek began at the Maxwell Meighan Centre run by the Salvation Army. The sliding-glass intake window was pulled back and a man with a kindly weather-beaten face told us that the shelter had no more spaces that night. The TV room had been turned into sleeping quarters, with mats taking over every inch of the floor. Bodies now occupied all the mats, wall to wall. The man wearily suggested we check with Seaton House up the street.

On the way, we dropped into the Council Fire Emergency Shelter, arriving about midnight. A couple of lost souls lingered in the doorway to the basement accommodations. Down the stairs we went and were met by a sight I'll never forget. Bodies lay shoulder to shoulder in rows of about thirty people each. Friendly and well-muscled young native men sat behind the modest table at the entrance to the single large room with its oppressively low ceiling. Behind them, in the dim light, lay the evening's charges.

"How many people are here tonight?" I asked.

"We're at 119 right now."

"But I thought the capacity limit was 100," I countered, looking around and realizing that there seemed to be no empty space.

"Well, we never really turn anyone away," the staff member confided. "Later, when more people arrive, we'll take down that table over there where people drink coffee. A dozen mats can go there. Couples or families we can take upstairs to the agency offices, where they can sleep on the floor and have a little privacy."

With one coffee urn and a few jugs of water, the volunteers and refugees of Canada's failed housing and health policies formed a partnership that harsh night, just to get through it. With TB running at dangerous levels on the street, risks were being taken with each breath and cough. Yet there were no sterile masks or hands-off attitudes. There was only the quiet dedication to coping.

Heading towards Seaton House, we passed a hodgepodge of run-down rooming houses whose landlords seemed none too interested in keeping their buildings in presentable shape. Squeezed between them, well kept and friendly, was the first low-income singles housing project built by the Metro Toronto Singles Housing Company. With over 100 self-contained units, the five-storey structure is, by most accounts, one successful result of Canada's national housing policy of the 1980s—exactly the kind of project we desperately need right now, I thought to myself.

Across the street, townhouses and an apartment complex houses low-income families mixed with market rental units. Several hundred homes occupy this once-vacant land and parking lot. Some years ago, rooming houses had been torn down here and tenants evicted, all in the name of land speculation. It worked—at least for the owners of the buildings who made a killing when their property was sold to the developers. However, City Council had insisted on affordable housing as a part of a rezoning deal. Because of the demise of Canada's national housing programs, the units were built using provincial housing program money. A lively, successful, mixed neighbourhood has resulted. Residents from all income backgrounds are housed in a decent, affordable community.

Only half a block north, we arrived at the doors of Seaton House. Built decades ago to receive itinerant workers arriving in the city looking for work, the place is nothing fancy. Now, with a population of much more needy people crammed within its walls, Seaton House was showing the strain. Inside, hostel workers tried to keep the 600-plus transients civil and safe—not an easy job in such overcrowded and emotionally charged circumstances. Seaton House has long been considered Toronto's last resort in the hostel hierarchy.

On this night, the affable staff welcomed us when we asked if we could come in and look around. On an old, yellowed computer behind the reception desk, data shimmered. "So have you any vacancies at the moment?" I asked. "Twenty open spaces at the moment—here, you can see them on the screen. There's a free bed in this room on the second floor—bed nineteen." We climbed the stairs. After midnight sounds at Seaton House are unique. Lots of coughing and wheezing from the darkened rooms as we moved down the long hallway. Occasionally a grunt of disapproval or protest. The air was very full of more than sound—sweat, but not gym sweat. A mixture of humanity and disinfectant filled the nostrils. In the darkened room with the vacancy, nineteen men slept on plastic double bunk-beds placed so close together that a large man would have to turn sideways to slip into his spot. The men were clothed, wearing what they owned. Two rows of five double bunks. "See, there's number nineteen—on the bottom at the end," said my guide, relieved that his tracking system was working and that there remained some shelter at Seaton that night.

I left with two impressions. First, I knew I would never want to have to spend a night at Seaton House. On the way home, I passed a man under a blanket over a steam grate at the University Avenue median just north of Dundas Street. I was unbelievably cold. I realized that he had made his choice. Yes, he could freeze, die, be run over, but he had his own space, he could see the stars, he was free. If I had any propensity to be frightened of closed, crowded, dark and strange situations, and I do, I would have taken his option. Second, I was impressed that working at Seaton House was a remarkable group of men and women who showed real respect for the huge crowd they had to deal with. This was different from the attitude I had seen many years ago as a freshman councillor representing the area. I attribute this to the new way that staff are thinking about homelessness, the leadership of the new manager, who had been a front-line worker in the hostel with a social-work background and new policies based on respect for the men who stayed there. But these workers are typical of the thousands who care for the homeless across Canada, day and night, on our behalf. Our tax dollars at work and I'm glad of it. I am sure many would prefer to be running housing projects in communities rather than emergency hostels, but with national housing policy as it is, a vacuum, that's not an option.

Toronto's homelessness crisis has simply continued to grow. Hundreds of new hostel beds are added each year, with a new hostel opening every month. Street homelessness continues to expand. Anger, terror, frustration—all the emotions build up. Keeping rational discussion of the issue going gets tougher and tougher. Fatigue has begun to strain at the edges of the discussion. Should police roust homeless people from parks? The once tolerant attitude is replaced by snarling rhetoric about how parks are for kids, not homeless people camping out. A colleague on council suggested that people would come here from Los Angeles once they learned they could camp out with impunity in Toronto.

Deaths in the street continued to mount through 1999 and 2000. Tales of horror of the kind that made the front pages when three men froze to death have begun to slip farther back in the papers and newscasts. What we all feared, the day when deaths due to homelessness would become like automobile crash fatalities—expected, part of normal life in the big city—has come to Toronto. Perhaps our city's ability to continue to provide the leadership, which it has done, will slip away. It's palpable, that slippage.

Every coin has its flip side. As callousness grows and homelessness normalcy begins insidiously to infect day-to-day Toronto, there's a reaction. It's ugly because it's angry. The homeless themselves see no results from the efforts of those who have advocated for them. Years of meetings and promises have passed, and yet friends still die on the streets and no housing is built. Seductive encouragement to lash out and resist "by any means" begins to sound reasonable to those with nothing to lose. Clashes, "riots" break out. This is encouraged, especially the rhetorical element, by the powers that be, because, finally, the homeless can be portrayed as undesirable again. People were starting to believe that the homeless were not responsible for their own situation. But then, as on June 16, 2000, the so-called Homelessness Riot at Queen's Park took place. Now, the homeless were the aggressors. Dozens of charging police on horseback scattered the hundreds of peaceful protestors like bowling pins. The church-group seniors (with whom I was standing) separated to avoid injury. Not all were successful as horses hooves broke bones. Paving stones were loosened from the walking paths and thrown in anger by younger men. The whole discussion of homelessness in Toronto had been reduced to this. Protesters and police were both injured. The fall-out lasted for months.

Ironically, the demonstration was held at Queen's Park, seat of the provincial government. Arguably the single most significant cause of increasing homelessness in Toronto has been the combined impact of the government's rent policy changes, housing cutbacks and social-service payment reductions. Yet Premier Harris is able to emerge from the fracas as the reasonable guy who wouldn't condone violence. A public-relations coup, to be sure. A setback to the debate.

At the same time, Toronto was, of its own initiative—and with little help from any other source—beginning quietly to build 220 new affordable-housing units, in four projects, scattered around the city on surplus city land. Making the point that we intend to lead by example here at city hall, the council, while it was still in the flush of the early enthusiasm to address the problem, provided financing from the revolving fund recommended by the Mayor's Task Force. Let's hope it can continue as the political tides and ebb tides begin to become more complicated.

The Prairies

Canada's first-ever national homelessness and affordable-housing disaster was declared on the Prairies. Ironic, because the cold cities of the Western breadbasket are, as the mayor of Regina told us once, "too cold for the homeless." They go inside; that's when the problems start. The poor quality of the places that people are forced to accept as home is a key issue for several Western cities. Winnipeg, Regina and Saskatoon all serve to illustrate the point.

Winnipeg

In the twenty-six months preceding the Big City Mayors' gathering, on the eve of the 1998 Grey Cup in Winnipeg, twenty-four deaths had occurred in slum-housing fires. The host of this historic meeting, the city's mayor, was someone I had known for his activism on municipal issues, including AIDS prevention. In fact, we are both Montreal–West Island expatriates and therefore immigrants to our chosen cities.

Glen Murray, the charismatic local city councillor who came to the mayor's chair in the fall of 1998, had experience as a counsellor of troubled kids. Young people he worked with often had no alternative to the substandard housing that Murray regarded as simply disgraceful. We drove together through some of the neighbourhoods that had experienced dozens of fatalities due to fires. Irish eyes betrayed his passion as he talked about absentee landlords allowing their buildings to deteriorate to such a point that they became fire traps. Pragmatism as well as a sense of justice motivated his approach to a solution. He pointed out, though, that the economics of housing were just not working in Winnipeg. Incomes of the poor were so low that they simply could not pay enough rent to provide the revenue needed by landlords to keep their places up to standard.

These problems have affected neighbourhoods like Main Street North, near Winnipeg's most famous intersection, Portage and Main. People are coping with straitened circumstances in this struggling area. More than half of the residents are of Chinese extraction, according to the latest census, and are living in straitened circumstances, by Winnipeg standards. With 39 percent of families receiving less than $10,000 in income (1996 census), paying rent for decent housing is a problem in this community. Fires have taken their toll there. As in many "Chinatowns" in Canadian cities, behind the surface enthusiasm of the flashing neon proclaiming prosperity often lie poverty and serious housing problems.

Throughout the 1990s, Winnipeg had a "soft" rental market. Vacancy rates ranged from a high of 6.6 percent in October 1991 and holding in the 6 percent range until 1998, when vacancies fell to 4 percent.[73] There was lots of housing available. Estimates are that the demand for rental housing could be satisfied with an additional 200 units a year until 2006.[74] However, the demolition of inner-city homes since 1994 (due to lack of maintenance by the owners) created pressures on the low end of the market. In 1998 alone, 123 single-family units were demolished.[75] Another indication of the general trend in the 1990s is provided by this unusual statistic: From 1991 to 1994, the number of placarded buildings in the inner city increased from 200 to 321. In the inner city, 12 percent of all residential dwellings were in need of major repair, according to the 1996 census.[76]

Still, since 1990 there have been fifteen organizations providing 550 beds, and they were reported to be generally full, with pressures rising. At the same time, the number of people on waiting lists for assisted housing has increased by 40 percent since 1993—for the Manitoba Housing Authority's units alone, and 47 percent of the households on that list were families representing 1,500 children in 1998.

A strategy was needed to bridge these gaps. Mayor Murray suggested that the national disaster be described so that the critical situation faced by his constituents in pathetic, poor-quality housing was included.

Encouraged by other Prairie cities facing the same problems, the Big City Mayors took his advice. A major part of their platform calls for federal expansion of the Residential Rehabilitation Assistance Program, to achieve 10,000 housing renovations for lower-income renters each year for a decade.

Critical housing issues face aboriginals in Winnipeg, as in many Canadian urban centres, especially in the West. There are modest off-reserve housing agreements between First Nations' organizations—like the Dakota-Ojibway Tribal Council and the Keewatin Housing Association—and the federal government, where the responsibility for housing for aboriginals lies. Important and unique issues are involved in addressing the pathetic aboriginal-housing situation, justifying a separate discussion later in this cross-Canada review.

Housing is, in Manitoba, a distinctly provincial matter—the province runs virtually all low-income housing programs, such as shelter allowances, and operates 17,000 social-housing units. But there was no indication that the provincial government, in the 1990s, shared the city's sense of urgency for action. So the city stepped in with initiatives of its own. Murray's council got behind the idea that special tax-experimentation and construction-permit-fee-waiving programs should be attempted to entice the standard of housing upward, through incentives to investment. With little happening provincially or federally prior to the end of 1999, the city itself created a $2 million housing-reserve fund to assist older neighbourhoods.[77] Finally, in response to the efforts of Winnipeg and other cities that had begun to act unilaterally, in December 1999 the federal and provincial governments announced a plan to provide $12 million in rehabilitation assistance to Winnipeg.

Regina

The City of Regina's response was brutally honest when I asked for a report on the state of homelessness and housing in that community: "Anecdotal evidence of hospital-service emergency wards and the police [holding people overnight] indicates their services are used in the winter to prevent exposure to the extreme cold."[78]

Just the kind of blunt talk that Mayor Doug Archer and FCM board member and Regina councillor Mike Badham typically bring to our discussions. Other cities have homeless people in their jails and emergency wards, but they're nervous about saying so, preferring to suggest that people in jails are there because they did something wrong, and wanting to steer clear of the notion that homeless people are taking emergency beds from those "truly in need." It's common talk on many Canadian downtown streets that sometimes it's best to commit a crime or get hurt—at least then you can get a bed and meal, maybe for a few days.

Regina's perceptive report on homelessness adds, "We also see increases in adult street prostitution and other gray-and-black-market, income-generating activities towards the end of pay or income-support-cheque cycles."[79]

You'll find few visible homeless in Regina, because homelessness is usually hidden. City staff reported, in the same memo: "In Regina we do have homeless, as evidenced by overcrowding [persons with no fixed or permanent address], camping out [people who have no permanent home who stay with friends and relatives and move from friend to friend or relative], and some housing units are unsuitable for habitation, but families must continue to live in them since there are no acceptable homes available, and transition houses are full."[80]

YMCA/YWCA and Salvation Army emergency hostels are found in many Canadian cities, and these organizations provide over sixty beds in Regina. Altogether, there were 42,000 "bed-nights" of emergency accommodation in the city in 1999, not including beds for women leaving abusive or family-violence situations.[81]

Indicators of the injustice that flows from inadequate housing situations emerges from data such as these:

- All fire deaths over the last ten years have been in neighbourhoods with the lowest-income families. All such fatalities in 1999 were in the inner city.
- Food-bank volume has doubled over the past ten years with a 6 percent increase in 1999 alone.

One fundamental in Regina has been the tumbling vacancy rate in private rental housing over the past decade—dropping from 6.5 percent in 1989 to 1.7 percent in 1998. Most recent reports from city staff indicate that vacancies have fallen to below 1 percent in mid-2000. With virtually no new rental construction and people coming into the cities as rural economies struggle during the farm crisis gripping the West, housing pricing pressures are inevitable. Lately, a large Calgary-based rental operator has been purchasing quantities of Regina's rental stock. Mayor Archer told me that this company may have acquired as much as 25 percent of the rental homes in the entire city. There are now serious concerns about the impact of this concentration of ownership—and of the refinancing costs of these purchases on the tenants who rely on these homes. Previous massive concentration moves in cities like Toronto in the early 1980s produced horrific pressures on rents, and Regina fears the worst.

Another ominous trend is poking its nose into the Saskatchewan capital: Demolitions are increasing in older, low-priced neighbourhoods. In fact, the number of vacant lots in the inner city has increased 50 percent over the past eight years.[82] Not only are affordable units lost in this process, but empty lots are like the missing teeth in the smile of a neighbourhood. Let's just say it's not positive. Developers often use this tactic—called "block busting"—to drive down the value of remaining properties, making way for parking lots and eventually some form of redevelopment for higher revenues. Rarely is there any provision for the displaced tenants. Property rights reign supreme over housing rights—even though neither is explicitly protected in Canada's Constitution.

Like most other cities, though, Regina is taking on the issue. In July 2000 the Mayor's Advisory Committee released a report that looked at all aspects of student, downtown, affordable-suburban, inner-city and social housing. Working with the co-operative movement, particularly the Regina Women's Construction Co-operative, the committee has encouraged new ideas for small projects. Without financial assistance from governments with access to growing tax bases—income, corporate and sales taxes—these promising initiatives will remain interesting "bench-scale" demonstration projects rather than needed full-fledged housing programs.

Saskatoon

The Saskatoon Real Estate Board paints a rather rosy picture of the housing situation on its website. According to the board, the annual family income required to carry a mortgage on a home in their city is just over $35,000 a year, contrasted with $65,000 in Toronto or Vancouver.[83] Also celebrated on this website promotion is the fact that apartment vacancy rates have declined due to in-migration caused by job growth, and a smaller supply of apartments due to conversion of rental housing to condominiums. Although the low vacancy rates have resulted in modest rent increases, rents are among the lowest in Canada.[84] In fact, the vacancy-rate graph looks like an Olympic ski jump, falling from a height of 8.8 percent in 1989 to 0.8 percent in 1998. Impact on tenant households from this situation will come right out of the food budget as rents begin their ascent. Although data for the most recent years are not yet available from Statistics Canada, the percentage of tenants in Saskatoon paying 30 percent or more of income in rent jumped by 15 percent between 1990 and 1995, increasing by almost 3,000 households. The number paying over 50 percent of their income in rent leaped from 5,205 to 7,045 in the same period.[85]

Along with a buoyant economy, insidious processes are at work. In 1996, 304 low-income housing units, financed originally under one of Canada's innovative national-housing programs called the Limited Dividend Program, were bought by investment corporations, and rents have subsequently been hiked to the tune of 45 percent by the new landlords.[86] Conversions of an estimated 548 units from rental to condominiums also took place since 1994, driving down the supply of affordable units.[87]

So despite the city's relatively lower rents when compared to many places in Canada, there are danger signs. The 1,600 households on the waiting list for social housing, half of whom are families, is one such sign. Almost 7,000 people stayed in Saskatoon's eight emergency shelters in 1998, over a quarter of these children. Hostel workers have noticed that people staying in emergency beds are staying longer.[88]

Aboriginals are especially hard hit in Saskatoon. Estimates suggest that 68 percent of shelter users are of aboriginal ancestry, although they represent only 8 percent of the city's population.[89] Proportions as high as 80 percent can be found among the incarcerated population.[90] Saskatoon was rocked by the freezing death of young aboriginal men, alone, in remote industrial areas. Rodney Naistus and Lawrence Wegner were found within five days of each other in January 2000. Neil Stonechild had met a similar fate a few months earlier. In the wake of the deaths, there were media reports of the possibility that police may have picked up the victims, driven them out of town and dropped them off in abandoned areas without laying charges—on these lethally cold nights. While not perhaps directly related to the housing issue, the incidents are stark reminders of what one account described as "a city of broken bridges, a city of two solitudes, prairie style."[91]

Saskatoon is blessed, though, with one of Canada's many creative minds in the affordable-housing field. Russel Mawby has the perfect job title in the Saskatoon bureaucracy: housing facilitator. Every city should have one. Most don't, because it sounds too threatening to usual practices. Hats off to Mayor Henry Dayday and his council for having the vision to be the first city I know of to take the step. Among the innovations that Mawby has brought to the debate in Saskatchewan, and beyond, is the Saskatoon Housing Initiatives Partnership (SHIP). This special fund will be seeded by provincial money and will promote start-up resources by attracting private donations through special tax provisions more flexible than the current charitable deductions. A multiplier effect of the initial government investment is created as a result, and more partners are engaged and involved in achieving the vision of new affordable-housing projects in the community. In the medium term, the SHIP proposal hopes to produce 200 new units a year—making a significant dent in the waiting lists and affordability problems looming in Saskatoon. This program is still being developed. Let's hope that the City of Saskatoon's website will feature a birth announcement soon.[92]

Calgary

Here are some quotations from a recent Calgary report.

- "Eighty percent of women with disabilities live on less than $5,000 a year."
- "Non-natives get work. We are different colours, but we still have the same blood."
- "I came to the city at 40 years old with no job or skills and a 5-year-old child."
- "[I became homeless because of] a lack of communication skills, work experience, and education [and poor] family relationships, lots of alcohol problems and lots of beatings."
- "When I am confused, I need someone to help me through to do things."
- "Why is it you treat me like a lesser human being?"

- "[To get off the street I need] some organized help as to options to get help financially and to find shelter accommodation. I have no idea where to look for help concerning long-term housing."[93]

These words, and many more like them, jumped off the pages of a modestly produced report on homelessness in Calgary, just before the soft-spoken alderman from that city took the podium at the FCM's annual meeting in Regina in June 1998. He was introduced as Bob Hawkesworth, co-chair of a committee dealing with homelessness in Calgary. As I listened, the penny dropped! Toronto was not the only place in Canada with a growing homelessness crisis! I honestly had not known this. No one in the media was talking about it. Homelessness was a dirty little secret, which each community was keeping to mayors and councillors from all across Canada itself. Well, Bob Hawkesworth had the guts to stand up and say that the mighty City of Calgary, home of oil barons and flamboyant stampedes, had homeless people! More than that, their council intended to do something about it.

Everything about what Hawkesworth said that day, and everything the Calgary committee did, was downright revolutionary. The report he spoke about had no page numbers. It's written in huge type, with drawings and point-form presentation, so that it's completely unlike a typical government report. Each section starts with shake-you-by-the-shoulders insights of homeless people themselves. Out of the mouths of people who've been there! No expert dissertations. No footnotes. Clear. Simple.

The first question the group asked was "Who is homeless and how many are there in Calgary?" They said that the earliest recorded estimate of "street dwellers" in Calgary, done in 1989 by the Horizon Society, a non-profit organization, was 100. The society added 5,000–7,000 "temporarily homeless/chronically hard to house and 10,000 more "at risk."[94] The opening chart of the report showed exponential increases over the years. Most recently, Calgary mayor Al Duerr reported to his fellow mayors that there were now 1,200 street dwellers—twelve times as many as a decade ago. The mayor's report (April 2000) also indicated that his city spent $200,000 to help the homeless in 1998, but had since increased that annual spending by ten times to $2 million (and counting).[95]

From today's perspective, the 1997 Calgary report is almost quaint: "Several churches are rallying their congregations to open their church facilities to shelter 10–15 individuals or families a night in need of emergency housing." Church basements in cities all over Canada now pack in 100 a night without thinking twice.

Lack of housing, unemployment, inadequate income, violence, addictions, mental-health issues and street life were common themes mentioned in the consultations conducted by the Calgary committee.[96]

But Bob Hawkesworth had started something that day. Councillors and mayors from across the country stepped to the microphones and said, "We have that problem, too, but we haven't looked into it the way you have. Let's work together."[97]

Frankly, Calgary's homelessness crisis is a bleak picture. Ten homeless people died in the twelve months preceding April 2000. "Shelters are operating over capacity the majority of the time with a low vacancy rate of 1 percent."[98] Calgary's 1998 homeless count showed an increase of 61 percent from 1996, amounting to 1,000 people a night.[99] (Calgary is the only city at present to do such a rigorous count at regular intervals.) Calgarian tenants have faced overall rent increases between 1997 and 1999 of 22.5 percent, with a forecast that rents would add another 3.5 percent in the year 2000, contributing to the happiness of the landlord subset of the population.[100] Tenant households forced to spend more than 50 percent of their incomes on rent climbed to 17,355 by 1995, and all indications are that this number has continued to rise.[101] No wonder that social-housing waiting lists grew between 1993 and 1998 by 64 percent—a conservative figure, as FCM researchers noted—because by 1998, despite qualifying under the government's social-housing criteria, "those with comparatively lower needs were discouraged from applying," a practice not in place in 1993.[102]

The fact is, in Calgary, people can often find work but housing is another matter. The market is just too tight. No wonder: An astounding 3,500 rental apartments were converted to condominiums between 1995 and 1998, while only 58 new rental units were started in 1998.[103] Rental units are completely disappearing—at sixteen times the rate that they are being produced. Those that remain are being priced out of the affordability range, through year-after-year rent increases well beyond inflation.

To the city's credit, community groups and the urban government did not sit on their collective Calgarian hands. They got busy. With the welcoming opening phrase "Remember, you are not alone!" the city's Information Office issued a comprehensive, easily pocketed booklet with all the information needed for survival and securing help when homelessness strikes—phone numbers, maps, services and friendly advice.[104] Drawbacks include the fact that the package assumed reasonable literacy, English as a first language and good eyesight, but it was a start.

Next, a Community Action Plan was developed by the ad hoc committee with the up-front goal of ending homelessness in Calgary.[105] Key to the plan were its goals of achieving "sufficient levels of suitable, adequate, safe, affordable emergency, transitional and permanent housing through closer working relationships among consumers, landlords, agencies and regulatory bodies."[106] The plan contained many practical suggestions, including transforming a disused military base into affordable housing, many municipal incentive initiatives and several provincial and federal regulatory changes. In the end, though, the strategy did not create the financial structure needed for the large number of new lower-priced rental units that would be needed to break the crisis.

That's why Calgary created the Calgary Homeless Foundation. With leadership from all sectors, the foundation suggests that "Calgary is unique in Canada in terms of the approach that has been taken—bringing together the not-for-profit, the private and the public sectors to work collaboratively on solutions."[107] A huge consultation and collaborative team was created on this basis, to develop the political will to gather the significant funds needed to build large amounts of housing. Its first report told gripping stories from Calgary's streets:

> Trisha is a young mother with two active children, ages 7 and 11. Recently divorced, Trisha works full-time as a cashier at Wal-Mart earning $7.50 per hour. With no financial support from her ex-husband, who is unemployed and unmotivated to find work, Trisha has a very difficult time making ends meet. She lives in a Calgary Housing Authority apartment that costs her $360 per month. Twice she's fallen behind on her rent, and has been threatened with eviction. The Salvation Army provided Trisha with emergency funds to bring her rent up to date. But, even when she keeps her groceries to a minimum and buys the kids their needs from second-hand stores, Trisha and her children are always less than one paycheque away from life on the street. It is such a struggle.

Curtis stands on the sidewalk outside of McDougall Centre. Wrapped in a large Canadian flag, Curtis distributes political leaflets. People walking by give him a wide berth, often staring at the ground as they hurry past. Curtis paces up and down. Occasionally, he shouts his agenda to anyone who will listen. The security people are aware that he is there, and they keep an eye on him, mostly to make sure he doesn't make a major nuisance of himself. Curtis has schizophrenia, and he has paraded up and down this block many times before. Later in the afternoon, he wanders down to the Drop-In Centre, folds his flag and leaflets and puts them in his backpack. Curtis is hungry, but he won't eat because the voices in his head tell him to be careful—someone is going to try to hurt him. He tries to stay awake as long as possible. Finally, he can hold out no longer and takes a mat between two suspicious people. The men who will sleep on either side of him hug the far side of their mats. Curtis wakes frequently throughout the night and thinks about going home. The problem is, he is not sure where home is.

Richard was a single, 42-year-old man who often spent his nights on a mat at the Drop-In Centre. A construction worker, Richard had struggled with alcoholism for many years—which of course made it difficult for him to hold down a job. But like most homeless people, Richard really wanted to turn his life around. So, he and a friend landed jobs as roofers and found a small basement suite that met their needs. The only problem was they couldn't come up with the money for the security deposit. Recommended [by a street worker], they decided to visit the Calgary Homeless Foundation. Because they were both working, they qualified for financial support and were approved for a security deposit loan. The Homeless Foundation immediately cut a cheque and called Richard's landlord to make arrangements to deliver the security deposit. But Richard's potential landlord now knew that Richard was homeless and might be more of a risk than he first thought, and decided to rent the suite to someone else. [Why did they not take the landlord to court under human rights legislation?] Richard took the news extremely hard and began drinking heavily. Two months later, he was found frozen to death in a park—just a few blocks away from the Drop-In Centre. "For Richard, losing the apartment was the final blow," said his social worker. "He just couldn't recover from the loss."[108]

In addition to the foundation's work to assist the homeless, Calgary has other initiatives, including the Sunalta Shelter extension and the Canadian Forces Base Lodge Barracks, with its eighty-eight units available until October 2001. (In Toronto, the loan of an armoury was terminated by Canada's military because it needed to accommodate the Y2K emergency team. The facility has not been re-offered, and it squats on the waterfront, empty, except for occasional marching cadets, despite hundreds of homeless in the streets.)

Edmonton

Bill Smith, Edmonton's mayor, was one of the first to join Mel Lastman's call for national action on homelessness. This surprised some. But Edmonton had been quietly grappling with growing numbers of people without homes. An Edmonton Task Force on Homelessness was established in late 1998, co-chaired by City Councillor Jim Taylor and MLA Gene Zwozdesky, mimicking the successful bi-level structure of Calgary's task force. With the help of that city's senior planner for housing, Daryl Kreuzer, the group issued its report on May 14, 1999.

The voices of Edmonton's homeless also spoke through the publication, which was enthusiastically titled *Homelessness in Edmonton: A Call to Action*. The surprisingly readable report is peppered with quotations. Reminding us of the obvious, Gary Trudel, a former homeless person, says "Don't forget the people."[109]

In fact, the Edmonton study included the following observation: "A count of people turned away by providers and crisis services identified 113, while an additional 32 individuals were discharged or ready for discharge from facilities but without a permanent residence."[110] So almost three dozen people were going to be set free from hospital or other institutions to rejoin the street population. A significant sign of a failing system. And another 113 people were given that familiar "no room at the inn" brush-off. In the Bible, that rejection at least produced some straw, cows' warmth and a roof. Not in Edmonton, on the day of the count, March 18, 1999.

At least Edmonton had the courage to admit the inadequacy of public policy. In my city, Toronto, despite co-chairing the relevant committee, I am unable to obtain the number of "refusals" on any given night. Apparently it's "too complicated" to obtain the number without the possibility of duplication in the counting effort! God forbid that we might duplicate a homeless person in our statistics! Apparently in Edmonton the committee felt it would be better to err on the side of overestimating the moral failure.

That study also included this statement: "For children, the majority (61 of 112) were absolute homeless compared to 51 sheltered [meaning that they had a bed in a shelter]." No wonder the subtitle of the committee's work was *A Call to Action*.

Edmonton's aboriginal community of 26,280 people represents only 4.1 percent of the city's overall population, but over 60 percent of them live below Canada's poverty line. That compares to 26 percent of the entire Edmonton population who are "officially poor."[111] This puts Edmonton in the category of communities with high poverty rates, and both declining absolute rental stock (condominium conversions and demolitions) and falling vacancy rates combine to add to the pressure on people who must rely on rental housing.

Here are other discouraging statistics about the housing crisis in Edmonton:

- An August 1998 study—mid-summer—found that the 827 emergency beds were 97 percent occupied.
- In two years, 1997 to 1999, the waiting list for Edmonton's largest family subsidized housing provider rose from zero to 865.
- FCM research estimated, in 1999, that Edmonton needed an additional 2,600 subsidized rental units with 30 percent of these being supportive housing for those coping with mental-health and addiction challenges.
- A Canadian record for the rise and collapse of rental-housing vacancy rates was set when Edmonton climbed from a low 1.8 percent vacancy in 1990 to a high of 10.2 percent five years later and back down to 1.95 percent in 1998—and still falling. No wonder rents began to rise, increasing 5.3 percent in 1998 alone. Estimates for 1999 are 4.1 percent, with forecasts of an astounding 6 percent increase in 2000.
- Over 1,800 low-rent units were lost, mostly in Edmonton's central city, as various federal program funding arrangements expired, allowing conversion of rental housing to condominium ownership.
- Over 20,000 households in the greater Edmonton area are paying more than half of their income in rent to their landlord.[112]

But what action has Edmonton actually taken in response? Their council joined with community groups to produce a list of initiatives (detailed in a memo from Mayor Smith to his colleague mayors):

- Council approved a Year 2000 expenditure of $1.3 million to assist with the implementation of recommendations of their task force.
- Vacated buildings, such as the Charles Camsell Hospital and lands no longer needed by the city, were to be considered for housing projects.
- Transportation needs of homeless people were to be considered through free bus tickets, special transportation allowances, etc.
- More drop-in child care was to be considered to help single parents access work.
- The position of Housing Initiatives Co-ordinator was created within the municipal staff to begin implementing the many recommendations of the study.

Although these moves are constrained by the limits of local action, Edmonton's City Council—and many Edmontonians—seem to have embraced the idea that a full-fledged national plan is required to tackle the shocking problem that has been documented in Alberta's capital city.

Wood Buffalo

We close out our Prairie review of homelessness with Wood Buffalo, Canada's largest municipality in sheer physical area. It's home to vast waves of immigrants who have come to participate in the oil-sands development and related industries. I was surprised to learn that there was a housing crisis in this quintessential boom town. How could a town with so much money have an affordable-housing problem?

Here are some excerpts from a fax from the mayor's office of Wood Buffalo to the Big City Mayors' meeting in April 2000:

> We have one shelter for men, which accommodates 32 and is currently 100 percent occupied; 75 percent of those staying are employed and cannot find rental accommodations. Another section of our working homeless resides in hotels due to the fact that the shelter is full. With the coming of spring in our region the campsites will

be occupied with people who are working and have no accommodations available to them. Today, there is a visual increase in homeless people living in vehicles.

We have one women's crisis centre, which will accommodate women and children living in abusive situations. The centre has had to extend the length of the stay [beyond the twenty-one-day limit] due to the fact that approximately one-third of its clients cannot find rental accommodations.

Indicators of homelessness and affordable-housing problems in our community are:

- Landlords less tolerant, therefore evictions are on the rise.
- Apartments are being shared by a number of individuals to meet current rental rates.
- Room and board housing arrangements are on the rise, use of illegal basement suites, increase in food bank services, increase in clients accessing the Thrift Store services, increase in panhandling, etc.
- There has been a decrease of rental property in our area. In the past five years the rental stock has decreased by 822 units, and another 272 have been proposed for conversion from rental to condominiums.
- As of March, 2000 our vacancy rate is 0 percent. Our rental rates are increasing every six months on monthly tenancies.[113]

Wood Buffalo's lively mayor, Doug Faulkner, brings his Newfoundland passion to the job of calling on the federal government to adopt a national housing policy to address these critical situations in his community.

British Columbia

Extremes and hyperbole seem to define the images of British Columbia—from its scenery to its politics. Geography provides the most beautiful of Canadian backdrops for the extensive homelessness and the affordable-housing problems experienced in the communities of Canada's West Coast, Rockies and interior plains. Yet the public policies to solve the problem are the most ambitious affordable-housing programs in the country.

Alone among Canada's provincial legislatures, B.C.'s government has approached homelessness from a province-wide standpoint, with hard-hitting awareness programs and accelerated, innovative housing for the hardest to house. The impetus for this approach came from the work of a network of community groups known as the Housing and Homeless Network of B.C., not a group to pull its punches: "Since 1993, when the federal government abandoned the national housing program, hundreds of thousands of low-income families, seniors, singles, people with disabilities, urban Aboriginals, new immigrants, and those with serious health issues have been forced to live in substandard third-world housing, temporary shelters and on the streets. The root cause of homelessness is clear: lack of appropriate affordable housing."[114]

To reflect B.C.'s provincial perspective I'll discuss homelessness in all of B.C. at once rather than adopting the city-by-city approach used in other parts of this cross-country review.

As she walks with me through the streets of Vancouver's Downtown Eastside, Linda Mix exudes the steady commitment and passion of one who has worked in the heart of the affordable-housing crisis for many years. What different eyes she and I possessed as we surveyed the Sunday morning scenes. There I was, buoyed by the sight of excavation equipment, hoardings and the cranes rising above them all, combining in the actual construction of hundreds of well-designed, low- and mixed-income homes, right in an area whose very visible homeless clearly needed it. I had not seen any such activity anywhere in Canada lately, except for a little in Montreal. (Back home, Toronto's affordable-housing cranes had been silent for years.) So on this April day in the new millennium, like a parched desert traveller, I found myself gulping in the optimism and hope represented by this housing under construction. Finally, some evidence of what we need right across the country, in every city and town!

Linda's eyes were seeing missed opportunities, terrains of struggle and all the work that remained to be done. Stepping respectfully past the pair of women in an alcove—who looked at us with the pleading, sunken eyes and skin-and-bones postures that gave away their heavy addictions—Linda told me about some of the unscrupulous owners of the old hotels in the area. These terribly maintained decrepit structures are where many homeless and at-risk people live, paying exorbitant rents to landlords who seem to have no respect for the buildings they own or the people in them. With B.C.'s long history as a primary resource-extraction economy, the hotels were the big-city home for the miners and loggers who flowed in from the bush after months at work camp. Thousands of these men queued up for rooms near the railway and docks in what is now called Vancouver's Downtown Eastside and neighbouring Gastown. They were single, flush with money and looking for thrills and company. In those days, the hotels performed a crucial service. Today, they are still essential, but for a very different reason—they provide the roofs over the heads of people who would otherwise be in the streets: the old, the desperately poor, the improperly provided-for mentally ill, the neglected addicts and fleeing youth. Many cities simply do not have a stock of this kind of "housing" and therefore experience much more street homelessness and use of emergency shelters. But in Vancouver, packed into the impossibly tiny rooms with their bare lightbulbs and disgusting washrooms at the end of the hall, people struggle to get by.

Ross lives in a hotel room in Vancouver. At 73 years of age, he is divorced and estranged from his two children. Ross spent nineteen years in the army, and he fought in the Second World War. He retired after many years of work in sales and construction. He tells his story this way:

> I was desperate when I took this room. I was tired and it was dark so I took it. It's steep for a little room. I'm paying $375.
>
> It's hot, smelly and noisy. It's filthy. Badly in need of a good coat of paint. No hotplate, busted fridge. Everything is busted here. The sheets and towels fall apart in my hands. Mirror is off the wall, can't shave. I found a hypodermic needle underneath the bed, so druggies have used it. It's noisy, buses and trucks all day and night. It's full of cockroaches. I don't know how they get away with that. Why aren't the inspectors around more often?
>
> I got robbed two weeks ago. My hip still bothers me where I got hit. He was about 23 and took off like a jackrabbit. Asking for help here is like asking for a miracle. I have no other place to go. If I wasn't here I would be homeless. Most of my friends are gone. I can't stay with anybody.
>
> Frankly speaking, 30 years ago if you were a war veteran you had no problems finding accommodation. I was hopeful that my years of active service might give me privilege to some place, but I'm pretty much forgotten. So are all the other people.[115]

There are an estimated 13,000 to 15,000 single-room occupancy (SRO) hotel and motel units across British Columbia, mostly concentrated in the larger urban centres.[116] Many of these are being lost, closed because they cannot pass building-standards inspections. Other units are destroyed by fire, are abandoned or torn down. Still others are demolished for redevelopment or conversion to upper-end housing. A 1995 B.C. report documented that "over 900 SRO units have been lost in the last nine years."[117] Since then, a concerted effort by housing activists has resulted in funding programs through B.C. Housing, which is purchasing and restoring some of these old hotels for use by the same people who have always lived in them—but with a measure of dignity. On our morning walk, Linda Mix took me on a tour of a recently reopened SRO hotel. The gentle giant at the front door, on duty as manager, was so friendly and quietly proud of what had been accomplished that I could see that this non-profit model had great potential. People living there told us how the new digs were helping them to turn their lives around. So impressed were we that my assistant at the time, Peter Zimmerman, has himself now moved to the City of Toronto housing staff, where he is responsible for building one of Toronto's first SROs.

Still, despite occasional important glimmers of hope, the housing situation in B.C. remains grim. Within the Greater Vancouver Regional District alone, there are an estimated 13,000 on the waiting list for B.C. Housing and non-profit housing providers.[118] City staff estimate that 300 to 600 people are sleeping on the street each night. B.C. Housing reports that the number of people living on the streets in Vancouver is estimated at between 600 and 1,000, with many in the surrounding municipalities, such as Surrey and New Westminster.[119] The city's Tenant Assistance Program reported observing an increase in absolute homelessness when they went out after midnight searching for homeless. All the shelters, which altogether have room for 300 to 400 people each night, are full and "had to turn away 4,000 people during 1998–1999. Both the number of people served and the turn-aways increased by 10 to 20 percent last year."[120]

"From 1995 to 1998, the number of 'sleep-overs' [people having to sleep on the floor as a last resort] at the Crosswalk Shelter in downtown Vancouver almost tripled, from 3,887 to 10,758."[121]

The coroner's service reported fourteen homeless people who died from exposure between 1992 and 1997 in Vancouver.[122] Community groups indicate that this trend is growing.

Almost half of the city's tenants (47.2 percent) spent more than 30 percent of their total household income on shelter costs, up 14.3 percent from 1991 to 1996. Contrast this to the Canadian national average of 27.6 percent (paying over 30 percent) and the stresses are clear.[123] And fully 31,000 Vancouver tenant households—one in four families—pay more than 50 percent of their income in rent costs.[124]

Vancouver's downtown core experienced a net loss of affordable units in the 1990s, although not as fast as other communities, because new homes were being built at the same time. Single rental units declined by 1,168 due to neglect, fires, closings, conversion to tourist accommodation, redevelopment and demolition. During the same 1991–1998 period, 700 new social-housing units were added to the stock, still leaving a significant net loss.[125]

In a campaign to protect the downtown area for those in need of affordable housing, the Downtown Eastside Residents' Association has put together a Community Housing Plan.[126] One of its recommendations is a "one-for-one" replacement policy and would require that the elimination of an affordable unit—whether it be a SRO hotel room or other low-income rental housing—would have to be replaced by the redeveloper. Had such a policy already been in place, downtown would be 700 new units ahead of the game in the 1990s, rather than 468 units behind. The plan also calls for the following: no net loss to the existing stock of over 10,000 low-income housing units; creating provincial legislation and by-laws to stop hotel conversions and ensure demolition control; enforcing standards; and achieving funding opportunities through regulations and other measures.[127]

I would not have imagined Victoria to have a homelessness problem—it just doesn't have that kind of image. I was wrong. Victoria has a similar number of homeless people to Toronto, taking into account the relative populations of the two cities.[128] Victoria's Cool Aid Society produced a report in 1997 called *And Miles to Go*, which was dedicated to those known to have died on the streets of B.C.'s capital since 1984. The dedication at the front of the document lists 102 names, which speaks volumes about the crisis in that city.[129]

The report's author, reflecting a broad consultation process in Victoria and twenty-seven years of his own front-line experience with marginalized populations, captured the emerging passion and concern in the community at the time:

> In its 1992 study, the New York City Commission on Homelessness reported that half of all homeless families placed in permanent housing returned to the shelter system. Similar rates were reported in Washington, D.C. Our research for this region supports what these cities discovered: housing alone is not the entire solution. For those in need of assisted housing, housing and support services are interrelated.
>
> But is it any wonder this concept has continued to evade us when we as a community remain largely blind to the homeless and refuse to really see the disengagement? They are like ghosts in our midst, adrift and lacking the resources to improve the conditions they live in.
>
> We live in a climate of poor-bashing and denial about mental illness, while blame for the consequences of bad management typically falls on those who are "managed." Many of us seemingly want the poor and vulnerable to disappear. Few of us want them in our backyards. Meanwhile, increasing numbers of people are being pushed into homelessness, many of them emerging from sectors of society not previously plagued by the threat of being without a home.[130]

Cool Aid's *Miles to Go* report is a stunning example of a community-based study filled with powerful and sophisticated data. Optimistic examples of innovative and successful local, national and international strategies are offered for moving us out of the homelessness crisis. Since this virtual call to arms, the Cool Aid Society has constructed what I would consider the best shelter in the country—and a longer-term, transitional housing project, building on the need for both housing and parallel-support mechanisms to help make the return from homelessness successful.

Optimism amid despair seems to abound in B.C. Serious social problems are flagged but then, instead of griping, community groups roll up their sleeves and get busy. When faced with financial institutions who would not allow the poor and homeless to have a bank account, Jim Greene and others in Vancouver's Downtown Eastside created the community's own—called the Four Corners. It proved to be the big banks' loss, because this small institution mushroomed, created jobs and is keeping money in the local community. At the same time, the simple ability to manage meagre personal funds is allowing people to stabilize their housing, support and employment situations. Across the street, the Carnegie Centre functions as the virtual living room for the SRO and homeless community. Nourishment and resources from a community kitchen (great, cheap food) to the learning and entertainment resources of a library are all included, as well as housing assistance and other community-run services.

There was victory in a long battle to preserve Vancouver's oldest block of houses—and their Victorian neighbourhood streetscapes—known as the Mole Hill community. Threatened by speculative demolition and redevelopment pressure, the oldest of this affordable housing dated as far back as 1888, less than two years after Vancouver itself was founded. Confrontation turned into negotiations, which were finally concluded, successfully creating a community-restoration, rehabilitation and redevelopment project in a partnership with the City of Vancouver and B.C. Housing. The goal achieved here was not to protect West End property values but to protect a mixed-income community.

B.C. has also taken the bull by the horns on the affordable-housing construction front. In the past six years, the provincial government has funded more than 4,100 units for families and singles through the Homes B.C. program. The province also provides funding and support for communities and municipalities, like Vancouver, to convert some of the old, private and problematic SRO hotels into high-quality but still-affordable SRO accommodation. Such a strategy ensures that re-investment and rejuvenation of downtown areas with new loft "lifestyles" and condominiums will not have the simultaneously destructive effect of driving out the poor—as so often happens through urban gentrification.

B.C. Housing's creative force, the irrepressible Jim O'Dea and his team, have even negotiated with developers of new condos to include significant numbers of lower-income units right in the new project, sometimes with whole floors devoted. Meanwhile, the developer picks up some assured financing, perhaps some relaxing of development rules, or other benefits. Win-win creativity is the watchword. Using these techniques, O'Dea may well double the number of affordable units actually created by the funding provided by the province in its 1999 budget, which had already doubled the support from 600 units a year to 1,200. Still, had federal funding for social housing not been withdrawn throughout the 1990s, roughly 11,000 additional affordable-housing units would have been built in B.C. by now. Homelessness would not be anywhere near its current level.

The housing ministry also took the unusual step of producing a practical and resourceful guide to deal with the resistance often found when low-income housing is proposed in any community. Resistance taking the form of a "Not in My Back Yard" attitude (NIMBY) has slowed down or killed many worthwhile projects, not only in B.C. but across Canada. It's just that across Canada, virtually no such housing is being built these days, so NIMBY is pointing at the street homeless and other targets of urban angst. The B.C. guide *Toward More Inclusive Neighbourhoods* gives examples of how NIMBY resistance has been effectively overcome, with positive results. Resources and strategies cited in this guide are helping community groups and non-profits to create positive ways of presenting their ideas and plans for low-income housing.[131]

Not everything is rosy, though. Right downtown the huge, full-block, historic, beautiful-but-vacant department store Woodwards sits wasting away in the hands of speculators. Community plans to transform these hundreds of thousands of square feet of space into housing, workplaces and community services have faltered. The resulting impasse has become a serious barrier to the injection of energy, capital and rejuvenation into this urban decay at the same time as affordable housing.

The North

"In the North, housing is a big, big issue!" Eileen Badiuk, past president of the Canadian Housing and Renewal Association and an employee of Saskatchewan Health working in Northern communities, was trying to make sure that I did not do the usual Southern Canadian navel-gazing exercise.

While many housing concerns in the North relate to native housing, to be discussed next, the emerging problem of overcrowding in lower-income households is now joining housing quality and energy costs as key issues. Some mayors of Northern communities are beginning to join forces and open dialogue. The servicing of land for housing development in the North can make new housing costs almost prohibitive. Rural and Northern poverty is also a debilitating fact of life. With half of the population of the North being less than 20 years of age and, therefore, not bringing in much income, families are finding that doubling-up, and tripling-up, is becoming a coping mechanism to match incomes to housing costs. Debilitating effects are inevitable with the enormous family stresses that result.

As in the rest of the country, federal housing programs in the 1970s and 1980s were working well to keep housing problems at bay. They focused on home-ownership assistance for low-income households under the Rural and Native Housing Program. Various options permitted leasing to purchase or other pathways to full ownership. Without banks and real-estate services in most communities, simple logistics to finance or buy and sell land to create housing are barriers not faced elsewhere in Canada.

Whitehorse has participated in the FCM National Housing Policy Options Team, but was fortunate to report few housing-affordability concerns at present.

Aboriginal Homelessness

Entering Council Fire, a native friendship centre in downtown Toronto, on a cold winter night was one of the most disturbing experiences of my twenty years as a city councillor. The facility, designated as a "drop-in centre," has become a de facto overnight shelter for at times as many as 185 people, 50 percent of whom are usually aboriginal.[132] On that night, Council Fire was absolutely full—mats covered every space on the floor; people lay, bodies touching, in rows. In only one other circumstance had I ever seen a similar picture that left such a visual impression—bodies laid out for identification after some horrible act of mass violence. The young Council Fire staff, rather than turn anyone away into the uncertainty of the night, even opened their small office upstairs to make more space available for a family.

This, I was told casually, was a pretty typical night in this cramped basement facility that is barely the size of two school classrooms.

The image of so many people crowded onto the floor of Council Fire is a fragment of a larger picture of homelessness in Canada. It is also a powerful reminder that the social policies and problems that have contributed to this terrible scene have had a frightening and disproportionate impact on this country's aboriginal people.

How many homeless native people are there in Canada? Sadly, as with non-natives, the path into homelessness is also a descent into a statistical void. There is no reliable national data as to the extent of this problem. In cities like Calgary, where some decent local data are being collected, the heavy weight of homelessness on native Canadians is abundantly clear. In this city, aboriginals make up 2.1 percent of the population but constitute over 18 percent of emergency shelter admissions.[133] This same magnitude of overrepresentation has also been identified in Edmonton (aboriginals are 4 percent of population but 40 percent of homeless population) and Toronto (aboriginals are 1 percent of the population and 15 percent of shelter admissions).[134]

Why are aboriginal people so overrepresented in our homeless population? If we look at some the general factors contributing to homelessness discussed in other chapters, a few key reasons become abundantly clear. Most significantly, higher rates of poverty and lower levels of availability of decent affordable housing drive aboriginal homelessness.

Table 4.1 provides just a few indicators of the housing difficulties faced by aboriginal people.

Table 4.1: Comparison of Canadian and Aboriginal Housing Indicators, 1991

	Canada	Aboriginal[1]	Aboriginal Position
Occupied dwellings	10,018,265	239,240	2.4% of Canadian households[2]
In need of major repairs	9.8%	19.6%	2 times as many in need of major repairs
No piped water supply	0.1%	9.4%	More than 90 times as many with no piped water
No bathroom facilities	0.6%	3.2%	More than 5 times as many
No flush toilet	0.5%	5.3%	More than 10 times as many
Average number of persons per dwelling	2.7	3.5	About 30% higher than the Canadian average
Average number of rooms per dwelling	6.1	5.8	Slightly smaller
Tenant-occupied dwellings	37.1%	48.7%	Almost 1/3 more tenants, not counting band-owned housing
Average gross rent per month	$546	$495	$51 per month lower on average

Notes:

1. According to the 1991 Aboriginal Peoples Survey (APS).
2. The actual figure is closer to 2.7 percent of Canadian households, owing to undercounting in the APS. Canadian data include only non-farm, non-reserve dwellings. The aboriginal data comprise all non-farm dwellings, including those on reserves, where at least one of the occupants self-identifies as an aboriginal person. Note that tenant-occupied dwellings do not include band-owned housing, which is treated as a separate category (see Table 4.2). Owners' major payment per month refers to the average monthly payments made by the owner to secure shelter.

Source: Royal Commission on Aboriginal Peoples 3, ch. 4.

In terms of poverty, income problems clearly weigh more heavily on aboriginal people than they do on the rest of the Canadian population. The Royal Commission on Aboriginal Peoples found that in 1991, 35 percent received less than $10,000 in annual income from all sources, compared with 26 percent of the non-aboriginal population.

5 The National Picture

The last chapter presented pictures—sometimes only glimpses—of homelessness in various communities. And you will have seen from the various data—about vacancy rates, about the number of tenants paying more than 30 (and more than 50) percent of income on rent, about housing available for low-income earners, the growth of shelters, affordable-housing construction reports, and much else—the problem is enormous, and it's growing.

But we have yet to look at the big picture. Why do we need to do that? Because any effort to design strategies to solve the problem—and any effort to create workable (realistic) social policy—is utterly dependent on fact.

So, what do we need to know about homelessness in Canada?

First, the numbers of homeless people:

- How many people are homeless?
- How many people are living in shelters, hostels, etc.?

- How many people spend 30 to 50 percent of their income on rent—the "Core Needs" group?
- How many people spend more than 50 percent of their income on rent?

Second, housing:

- What is the quality of our housing?
- What is the vacancy rate for affordable units?
- How many affordable units are in need of repair/renovation to bring them to acceptable standards?
- How many low-rent units are being demolished or renovated for the high-priced market?
- What about new and co-op housing at modest rents?

To complicate matters, Canadians are blessed (or cursed) with three levels of government: municipal, provincial and federal. But which level has responsibility for housing? The answer to that question depends on whom you ask or how you phrase the question. However, in recent years, municipalities have been forced to deal with the issue, because the "higher" levels of government have, for the most part, washed their hands of the problem. And municipalities don't have the money to create solutions.

Now, that is the context in which we have to do battle. It isn't pretty, but it's the reality.

In November of 1998, the mayors (or their representatives) from the biggest cities in Canada passed a resolution declaring homelessness and the affordable-housing crisis to be a national disaster. To back up their rhetoric, they created the National Housing Policy Options Team to design options for a national housing policy for Canada to take the country out of the crisis.

Imagine that we going to create a plan to eliminate homelessness in Canada. And we'd better add to this project the goal of reducing the affordability crisis in housing, which hundreds of thousands of Canadians are facing.

NHPOT's first major challenge was to determine the size of the homelessness and affordable-housing problem in Canada. But there were no solid national data—perhaps the best proof of the absence of a national housing policy.

We had five months (before the June 1999 National FCM Convention in Halifax) to create a full set of recommendations for the 700 communities that then made up the FCM (now, over 1,000 municipalities are members). We decided to collect the information in two ways: (i) national data were pulled together from a variety of sources and standardized;[1] and (ii) city-by-city profiles were created.[2]

The group could have attempted to create a snapshot of the number of roofless people in Canadian communities on any one day. As we have seen already, most communities simply do not have this information. The individual profiles of some of Canada's larger cities are all we had.

The variations across Canada are clear. A shocking increase in homeless families and rapidly growing affordability problems are the dominant features of the picture in Toronto. The boom in Calgary brings people who have or want jobs but have no housing. Aboriginal peoples' housing needs press upon the communities of the Prairies. Montreal neighbourhoods attempt to deal with the consequences of concentrations of poverty. Elsewhere, seniors' housing and homecare needs are rising fast while budgets and services are being trimmed. Housing for the disabled, once making headway, is slipping as programs are downloaded or phased out. Overall, the rental share of new housing is rapidly shrinking, while the number of tenants in need of this kind of housing has risen and is expected to continue to rise. Baby boomers becoming seniors will need rental housing, including specialized seniors' accommodation. As the "echo-boom" generation hits the housing market, the demand for affordable rental housing will continue to grow.

So, the pressures on the housing stock are significant. How many Canadians will need housing in what price ranges? Those that cannot afford what is available will be the Canadians who will become homeless, or who will live at the edge of this precipice.

Faced with this worrisome picture, the team looked at various dimensions of the problem.

Street Homelessness, Shelters and Hostels

Our review of the national picture found that the "use of homeless shelters on an average night is about 300 people in Vancouver, 1,200 in Calgary, 460 in Ottawa and close to 4,000 in Toronto. Since then, numbers have increased sharply in Toronto and Calgary and significantly in Edmonton, Hamilton and Mississauga."[3] We learned that one downtown Vancouver shelter turns away twice as many people each night as it did five years ago. Toronto has been opening almost one new shelter each month for the past year in an attempt to stay ahead of the rising needs. At up to 500 new beds a year, with costs of approximately $40 per bed per night, this expansion program is adding $6 to $7 million in annual expenses to the city's budget.

Toronto's own analysis shows that four to five times as many people could be provided with permanent housing for the same costs, but the provincial government, which pays 80 percent of the emergency hostel bill, will not allow their funds to be used to create new social housing. Recently, the mounting pressure for better solutions prompted the province to allow some creativity in the use of hostel service funding, and the city council is attempting to sneak some forms of more permanent housing into the mix.

Meanwhile, as we have seen from our earlier cross-country review, emergency-shelter services in Edmonton and Calgary, Moncton and Halifax are close to 100 percent capacity nightly, with demand rising. And just about everywhere across the country, shelter users are staying longer in the emergency facilities. Alternative housing options are tougher and tougher to find in the middle of the housing crunch.

Core Needs

But these data and stories were iceberg tips compared with the looming mass of households facing severe housing affordability pressures. Beyond the numbers of street homeless and shelter users, evidence is accumulating of a much broader population of Canadians at significant risk of losing their housing at any time. From this much larger group, the homeless of tomorrow are drawn.

Core Housing Need is a term developed by the CMHC to count the households unable to afford a suitable, adequate, median-rent unit in their community and that have one or more of the following concerns:

- affordability—their home costs more than 30 percent of their gross income;
- suitability—their home is too small for the household size and composition;

- adequacy—their home lacks full bathroom facilities or needs major repairs.[4]

The most recent data (from CMHC) are shown in Appendix C. From this table, we found some alarming and striking trends.

Here's what Core Need means in 1996 dollars: The over one million Canadian tenant households who live in Core Need situations have average incomes of $14,600. (There is a range by province from $11,600 to $17,500.) These tenant households pay, on average, 47 percent of their income in rent. This translates to $6,862 a year or $571.83 a month. This leaves, again on average, $7,738 for all other living costs, including food, clothing, health products, education, transportation, insurance, utilities (where these are not included in rent). The average Canadian tenant household has 2.6 persons. How does this affect daily living? Core Need tenant households have, on average, $4,552 per person per year, or $87.50 per week, or $12.50 per day per person for all living expenses other than rent.

What does this mean? At a couple of loonies for transportation a day (more if these tenants have to drive a car), seven loonies a day for food—no fast-food allowed on this budget—there's $3.50 a day for everything else. No wonder food-bank use has exploded and that those who resort to food banks cite affordability as the key factor. Add a dollar a day for phone service. Phoneless Canadians are an increasing group. It's hard to deal with emergencies, get and keep a job, stay socially engaged, avoid loneliness, not to mention have fun when you have no phone. Forget the dollar a day Internet service for your children trying to keep up with the Joneses whose kids are "plugged in."

Now, remember, we talking about "average Core Need tenants." Roughly half those households are worse off than the average we've described. That means 600,000 households (approximately a million Canadians) are facing even greater daily financial challenges.

We wanted to find out if things were getting better or worse, so we looked at the changes in just five years, comparing 1991 and 1996 data. The table in Appendix C shows that the number of tenant households in Core Need increased from 1,273,175 to 1,670,770. Since 1996, all indications are that the trend has continued because raised rents have outpaced incomes—particularly in post-1998 Ontario, where previous strict rent controls were largely removed, producing double-digit rent increases when tenants moved and well beyond inflation increases in almost all other units.

If we look province by province, between one-third and one-fifth of tenant households were in Core Need in 1996. In all but Alberta and B.C., this number had risen sharply between 1991 and 1996. Indications are that the rate of increase continues. All studies of the rise in homelessness across Canada show that inability to pay rent as well as cover other living costs is a principal cause of people's losing their homes. Other factors play a role, such as the need for supportive mental-health care, addiction treatment or refuge from abuse. However, affordability and rising poverty always emerge as ubiquitous foundations of the homelessness crisis. For this reason, our study for the FCM spent considerable time documenting and analyzing this growing feature of Canadian life. (See Appendix C.)

The problem with these statistics is that we're looking back at a crisis that is still unfolding ahead of us. To create an effective national housing policy, we need realistic projections about where these trends are headed so that we can calibrate our response appropriately.

Let's look more closely at the affordability issue for tenants.

In 1996, 1.7 million tenant households (nearly 2.9 million Canadians, or 43 percent of all tenants) paid 30 percent or more of the their income on rent.

As we know, the 30 percent cut-off point was considered the appropriate income proportion to determine Core Need. Canadian housing policy expert Jeremy Carver wrote in the late 1940s that families should not have to spend more than 20 percent of their income on housing.[5] He argued that Canadian housing policy should be directed towards ensuring that no one had to pay more than that amount. In the 1960s, without any apparent rationale, 25 percent began to be considered by CMHC as the appropriate number to use. This crept up to 30 percent in subsequent years.

This statistical creep had the effect of apparently reducing the magnitude of the problem each time the adjustment was made. An additional and cruel factor is also ignored: The incomes of the lowest-income Canadians generally fell for the past twenty-five years. This fall accelerated in the 1990s with government policies at all levels causing transfers of funds to individuals to be reduced.

People Paying 50 Percent of Income for Housing

Despite all these caveats, our team decided to illustrate the new level of critical housing affordability by adding a further cut-off—the number of Canadian households paying more than 50 percent of their income in rent. This 50 percent number has only just recently begun to be used in policy analysis. Prior to this time, such a level of rent was considered such an aberration, such an exception, one that simply couldn't be sustained by enough people to warrant serious attention.

The biggest jump, in terms of the number of people affected, has happened in Ontario, with Quebec not far behind. Ontario had 194,920 households exceeding the 50 percent threshold in 1991, but this increased to 300,645 by the 1996 census information (based on 1995 incomes). This increase means that over 20,000 households a year were added to that list. That's the size of a small Ontario town every year for five years, in Ontario alone. And all that was happening before the Conservatives took power. Data on what has happened since are not yet available.

However, we do know that incomes for those on social assistance were cut by 21.6 percent early in the Harris mandate, which drove up the ratio of rent to income for lowest-income tenants in one fell swoop. As well, inflation has outpaced the minimum wage. Total employment income in the province has risen but the distribution has not been even. As we've seen, rent-control relaxation has allowed income to the landlord subgroup of Ontarians to rise, drawing cash-flow from tenant incomes. Higher-income groups benefit from tax dodges, while increased user charges for services such as transit have a disproportionate impact on lower-income earners.

Quebec's 50 percent club showed an increase from 194,220 to 273,825 tenant households—a huge five-year jump. Other large increases (in the 50 percent-housing-costs group) were found in British Columbia and Nova Scotia. Yukon more than doubled its relative small number of tenant households in these straits (from 225 to 560) between 1991 and 1996.

When numbers of households are converted to people, we have over a million people in the deepest housing crisis—in danger of losing their homes—and we are approaching three million (one in ten Canadians) in serious difficulty.

Who's "At Risk"?

Canadian housing-affordability crises strike both families and individuals. It's amazing how single-parent families get hit so hard, though—far in excess of their proportion of the population. And no one needs to be reminded that the lone parent in these families is much more likely to be a woman.

At the National Housing Policy Options Team, we wanted to know what kinds of people were living in these high-risk situations?

Children—thousands of them—were the startling revelations: Families with kids constitute 565,810 of the people who spend more than 30 percent of their income on rent, and 289,470 of these families spent more than 50 percent of their income on rent. And this was based on 1995 incomes.

The data will not allow us to forget the singles. While singles may not be politically sexy, the fact is that many live in difficult financial circumstances.

Many single women in their senior years are facing housing situations they never imagined. Perhaps they never expected to live as long as people do today. If they were married and have been predeceased by their partners, the pension plan that they or their husbands may have had did not likely anticipate twenty years or more of retirement life.

I remember when my father introduced us, in the teens group at church, to the word *octogenarians*. These were the frail elderly we visited and sang carols to. I recall the distinct impression I had at the time—these women were rarities. Now I realize how wrong that was. The central city communities that I have represented in the past twenty years include innumerable senior women, many over 80. What is extraordinary, and shameful, for all of us is the number who live in pitiful poverty. Fortunately, most of those in my riding live in seniors' housing built during an era when we believed it was important to provide our elderly with a decent environment. Now, most of these programs have been cancelled or reduced to unrecognizable shadows of their former selves—this despite the growth of the senior population.

Our team found cities in Canada reporting homeless seniors showing up at hostels. Many more seniors are at risk of being homeless, as the value of government pensions erodes and rents continue their inexorable climb. When we see statistics like the 808,210 single tenants who spend more than 30 percent of their income on rent, or the staggering 416,660 who put more than 50 percent of a meagre income into housing costs, we need to think of the seniors, the disabled singles and those at home alone on very limited incomes, often trapped with few options.

Late in 1999, news stories and investigative reports initiated by the *Toronto Star* showed the deteriorating conditions in which seniors were having to live. Poor-quality private-sector seniors' housing was springing up in the vacuum created by governments' withdrawal from funding new projects. As seniors suffered, predictable calls for regulation and control followed. However, the underlying problem of low incomes combined with the absence of affordable-housing options made lots of room for charlatans and sharks to cruise these profitable waters and take advantage of vulnerable seniors.

Another group of singles is the student population. Living largely on borrowed funds and faced with rising tuition fees, book costs, user charges and rents, students also find that their choices for accommodation have narrowed to a slit. Desperate for any room they can find, they grab cockroach-infested, poorly maintained, dimly lit and badly heated rooms. Inexcusable rents—particularly where there is no control—can be the norm for vacant units. In Ontario, when vacancy decontrol began to show its effects, in the fall of 1999, low-income long-term roomers were often evicted in favour of the more lucrative student market, from whom desperation rents can now legally be charged. Increased homelessness resulted. At the same time, students suffered under shabby living conditions and piled up debt.

The Quality of Housing

Our study also took a close look at the physical condition of housing already built in Canada—housing that is accommodating many people with low incomes across the country. Canada-wide, the problem of substandard housing—dangerous, badly heated, inadequate or deteriorating housing stock—was flagged as an important part of our country's housing problem. Particularly in Western cities where vacancies are high and landlords seem unwilling or unable to invest in maintaining their buildings, there are serious consequences for residents, which threaten the stability of their housing situation.

Census data showed us that throughout Canada, 361,000 dwellings were in need of significant repair—over one-third of a million homes.

Excluding single-family houses, which are not as often rental properties, there were 267,000 dwellings that needed repair. The rates of disrepair ranged from 6 to 11 percent of all non-detached homes.

We were actually surprised that the highest levels were in Ontario: A staggering 9.8 percent (116,975 units) needed major repair. This finding ran counter to conventional wisdom like that expressed by Canadian analyst John Miron, based on 1986 research, when he claimed that "substandard housing is still generally more common in rural areas and the less-affluent Atlantic provinces and to a lesser extent the prairies."[6] However, Miron is right when he says, "Canada's Aboriginal peoples, whether Inuit, Indian, or Métis, also tend to be housed less adequately."[7] Miron's data showed that First Nations' households had roughly double the rate of major repair needs, triple the need for central heating, eight times the level of over-crowding, and over ten times the percentage of homes with no bathrooms as other Canadians. This helps to explain why, in the Territories, we found significant percentages of problem housing. We found major repair requirement levels of 10.5 percent of units in the Yukon and 9.8 percent of units in the Northwest Territories.

We often associate run-down, ramshackle homes with times past. And, indeed, there have been serious problems before. The Curtis Report of 1944, using 1941 data, found that "using three indicators (needs external repairs, lacks exclusive use of indoor flush toilet, and lacks exclusive use of installed bath), 31 percent of the total stock were classified as substandard."[8] The same report also found that nearly 50,000 (28 percent) of low-income renter households were crowded (based upon an occupancy standard of one person per room, including the kitchen).[9] And while building standards and technologies have improved over the decades, there are still significant problems.

When we examined CMHC's Core Need estimates for 1991, we discovered that about one-third of households in homes needing major repairs were in Core Need; the rest of the households in these homes could likely afford an alternative, more adequate unit in their community. Nationwide, 3.5 percent of tenants are in inadequate housing and are in Core Need, based on 1991 figures from CMHC. Using this ratio and applying it to the 1996 tenant household figures results in between 115,000 and 137,000 households in Core Need and living in units in need of major repair.

An obvious truth in housing is that the rents payable have a major effect on the extent to which improvements in housing can be provided by the landlord. Financing an investment of $20,000 to upgrade a unit to a reasonable standard requires well in excess of $100 a month in additional rent, even at today's relatively low interest rates. When an income left over (after the existing rent is paid) is measured in tens, let alone hundreds, of dollars, such rent increases simply cannot be absorbed by low-income tenants. So there are essentially two options.

One option would be for landlords to find tenants with greater rent-paying capability—to replace the low-income earners, so that the housing can be upgraded using the increased rental cash flow. This option creates more homelessness, but it's underway almost all the time, to one degree or another. Some landlords consciously pursue an upgrading of their housing stock to improve long-term cash flow.

Another option would be to continue to allow the housing to deteriorate to the point that it has to be shut down by municipal authorities for building-code violations. This course of action, too, leaves the tenants homeless. Most cities are reluctant to take action that throws people into the streets as a result of the irresponsibility of their landlords. Still, pressure from surrounding neighbours, councillors, or the building and health inspectors who are concerned, often with good reason, about the health and well-being of the tenants in these situations can result in evictions.

Typically, the city staff will work with the tenants to assist with relocation, if they are organized to do so. But where is the relocation to happen if the supply of affordable rental housing is very low and waiting lists for assisted housing are long?

Neither of these options, however, involve direct financial intervention by governments. Costs to the taxpayer from these options lie in the emergency hostel expenditures, and the associated implications for the municipal budgets: increased emergency-room admittance, policing costs, incarceration costs—on and on down the operational budget lines of government services.

If governments would assist in upgrading substandard housing stock, another option is possible: a strategy to help landlords to improve their units with financing (or grants) in exchange for guarantees that rents would remain within the range of the lower-income tenants in need. Programs like this have been pursued from time to time by the federal and various provincial governments. As a scheme to prevent homelessness and improve the quality of life for tenants in Core Need, it could turn out to be one of the most cost-effective measures. Pressure from communities and FCM's Big City Mayors' Caucus produced an increase of $50 million a year for a program called the Residential Rehabilitation Program. Forgivable loans to fix up rental homes are made available in exchange for a guarantee that rents will stay low. Long term funding of $150 million a year could achieve FCM's targets and make thousands of homes safe and affordable at the same time.

Loss of Low-Priced Rental Housing Stock

The quantity of housing that people with low incomes can afford is constantly shrinking. Poverty is on the rise, while modestly priced housing is disappearing in most communities, with no equivalent replacement in sight. A steady increase in the number of affordable units is needed to actually reduce the existing crisis levels of homelessness and Core Need households; to respond to the falling incomes of the bottom third of the Canadian population; and to match the growth in the Canadian population, some of whom will be unable to afford market rental or ownership housing.

Canada's urban centres also lost a minimum of 13,000 units of rental housing between 1995 and 1999 owing to demolition of often perfectly sound housing, or its conversion to condominium ownership out of the range of those in need of affordable housing.[10]

The mantra in government was to do more with less. It's a useful concept, when applied properly. But in Canada, we have done less with less. This philosophy has left basic needs out in the cold. Housing is one of these. And thus there are demands for a renewed federal engagement in affordable-housing policies to wrest us from the grip of homelessness and its social shame and despair.

Canada's Big City Mayors have sounded the alarm that "a bigger housing crunch is coming."[11] As Canada continues to grow, somewhere between 38,000 and 50,000 new rental units will be needed each year. Because of the way demographic change occurs—younger people moving out, new immigrants arriving and starting over again— "roughly half of all demographic change is expected to come from lower income tenant households requiring affordable housing."[12]

Vacancy Rates and Rising Rents

A cross-Canada scan of the affordable-housing picture shows some bright spots in a couple of provinces.[13] The Parti Québécois government and British Columbia's New Democrats have taken the position that the federal withdrawal created a vacuum and that a provincial response was required. Quebec says to municipalities and communities that it will join with them to fund over 1,000 new units of housing focused on low-income communities each year. The key program, known as Accès Logis, focuses on community groups whose primary function is to provide rental housing to low- and moderate-income households.[14]

B.C. launched its comprehensive program called 1999/2000 Homes B.C. Developed with lots of input from the remarkable duo of Jim O'Dea and Jim Greene—two wonderful Canadians who really can be called housing revolutionaries—the commitment has been to build 2,400 housing units over two years for low-income earners and those with special needs such as mental-health challenges, addictions and experiences of abuse. They have parlayed this commitment, through creative leverage and partnerships, into even more units than the government thought possible. Even though the federal government pulled out of new housing altogether, total provincial allocations for their go-it-alone projects in the 1998–99 fiscal year were almost $60 million.[15]

Elsewhere, the pickings are slim at the provincial level. Most other legislatures have accepted the national government's judgment to withdraw, and have been unwilling to put "100 percent" provincial dollars forward for affordable-housing initiatives.

A contributing factor to rent increases is the vacancy rate. The fewer apartments vacant, the less competitive the rental market becomes. Less supply increases demand, which drives up prices. The competition is between tenants to secure the few units available on any given day. Landlords are the only winners.

Figure 5.1 shows trends in vacancy rates in communities across Canada from 1996 to 1998. Remember that these are the vacancies for all private rental units, no matter what the price. Usually, much higher vacancies exist for higher-priced luxury units. The lower the price range, the lower the vacancy rate.

Vacancy rates can fluctuate markedly as communities go through the ups and downs of economic and employment cycles and housing-construction

Figure 5.1: Rental Unit Vacancy Rates by Community, 1996–1998

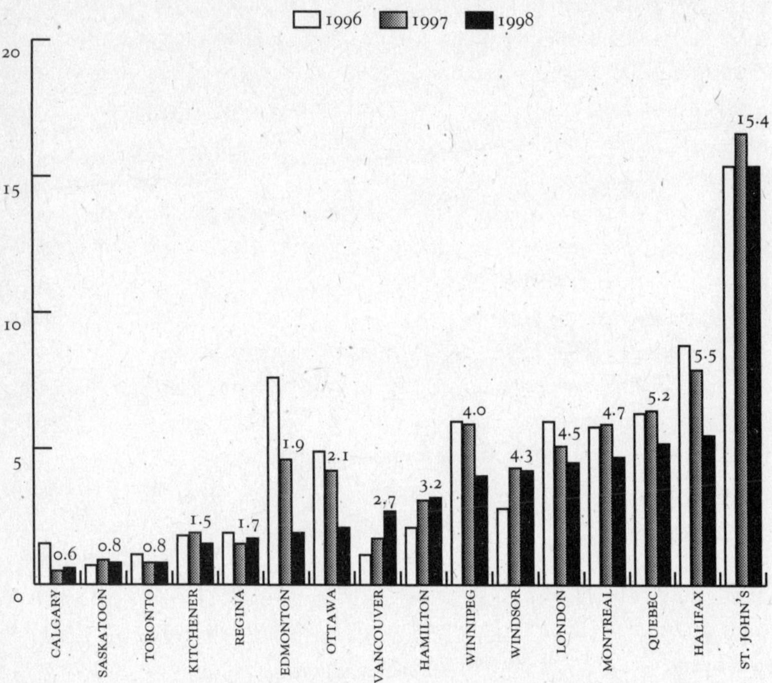

Source: FCM, *National Housing Policy Options Paper: A Call for Action*, June 1999, p. 77. Data are for Central Metropolitan Areas.

trends. St. John's, Newfoundland, ranged from a low vacancy rate of 1.8 percent in the construction boom of 1990 to a high of 15.4 percent in 1997. Others dropped from low to even lower levels throughout the decade as in Toronto (2.2 to 0.2 percent) and Vancouver (2.7 to 0.4 percent). The tightest vacancy situations were found in Calgary, Saskatoon, Toronto, Kitchener, Regina and Edmonton, all showing under 2 percent vacancies in 1998.

Across the provinces, rent-control legislation caps these increases to a greater or lesser extent, depending upon the province. Some have no controls at all; others have significant controls, which moderate the effect of tight housing markets; most have some controls, with extensive loopholes and options for landlords to end-run the regime, with the case in point being Ontario.

The rent problem

There is a basic problem with looking to private rental housing to close the gap between the low and falling incomes of tenants and the high and rising costs of existing or new rental units. To illustrate, I have created Figure 5.2.

Figure 5.2: Costs, Rents and Affordability: Why the Market Cannot Provide Housing for Low-Income Canadians

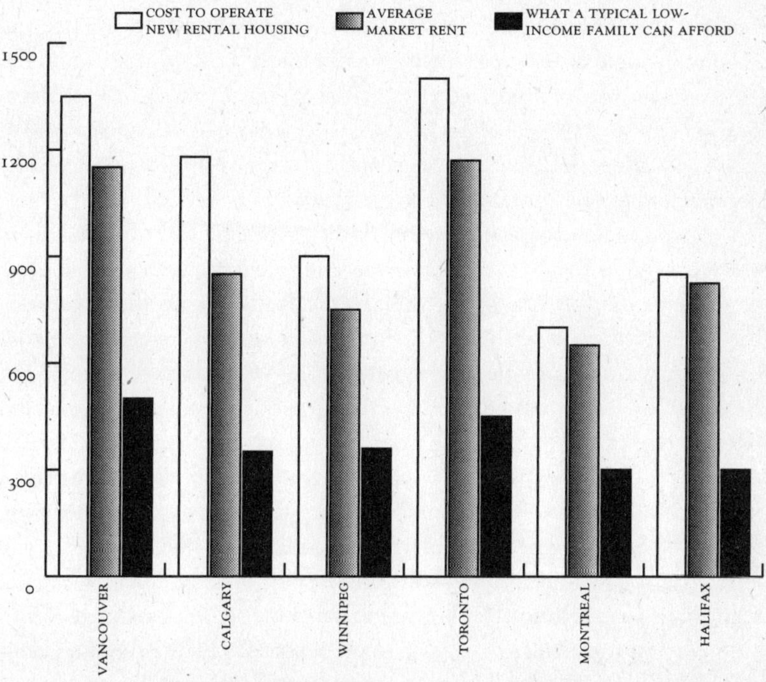

Source: Created by author for this book.

This figure illustrates perhaps the most compelling argument for the need for a national housing program. Simply put, the cost in Canada of building and operating rental housing exceeds market rents in every major centre. In other words, for a private developer, building rental housing as an investment is a losing proposition.

When we look at what low-income Canadians can afford (based on the standard of 30 percent of gross income for rent), building housing for them as a straight private enterprise is absolutely out of the question. What's the incentive, when vacancy rates are 2 percent—or less?

This problem is not uniquely Canadian; it is a part of the economic fabric of every industrialized country. The big difference between Canada and the other countries is that Canada stands alone in its failure to recognize the issue and respond with a national affordable-housing program.

Rent changes in the past decade have not affected Canadian communities equally. In fact, the differences are quite marked. Highest rent increases were posted by cities that, by the end of the decade, were experiencing the most severe street homelessness problems, longest housing waiting lists and lowest apartment vacancy rates.

Most politicians and media commentators portray the economic situation as a win-win scenario—everybody's doing better as we lick the deficit and as jobs are created. But the deficit-cutting policies have focused on reducing the social safety net by cutting back payments to needy individuals—seniors, disabled, students, single parents (mostly mothers) and those unable to find work—thus reducing their incomes. And the job-creation process has, as we've noted, often replaced well-paid full-time work with part-time lower-wage work, thus reducing the incomes of working Canadians.

This ran directly counter to the prevailing economic orthodoxy. The fashionable position has been that as things got better and as Canada continues to be ranked number one in the world, these benefits would flow to everyone. It was always assumed that some would benefit more than others, but surely all would see some positive results of the economic turn-around that has been touted by national political and business figures.

At the same time as rents were increasing, incomes for low-income Canadians were falling. The bottom 10 percent saw their incomes fall by 18.8 percent from 1992 to 1996 (see Appendix C), while rents typically rose significantly before, during and after that period.

In Toronto, in the same period, rents increased by 32.3 percent while incomes of the bottom 10 percent of households fell a staggering 23.6 percent.

The central message is this: It is not enough to examine changing rent levels alone in determining the affordability of housing.

Modest GST adjustments for new rental housing were announced in the 1999 federal budget after years of pressure from builders and municipalities. Combined with other measures, this move could help produce thousands of rental homes. However, run-down housing with potential for renovation into decent homes for lower-income folks faces a more optimistic future.

Decrepit housing is now able to be brought back to life by the little-known but useful federal grant system called RRAP, the Residential Rehabilitation Assistance Program.[16] Government stepping in to help in this way can help rejuvenate decaying neighbourhoods, heeding the call of such people as the mayor of Winnipeg, who reported that whole neighbourhoods in his city were at risk of being abandoned and left to rot. Fires, as we have mentioned, were the most shocking evidence, and many of these were fatal.[17]

National data reveal that 360,735 units in Canada are currently below acceptable standards, and that almost half of these are currently occupied by very-low-income households.[18] At the current rate of funding, it will be many years before these people can benefit from their landlord's substandard offerings.

Canada's housing programs from the 1970s and 1980s are a continuing funding obligation for the federal government. Although much of this has been downloaded to the provinces through a complex exercise begun in the mid-1990s, Ottawa still provides ongoing financial support to housing projects initiated under the non-profit and co-op funding programs of the 1970s and 1980s. The national accounts show that Ottawa was distributing over $1 billion in housing subsidies. As a percentage of the national revenue, this has fallen steadily over recent years. Rules have been changed in the 1990s within these programs to reduce the number and affordability of the homes funded by the federal government in co-ops and non-profits.

Condo Conversion, Demolition and Luxury-Unit Creation

The most direct way of reducing the number of low-rent homes is simply to tear them down.

Demolition of older rental accommodation is a consistent threat to the affordable-housing stock. We found that Winnipeg, for example, lost 615 rental units to demolition in 1998.[19] But cities do not keep clear data on demolition, making it hard to know the size of the problem. Generally, when the redevelopment potential of land becomes sufficiently attractive, developers will press for permission to take down older, smaller buildings and seek permission to rezone the land to permit "development." Multinational property owners like Lendhorff—the owners, with partners, of the 325 Bogert Avenue complex in North York—have been trying for years to tear down this lovely low-rise rental complex and replace it with luxury high-rise condos with views over the ravine. The tenants have been masterful and tenacious in their opposition to the tactics by the landlord—from threatened evictions to major annual rent increase applications. Fortunately, for many years, the provincial government had protection for tenants in place, preventing condominium conversion. An early act of the Harris government removed these protections—throwing the issue of condo-conversion limits back to the municipalities to decide. As a result, the fate of the hundreds of tenants at 325 Bogert Avenue is now sealed—they'll lose their homes. Local councillor John Filion won some assistance for the displaced, but those affordable apartments are gone for good, like thousands of others across Canada.

A rapid way for landlords to reduce the amount of affordable housing is to convert rental units into condominiums. Households which can afford to purchase have a number of advantages. They are not likely to be low-income earners. They can afford the typical 25 percent down payment. Since securing a mortgage is key to the purchase of even a modestly priced condominium, mortgage lenders are unlikely to provide funds to low-income individuals or families. They prefer to see a certain ratio of income-to-mortgage payments. And people with lower incomes are simply not able to provide that ratio. The result? Low-income renters are pushed out of the condominium market.

Some provinces have controls and restrictions on condo conversions. Perhaps the largest meeting on the subject I attended was when the infamous Cadillac Fairview "flip" took place in 1981—affecting over 25,000 rental-housing units in Toronto—and 500 residents showed up in a baking-hot school auditorium to fight for their homes. In the end, we succeeded in preventing the conversion. Enlightened city and provincial policies in the 1980s allowed those homes on Church Street to become an affordable housing co-operative, preserving almost 1,000 low and moderate rental units in perpetuity.

Limited data are available to document how large a problem condo-conversion is. Some statistics show that during the 1990s, in eleven cities, almost 12,000 units of rental housing were converted to condominiums. Calgary led the field with an average of 877 units converted a year.

Luxury renovation also eliminates affordable-housing units. Sometimes a well-heeled landlord will "renovate" an entire building, putting in fancy new lobbies (although rarely, it seems, fixing the elevators), security systems, amenities of different kinds, new carpets and improvements within the suites such as new countertops, appliances and other features. These changes require the previous tenant to leave or live with the changes and the increased rents that result.

A more subtle approach takes place in neighbourhoods that traditionally had many rental rooms or flats. Often called "gentrification," the process involves trendy neighbourhoods being invaded by well-meaning urban professionals, who then begin to upgrade their newly acquired homes. Before you know it, the neighbourhood gets a reputation as being particularly "cool"—which makes it "hot" in the real estate market. Speculation, increased numbers of renovation applications and lots of moving trucks become the norm as the lower-income roomers and tenants are replaced by the new gentry.

In a way, these processes are the natural ebb and flow of urban change. They also bring reinvestment to an aging housing stock. Indeed, some neighbourhoods have been through the cycle several times. But we need to recognize that affordable housing is lost through this process. Were it being replaced at an equal or greater rate elsewhere in a city, there would be no problem. This is not happening, though. Zoning restrictions often prevent the creation of new rooming houses or second-suite housing. So as gentrification moves through communities, there is a net reduction of low-cost housing in the urban area. Studies have shown that thousands of scattered rooms and affordable units in neighbourhoods have been lost and not replaced in Canadian cities over the past two decades. Increased homelessness is a direct result.

What about New Housing with Modest Rents?

Housing construction is big business and a major economic activity. In the past ten years (1989 to 1998) 1,335,369 new housing units have been built in Canada. Surely some of these can meet the needs of low-income people. Once that might have been the case, but no longer. From 37,279 new rental units in 1989 to only 7,287 new rental units in 1998 is a drop of over 80 percent. (See Appendix D.)[20]

Co-operative rentals, another form of low-income housing, is separately counted by CMHC. Over the years co-op housing was recognized and often received awards because of the successful way it addressed the housing needs of low- and moderate-income Canadians. Mixed incomes were encouraged in co-op communities. This provided an alternative to separate housing for low-income households—the pattern of earlier years. It also ensured that there were tenants paying market-level rents as well as those receiving subsidies, creating a diverse economic base for the sustenance of the project's financial requirements. However, construction of new co-operative housing units, mostly funded by federal programs, fell from 3,839 units in 1989 to a paltry 71 units in 1998. This was a drop of 98 percent in co-op construction.

Although general economic conditions led to an overall reduction in new housing completions over the past decade, the declines in rental and co-operative housing production were much more rapid and larger in magnitude. At the end of the decade, houses built for ownership were down only 20 percent, but condominium construction dropped 31 percent.

For many years, the feds and the provinces worked with cities and communities to build social housing to backfill the loss of affordable housing, which was occurring steadily. This new social housing took the bite out of the housing crunch by providing a steady supply of units at modest rents. The programs that funded these projects were part of Canada's social safety net. However, there was always a significant "lag" between the funding and building processes. Government funding was usually awarded about four to five years before the projects were completed, but social housing often took longer. The communities into which the projects were going to be placed often had things to say about their potential neighbours. Public hearings, rezonings, development permits and so on had to follow the sometimes-lengthy land-acquisition process. So when we look at social-housing completions in the early 1990s, this reflects the funding by the federal government and some provinces in the mid-1980s. When Mulroney's government began to cut new housing programs, the implications for social housing were not seen until several years later. When they were seen, they left the social-housing development sector as a mere shadow of its former self. And the private sector did not step in to pick up the slack, as the market economy ideology had suggested it would.

Social-housing completions reached a high of 19,621 in 1992, but plummeted to only 1,439 units in 1998. (See Appendix E.)

With fewer units coming on stream, and with those living in the existing units becoming less likely to move from the non-profit or co-op homes where they currently live, there were fewer openings. More names on waiting lists and fewer openings meant that people were staying on the lists longer and longer. Our FCM study found that there are "an estimated 96,000 households on assisted housing waiting lists in large urban centres across the country."[21] Nationally, the total list is likely approximately double this number.

Conclusion

The evidence presented here is only the tip of a huge iceberg of housing problems. Some community-level studies have documented this powerfully and well. The FCM's effort to pull together the national picture was enough to convince the annual meeting to unanimously endorse the findings of the National Housing Policy Options Team and to call for a national housing policy. The rest of this book explores some strategies for developing affordable housing and other ways of addressing the crisis in homelessness. By now, the growing impact of the vacuum in housing policy on the lives of the most vulnerable of our compatriots should be clear. It should move Canadians to act, to demand action from their governments.

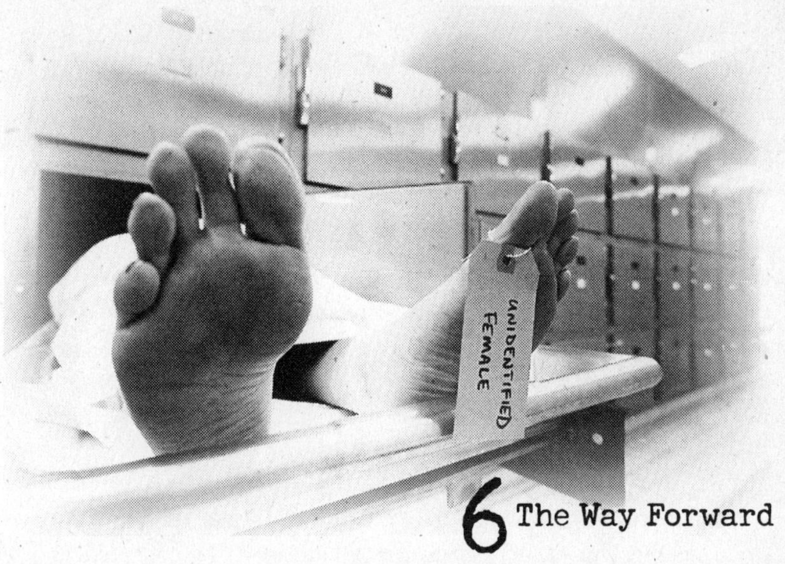

6 The Way Forward

Let's build this house!

Let's end homelessness and Canada's affordable housing crisis by building a national housing policy. First, as sensible builders, let's check what is already in place. What tools do we have now? What foundations in public policy exist, ones that might help us to build this project? Let's find out which policies, programs, good ideas, tools and people with expertise have atrophied from disuse. Is rehabilitation possible?

All is not bleak. We find that the federal affordable-housing toolbox, for example, has some useful items already tucked away. When we look at the laws governing public policy, for instance, we find that the National Housing Act of 1954 says that the Government of Canada is supposed to take action on affordable housing. Amendments to this Act, in the early 1970s, created a mission for the government to provide affordable housing for Canadians. Many of the same words still reside in the mandate of the federal government in today's version:

> The purpose of this Act, in relation to financing for housing, is to promote housing affordability and choice, to facilitate access to, and competition and efficiency in the provision of, housing finance, to protect the availability of adequate funding for housing at low cost, and generally to contribute to the well-being of the housing sector in the national economy.[1]

It's not exactly a call to arms, and it has clearly been softened through recent amendments. (The Canadian government does not want to suggest that it has an obligation to house Canadians.) But this National Housing Act could still be interpreted as for a mandate for the Canadian government to get involved. And, try as they may, federal cabinet ministers should not attempt to hide behind the idea that housing is only a provincial responsibility.

Deep in the toolbox, we also find that Canada signed the following article from the Universal Declaration of Human Rights, adopted by the United Nations in 1948.

> Article 25:
>
> 1. Everyone has the right to a standard of living adequate for the health and well-being of himself and of his family, including food, clothing, housing and medical care and necessary social services, and the right to security in the event of unemployment, sickness, disability, widowhood, old age or other lack of livelihood in circumstances beyond his control.

Perhaps, after fifty years, forgetfulness has set in. Perhaps the conscious drift towards the idea that the free market can best achieve these goals has been at work. Whatever the cause, many of the tools in Canada's affordable-housing public policy kit have not been used in years.

A good example: Social-housing programs built tens of thousands of units for low-income people until the focus on deficit reduction and tax cuts knocked the wind out of those sails—sails that were judged too expensive by both Brian Mulroney and Jean Chrétien. These were some of the same tools that put Canada on the international map, for those who studied and wanted to know how we were able to build such marvellous new housing. At the time, Canadians were building lots of mixed-income communities, avoiding the ghettoization often found elsewhere.

In one of the ultimate ironies, the Habitat II world convention in Istanbul in the early 1990s gave Canada an award for its remarkable housing programs. At the same time as the award was being presented, in front of the whole world to Canadian representatives, Paul Martin's federal budget was axing the award-winning initiatives.

The Canada Mortgage and Housing Corporation was the instrument that delivered these programs in their heyday. But CMHC has since been forcibly divested of the budget and the mandate to do this sort of work. The National Housing Act was amended several times to limit CMHC largely to conducting and funding experiments in building design, including energy efficiency and cost-saving construction.

A few small programs remain in the affordability area—and perhaps these will be the seeds from which a new forest can grow. One is called ACT—Affordability and Choice Today—a grant program run jointly by CMHC, the Federation of Canadian Municipalities and the Canadian Homebuilders' Association. Under this program, grants of $20,000 are given to groups, developers or municipalities to come up with innovative ways to cut through the cost barriers, to create new housing that is affordable to lower-income people.[2] Once an idea is in place, the difficulty then becomes repeating it. Grants are only available for the first version of the innovation. Over 100 fascinating projects have been funded, and many new ideas have proven successful. Sadly, though, no funding is available to spread the findings of these ACT projects. These seeds are not being allowed to grow.

Once a hotbed of affordable-housing creativity—and possessed of an exciting sense of mission—CMHC is struggling these days to hang on to remnants of credibility in the affordable-housing field. A sad fact is that today CMHC's mortgage-insurance program actually makes affordable housing more expensive. This key program was originally designed to help by insuring mortgages on housing projects, thereby enticing banks to lend funds to lower-income housing projects. Now, the CMHC charges such high mortgage-insurance fees to any non-profit community group wanting to build that the housing becomes significantly more costly. (Federal coffers are currently being enhanced to the tune of well over $250 million a year through these insurance schemes.)

When the City of Toronto attempted to assist the community organization at Dixon Hall to replace its homeless shelter with very-low-income housing, the CMHC gave a small grant to help. Everyone then discovered that CMHC's fee for mortgage insurance was five times the grant. A private philanthropist had to dig deep for an additional $150,000 to make the project work financially. The good news is that the houses are now built, and some formerly homeless people are making their way back to a happy and productive life. As one of them told me, "Without a home, you can't get started on the road back. The costs to yourself and the community are so great compared with the costs of this fresh start."

Stories like this show how Canadian housing strategy has been distorted beyond all recognition. Can it actually be repaired, or do we need an entirely new national program? We'll come back to this question.

Thirty years ago, two analysts wrote that Canada's housing programs were disconnected and haphazard—programs, as they put it, "in search of a policy."[3] The upshot of their book by that title—and the debate at the time—was the creation of the remarkable non-profit, municipal and co-operative housing programs that gave Canada its glowing reputation. We should be so lucky today.

Homegrown Solutions and Affordability and Choice Today are two small but promising national programs. I say promising because both are built on the concept of partnerships among community groups, government and national groups (like the FCM, which runs the ACT program).

Needed now are ways to take the positive results of these small initiatives and extend them across the country in a concerted effort. Ottawa's Better Way task force brought all kinds of players into one room and worked out how to speed up planning approvals for housing so that costly delays could be radically cut. Lessons they learned could and should be brought to all cities now. Instead, each municipality invents its own version of the wheel. For example, in Vancouver, a "convertible house," designed by a firm called Dovertel and assisted through the city's approval, shows how a home can be built with a secondary rental suite included from the outset, even in a traditional single-family neighbourhood. The extra $10,000 cost is quickly recovered from rent and lets first-time or lower-income homebuyers qualify for mortgages. This terrific idea should be shopped all over Canada, but little headway is made in the absence of a national plan to actively disseminate good ideas.

Charlottetown brought together the Atlantic People's Housing company, the Prince Edward Island Home Builders and CMHC to figure out how to put more homes in the same space—housing intensification, as urbanologists would say. But who else knows about this?

Just outside my second-floor office window at City Hall, where I can look out on Nathan Phillips Square, is a group of three homeless people bunking down on the hard concrete. Ironically, their "home" is right next to the city's building-permit department—where people go to receive the official go-ahead for housing construction. Around the famous plaza, there are many homeless people. Tonight, in late September 2000, I count roughly fifty. Many seek the safety of the open, lit areas, lying on the many benches in the square. Still others have claimed space between gardens and walls. A few, needing a little heat, construct cardboard enclosures over the noisy air-conditioning exhaust ducts. The most shy or frightened hide in stairwells and various other municipal nooks and crannies. When I began writing this book a year ago, I remember counting almost twenty homeless fellow citizens. It shocked me then. None was so bold as to lie right under my window. But now, all the benches, vents and corners are taken. I've checked the web-based service that tells me which of the fifty hostels in Toronto has beds at this hour. There are only a few spaces available, scattered across facilities that are sprinkled across the mega-city, but not enough to take all fifty of these people, should they seek indoor refuge.

These people gravitating to City Hall are silent testimony to their search for solutions from their governments. So what—based on the evidence presented thus far—is our strategy?

Targets and Goals for Housing Canadians

You can't design a strategy for housing Canadians in dignity without defining what would be a successful effort.

It's easy to say that we should not rest until there are no homeless people in our streets. The problem with that goal is that it's too easy for people to say, "Well, you'll never accomplish that—go away!"

Recognizing this danger, many who have tackled the homelessness problem have articulated a goal.

For instance, Anne Golden, in her report to the mayor of Toronto, outlined a program that was based on stopping the growth of homeless in that city. Her task force designed the program so that homelessness would not continue to grow and so that many currently homeless people would be helped. She urged politicians to take the steps she outlined "just to tread water" on the issue.

Figure 6.1: Rental Starts and Apartment Vacancy Rates

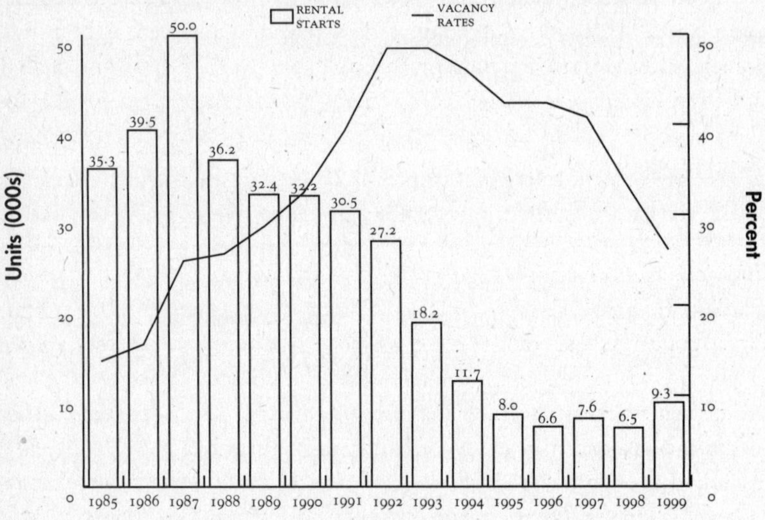

RENTAL STARTS
VACANCY RATES
Units (000s)
Percent
35.3 39.5 50.0 36.2 32.4 32.2 30.5 27.2 18.2 11.7 8.0 6.6 7.6 6.5 9.3
0 10 20 30 40 50
1985 1986 1987 1988 1989 1990 1991 1992 1993 1994 1995 1996 1997 1998 1999

Source: from CMHC data compiled by Focus Consulting for FCM, September 2000.

John Sewell, in his 1994 book on housing for Canadians, suggested that 150,000 units a year for ten years would be needed to house the 1.5 million Canadian households with affordability problems (spending greater than 25 percent of their income on housing). He then suggested that this number "is far beyond the number of affordable units supplied in any of the past twenty years, and can be considered an unachievable target." A more realistic target, according to Sewell, "achievable although still high, is the creation of an additional 50,000 units of affordable housing a year. This number of affordable units was achieved in the fiscal year 1987–88."[4] This approach would reduce the affordability problem by approximately one-third in a decade.

Our team at the FCM wanted to cut homelessness and the number of people at risk of homelessness by half over a decade. We reasoned that it would be difficult for anyone to disagree with such a conservative objective.

In fact, in the years since this target was formulated, it has not been significantly reached. Here is how the FCM estimated what level of new housing would be required. (There are a number of targets to set if our overall goal is to be met.)

New affordable-housing units

We need an additional 45,000 rental units annually over the decade 2001–2010.[5] If we do not achieve this level of new rental housing, homelessness will rise much faster in Canada, as we will see in the analysis below. Compare this with what rentals builders have actually built in Canada recently, and we see that it falls far short—like the 7,287 new rental housing units added to the stock in 1998. Very few of these could be classed as "affordable."

How did we determine this "demand"? Our team drew on several of the situations explored by Roger Lewis in his study, *The Long-Term Housing Outlook: Household Growth in Canada and the Provinces, 1991–2016*.[6] And Linda LaPointe, one of the most brilliant housing researchers I know, helped us with careful revisions, updates and refinements.

Let's remember that estimating housing demand does not estimate the supply of housing. Far from it. If supply does not match demand, good old-fashioned Economics 101 tells us that prices will rise. One of our goals is to develop strategies to help the supply to meet the demand, at the price that various groups of Canadians can afford.

We constructed projections based on the expected growth of population in Canada, and how much housing will be "consumed" by different age groups over time. We found some surprises. For example, forecasts tell us that rental-housing demand will rise faster than demand for ownership housing during the next ten years. (This would be difficult to discern from the size of the real-estate section of the daily papers, complete with new suburban subdivisions and condominium sales, contrasted with the tiny section devoted to the "for rent" category.) The reason for our forecasted shift towards rental, as in the Boom-Bust-Echo phenomenon described so well by Professor David Foot at the University of Toronto, is that Canadians are aging, and elder Canadians are selling their homes.[7] As well, younger Canadians are not able to buy homes as early as they might have twenty-five years ago. The baby boom's echo (offspring) is entering the "household-formation" phase and the housing market. As I write this, both my kids (in their twenties) and my mother-in-law are living at home. Don't get me wrong, it's great! Really! But my children will no doubt be moving out one of these years and adding to what the statisticians call the "echo" demand in the rental market. They won't be able to afford a down payment. The combination of today's job market and housing market, and student costs, just make home ownership more difficult for those in their twenties than it used to be.

Immigration to major cities brings increased rental demand as well, because a significant portion of people arriving cannot afford the prices of homes for sale.

A disturbing consequence of the polarization between Canada's rich and poor shows up in the projections. Comparing the renters of the past with those of the next decade, we see that a larger share of the additional renters will have lower incomes. Falling incomes of tenants generally—and rapidly falling incomes of poorer tenants especially—is creating this trend. Middle-income tenants will tend to buy homes but be replaced by lower-income tenants. Cutbacks in transfers to low-income people, through the reduction of social-assistance payments in several provinces, accelerates this trend. Employment-insurance entitlements have been reduced, further reducing the incomes of the renters of the next ten years. Some say it is taking longer for immigrants to establish themselves with sufficiently lucrative jobs to afford ownership, by comparison with past decades. All these factors add up to create a steadily increasing proportion of renters with lower incomes than we have seen in the past.

When all these factors are taken into account, our FCM study concluded that Canada will need roughly 450,000 new rental units between 2001 and 2010.[8]

The need for new rental units will not be evenly distributed across Canada. In the North, there is practically no demand for new multiple-unit rental apartments. Our analysis showed that Manitoba and Saskatchewan produce a modest annual rental housing demand of about 1,000 units. Where urban centres are growing rapidly, the highest demand for new rental units exists. Therefore, it is no surprise that Quebec, with its growing cities, could need 11,000 rental units a year—although this number was adjusted to take into account the high-rental vacancies we've seen in Quebec cities in previous data. Then, Ontario produces an annual rental demand of 21,000 apartments, Alberta 4,000 and British Columbia 7,000.[9]

What do all these projections mean? Data like these should be incorporated in all government planning concerning housing. If not, it's like pretending we are standing still. The numbers also signal a huge, looming problem: Because we are not producing anything like the number of rental units required to meet the needs of Canadians as expressed by these estimates, inevitably this lack of supply will drive rents much higher and leave more Canadians in housing-rental-cost-induced misery. This research proves that *more* Canadians will end up homeless.

So our data show powerfully that an acceleration of homelessness is now on Canada's horizon. Something must be done soon. To quote our study: "The sharp rise in affordability problems in the 1990s tells us that relief is needed if low-income Canadians are to regain the quality of life they had a decade ago. . . . The expected increase in rental demand suggests that national housing policy needs to shift from its focus on ownership housing."[10]

So these are "rental-housing-demand projections." How can we refine them to help us know what we need know about the need for *affordable* rental housing?

Affordable rental housing

The way we used this term in our research refers to housing that is affordable to tenants below CMHC's Core Need Income Thresholds. These thresholds vary across the different areas of the country, because living costs vary from place to place. So CMHC defines households in Core Need across Canada as those tenants and their families with annual incomes under $15,000 who require average rents under $400 monthly in order to have enough resources to cover other essential living costs. Paying more in rent would mean that in excess of 30 percent of the income of these households was being absorbed by their housing rents. This average number would have to be adjusted for different regions in Canada, because actual incomes and rents to determine Core Need also vary across the country.

Each year in Canada, population growth, immigration and household formation all create an additional demand for rental housing. Best estimates indicate that about half of the net new demand comes from low-income households.[11] Besides, we found that "not all of the added low-income demand requires new units."[12] This is because some of the assisted-housing need could be met through acquisition of less-expensive existing apartments or flats by housing or non-profit agencies that would then make these units available to tenants with low incomes, according to their mandate. This is possible because existing units are sometimes available for sale at a lower price than the construction of new units.

But let's not be carried away with these possibilities. While cities and agencies should grab them whenever they can, only a modest portion of the added low-income demand will be met by buying up low-priced rental properties that might come on the market from time to time. In today's urban Canadian housing markets, there will not be much "filtering down" of existing rental units at lower prices. Most rental markets have such low vacancy rates that prices will generally be driven up, not down. Still, in some communities, this will be a worthwhile strategy, and some portion of the need may be met this way. The sad fact is that affordable units being lost to condominium conversion and demolition often outweigh any possibilities here. As well, rents in most markets are rising, in some cases terrifyingly fast.

Our team at FCM concluded that about 50 percent of the added rental demand each year is from households unable to pay market rents. This was a rough estimate, because we really don't know, with precision, the incomes of those households that become "new renters" each year. Here's our conservative estimate: Half of the new rental apartments that could be absorbed by the market every year would need to be subsidized so that those who need them can afford them.

The result of this analysis produces a target of 22,000 new assisted rental units every year—affordable to tenants below the Core Need Income Thresholds (CNIT). We assumed, for the sake of argument, that 10 percent of these could be met through the purchase of lower-rent units by community agencies, for rent to needy tenants. This left a target of 20,000 units of new assisted rental housing units each year to meet the requirement of Canadians for affordable housing—and to reduce the affordability crisis by 50 percent.

Numbers of rehabilitated units needed to reduce the affordability problem for households "at risk of homelessness"

We've seen that between 115,000 and 137,000 households in Core Need are living in rental homes that need major repairs. Assuming that our goal would be to substantially eliminate this situation for Canadian tenants, we should target at least 10,000 units a year for ten years to clear the backlog.

If you have been keeping track, you'll see that our National Housing Policy Options study is recommending, so far, 20,000 new units and 10,000 rehabilitated units a year for ten years. These 300,000 affordable homes will be key strategic elements in solving the homeless and housing-affordability crisis, but they clearly will not address the needs of the 1.7 million households who are facing severe risks of losing their housing.[13]

As soon as our team realized this, we had to look for other ways to bridge the gap between what these people could afford to pay for their private rental housing and what rental housing in Canada costs today. This way, the high risk of homelessness and other forms of deprivation that these families and individuals are facing could be reduced.

Building new units of housing is much less expensive than putting or keeping people in emergency shelters (four to five times less costly, according to a Toronto study). Still, new housing is costly. While there are some ideas (suggested later) that would reduce costs significantly, even at $70,000 per unit, the monthly amortization, taxes and operating costs for new housing is in excess of 50 percent of the income of many—and would be well above the 30 percent threshold for Core Need. Average market rents remain below the costs of newly constructed housing. The kind of apartments in which Core Need households are living tend to have a lower rent profile than the total rental stock. Therefore, the rents for Core Need households, the ones we are concerned about, are significantly lower than the carrying costs of new housing.

Besides, it will not be possible to build enough new homes in a reasonable length of time to address the crisis. So it makes sense to see how we could address this gap with direct transfers of support funding. That is why we decided to recommend direct payments to bridge current rent levels and current income levels in the form of rent supplements or shelter allowances. These initiatives, in combination with new housing construction and rehabilitation, creates the best mix of solutions.

How large a program is needed to relieve affordability problems?

Our FCM Paper came to this conclusion: "Affordability problems are defined in terms of rent exceeding 30 percent of income. Affordability problems are so widespread that there is a need to focus on where the problem is most acute. Addressing the issue on a comprehensive basis would go beyond housing policy and into income policy."

Table 6.1: Summary of National Targets for Rental Construction, Repair and Affordability

	New (Assisted)	Renovation (Assisted)	Relief of Affordability Problems
10-Year	200,000	100,000	400,000
Annual	20,000	10,000	40,000

Source: FCM, *National Housing Policy Options Paper: A Call for Action* (Ottawa, June 1999), p. 77.

As the team discussed how to approach this situation, I suggested that no one would believe that we could solve the problem in one fell swoop. This simply would not fly. But if we committed Canada and all its governments to work to reduce the housing affordability crisis by *half* in a *decade*, and if we could conclusively show how many units would have to be built, rehabilitated and subsidized to accomplish this goal, many Canadians would come on board and support the program. Of course, this is a somewhat arbitrary target, but surely most people would accept it as a minimum objective. Would anyone argue that we should attempt to improve the situation by only 25 percent or 10 percent rather than 50 percent over the next ten years? Or would someone argue we should stage the program over twenty years rather than ten? Perhaps, but our group determined that the concept of reducing the problem by half in a decade was as reasonable as we could imagine. Therefore, our policy statement continued: "A national strategy should aim to reduce the severe affordability problems by 50 percent over a 10-year period, from about 800,000 to about 400,000 households. This implies a target for relief of affordability problems of 40,000 households annually. This is a cumulative annual increase each year."[14]

Supplementing the income of these 400,000 households to bring their rents below the unacceptable level of 50 percent of their income is what the FCM is pushing. This rent supplement program would allow people to stay in their homes. There would be no disruptive moves into shelters, no need to move into a newly built or renovated affordable home. Such a program would be good for families, communities and government's bottom line.

These targets were embraced by the June 1999 convention of the Federation of Canadian Municipalities in endorsing the document as the basis for FCM policy.

Numbers needed for people with disabilities

Those Canadians with mental-health disabilities and challenges, who make up about one-third of the roofless population (higher for women on the street) need to be considered with care and attention, not just lumped into generalized targets. Anne Golden's task force argued strongly and effectively that we should address the needs of these high-need users of the hostels and drop-ins so that we could quickly ease the daily pressure on these facilities. Quick, focused action to provide supportive housing could significantly reduce the population of vulnerable homeless people. At the same time, it would contribute to the care and support that these individuals need so badly. People coping with mental illnesses, sometimes compounded by addictions, typically have to use the emergency shelter systems for much longer time periods than others. It's just a lot tougher for them to obtain other housing and to hang on to it.[15] So housing that works for them will free emergency beds for short-term stays.

Each community should set targets for specialized supportive housing based on assessing its own need profile. The overall targets proposed here can include these special units.

Aboriginal housing in Canada

The sad state of First Nations' housing in Canada has long been known—and ignored. To recite the litany of shortcomings here seems an insult. Perhaps all I can do is remind certain government ministers and their staffs what a Royal Commission said almost *ten* years ago. The following is only a tiny part of that forgotten report:

> The Commission recommends that Federal and provincial governments address Aboriginal housing and community services on the basis of the following policy principles:
>
> A. Governments have an obligation to ensure that Aboriginal people have adequate shelter, water and sanitation services.
>
> B. Governments have a responsibility to restore an economic base to Aboriginal people that enables them to meet their needs.
>
> C. Aboriginal people, individually and collectively, are responsible for meeting their housing needs according to their ability to pay or contribute in kind.

D. Governments must supplement the resources available to Aboriginal people so that their housing needs are fully met.
E. Aboriginal nations should assume authority over all housing matters as a core area of self-government jurisdiction.
F. Acute risks to health and safety should be treated as an emergency and targeted for immediate action.

3.4.2
The government of Canada clarify with treaty nations a modern understanding of existing treaty terms regarding housing.

3.4.3
The government of Canada make resources available over the next 10 years to ensure that housing for Aboriginal people on-reserve is fully adequate in quantity and quality and engage the governments of the provinces and territories to reach the same goal in rural and northern communities and in urban areas.[16]

Loss of affordable housing

Finally, we have a rather non-quantifiable target to bear in mind. Somehow, the loss of the relatively few affordable units that remain in our communities *must* be stopped. At a minimum, the rate of loss of affordable housing should be reduced so that our solutions strategies can work. If the housing stock leaks affordability out of the bottom of the barrel while our new strategies are adding units to the top, our efforts will be fruitless. Stopping the leaks is as important as bringing in new supply.

Solving Canada's Housing and Homelessness Crisis—Who Does What, When and How?

With objectives as ambitious and critical as those outlined above, teamwork and collaboration will have to be central to the solutions. We need a co-ordinated approach, involving all levels of government, community groups and the private sector in realizing the right of every Canadian to have decent affordable housing. Given that the cities, towns and municipal governments generally have been handed the responsibilities for housing, it is logical to start with what cities can do. Besides, if we hope to convince the other orders of government to join municipalities in moving forward, we had better show that municipalities are doing all that they can. Much is being done, but there's more to do.

Solving the crisis: Cities

Municipal councils know their communities best. They have or can quickly develop the abilities and skills to implement effective, community-based projects and solutions.

While some affluent suburban councils are tempted to say, "It's an inner-city problem," when one of their own dies in a far-off city or the homeless begin to show up in their community—which eventually they do—they change their tune.

On the homelessness and affordable-housing fronts right now, Canadian municipalities are fighting a losing battle. They are applying Band-Aids to a wound that is haemorrhaging.

So what can municipal governments do? What is their part in a national action plan to eradicate homelessness?

Land-use laws and development management

Councils can pass laws. This may sound easy and basic. Far from it. When councils consider new laws, there are always opponents—people and interests who liked the old way of doing things. However, most municipal governments have public hearings, and while this allows opponents to turn out, it also gives homeless advocates and the homeless themselves an opportunity to speak. It's powerful when it happens. I wouldn't say it's always pleasant, but then what is pleasant about homelessness? Homelessness is not inherently a win-win situation.

One of the most powerful tool that cities have is land-use control, usually found in laws known as Official Plans and Zoning By-Laws. Few cities use these tools systematically and effectively to create affordable housing, even though they could do so. Let's consider the possibilities.

Cities could insist that new developments contain a specified proportion of affordable housing. In fact, some cities have attempted this, as have some provinces. Developers, predictably, object. "Why should I have to absorb this obligation when previous developers did not have to do so?" they typically moan. Still, cities should insist that newly developed communities should provide housing to meet the needs of a broad spectrum of household incomes.

To make this kind of planning policy work, there has to be a linked program of financial support to the tenants moving into the affordable units within these developments. We've already seen that low-income, core-need tenants in Canada simply cannot afford the rents for even a modestly built new rental apartment today. But there is absolutely no point in having by-laws that just cannot be made to work. Toronto found this out when its wonderful Central Area Plan of the mid-'70s proclaimed the goal that 25 percent of the new housing in the downtown should be affordable. For a while this worked, because there were programs to assist low-income tenants and non-profit housing developers, to bring all the economic factors together. Then federal and provincial governments withdrew from these housing-support programs, leaving the city with a policy that sounded good but wasn't producing results. By the early '90s, affordable-housing construction in the central city was grinding to a halt. New housing was still being built—but as we have seen it took the form of ownership condominiums, not affordable to low-income families.

Another classic example was Toronto's railway-lands development, next to the SkyDome and CN Tower. After a protracted debate, stretching well over ten years, council insisted that a portion of the 200 acres be reserved for affordable housing amid the forest of office towers and luxury condominium high-rises, the preference of the big development companies. Today, those reserved lands stand vacant. There is no sign of a government program to pay for the construction or to help low-income tenants with the rents. Yet right next door, on the waterfront, low-income non-profit housing and co-operatives were built at the same time and adjacent to the condos lining Queen's Quay. Constructed in the 1980s, these successful mixed-housing neighbourhoods came into being when federal and provincial low-income housing-construction programs existed. Absence makes the heart grow fonder. Toronto City Council is now calling for the reinstatement of programs like the ones that made the waterfront development relatively successful at achieving affordability in the housing mix.

It is time for the cities to create Official Plan and Zoning laws that integrate the land-use provisions with funding programs more directly. As with everything municipal, the provincial governments would likely have to give their assent to such a new approach to land-use regulation. Montreal and Vancouver, with their "city charters," have more legal freedom to act and may be able to set the pace.

There are other ways in which the price of housing may be affected through land-use controls. One way is to reduce the cost of providing services to new houses by requiring them to be built closer together. "Residential intensification" is the technical planning term used these days to capture this idea. Sprawling suburban housing is expensive to service. When development sprawls, underground water pipes, sewers, roads, sidewalks and public-transit vehicles all have to go farther to reach the next house. As a result, costs are driven up. Eventually, the resident pays for these costs through development charges or through property taxes—usually both. More densely planned housing can save money.

However, there is no guarantee that the savings will go to the residents, because the demand in the new-development area may permit high prices. This is another case where complementary development and financing strategies have to work together. If each development has an affordable component built by the municipal housing agency or a non-profit group or co-op, there can be some certainty that the savings will produce more affordability. Arrangements such as this need to be factored into the new community plan from the outset. This means that municipalities need to know that there will be funding programs from the partners—the national and provincial governments—in order to make this strategy succeed.

Providing additional density in exchange for new affordable units is one rather crude way of providing a financing mechanism for the low-income units. Because the developer can realize more profit if additional density is allowed on a site, this can be shared with the housing program of the municipality in various ways. Some units in the project could be dedicated to a city or non-profit agency, at no cost, to be used for the life of the building, to meet the needs of low-income households within the project. This is a relatively painless and cost-effective strategy from the city's standpoint. However, there is always a trade-off whenever densities are increased, because the building bulk, massing and design characteristics affect the locale. But as long as the urban-design objectives are carefully balanced with the affordable-housing goals, creative win-win situations will result. Still, the number of affordable units that can be built this way will be very small, unless there are compatible funding programs to stretch the effectiveness of the density-bonusing strategy.

Another way to use municipal planning powers is to outlaw policies designed to prohibit affordable housing in certain communities. Subtly, zoning laws can act as invisible walls that effectively exclude certain people from communities. When the exclusive Rosedale neighbourhood in Toronto enacted one of Ontario's first zoning by-laws many years ago, it prohibited Chinese laundries. Exclusions in those days were rather specific and were not outlawed by any Charter of Rights. These days, the exclusions are indirect. By defining lot sizes and other criteria about the homes that can be built, a neighbourhood can virtually prohibit many low-income people from ever having a chance to live there. Usually, there is a strong community concern to "maintain the character" of the neighbourhood. Maintaining a neighbourhood feel and character is important. But most neighbourhoods are changing steadily. The key for municipal policy should be to ensure that the changes open possibilities for all residents, not just some.

Here are just a few specific techniques to accomplish this: permitting second suites, stimulating main-street redevelopment and enabling infill redevelopments. All are ways to allow changes that can help the housing crisis while preserving the essence of a neighbourhood's physical characteristics.

"Second suites"

Many homes in Canada have a second unit for a renter, an in-law, an aging grandparent or a young family getting started. Some have more than one unit. Technically, such an arrangement usually requires municipal government approval, but many people simply set up the second suite and get on with providing the housing. In a way, it's a good thing that people take this particular law into their own hands: Second-suite housing has added many very affordable units that were not being created in any other way. Second suites usually have rents that fall well below the open market's rates. They require no government subsidy to be affordable to many tenants otherwise at risk of homelessness. Because second suites are usually in homes where the owner lives as well, the quality and safety of the accommodation is usually not too bad—and is sometimes very good. The second suite also makes the home more affordable to the owner as well—indeed this is often how a new owner is able to cover the mortgage payments.

The downside is the possibility that the second apartment will be substandard, dangerous or unhealthy, because it has not been permitted in the zoning by-laws of communities and may therefore may not meet municipal codes.

The answer to this problem is to permit second suites as a matter of course, anywhere. This makes sense for another reason. Decades ago, when most of the housing in Canada was built, families were larger. There were more kids at home. The number of rooms per capita was much lower than it is today—the same floor space used to house more people. Do we need all this extra housing space with an aging population—especially when empty nesters' children have flown the coop, and with new families having fewer children than the baby-booming families of the post-war era? Probably not. Why not let people in their homes decide themselves if they want to re-fill their residence with people, the way it was when it was initially built? In this sense, the second suite is really just a reorganization of the living space to handle a similar number of people for whom the house was originally designed, but in two living units rather than one.

This very sensible and remarkably inexpensive plan—to permit second suites as a matter of course in all zoning by-laws—was put in place in Ontario in the early 1990s. Then a newly elected Mike Harris Conservative government rescinded this permission, forcing each of the several hundred municipalities in that province to have to consider reinstating the open zoning for second suites. The new provincial policy was supported by some of the most exclusive neighbourhoods whose leaders opposed "tenants" in their communities. The major private landlords were not pleased with the permissive second-suite laws either, because these apartments were renting at rates below their apartments—pulling down the rents they could charge. The last thing these private rental organizations wanted was competition from hundreds of thousands of enterprising homeowners putting up dry-wall and installing additional bathrooms to allow a tenant to be housed at reasonable rates.

Toronto City Council recently approved introducing second suites into every neighbourhood with a very strong majority vote. Many people were surprised that council was willing to face the wrath of the residents' groups who were leading the charge against the idea. I like to believe that it was because of the commitment that council has made to address the homelessness issue. Mayor Mel Lastman, who had once opposed unrelated people living together in homes in North York, came out in favour. The city's planning staff had estimated that this initiative could produce 2,000 additional affordable units a year—without a penny of government funding. I argued that this amounted to 160 units a month! "Imagine," I challenged my fellow councillors, "we are willing to open fifty new hostel beds each month, but we are being urged by some not to pass a by-law allowing 160 new affordable apartments to be created by our fellow citizens in their homes at no cost to government!" The by-law passed. A few residents' associations leaders from affluent areas challenged the by-law through the Ontario Municipal Board. They failed and second suites should start to blossom.

Main-street redevelopment

When I had a chance to visit European cities, I was blown away by how their main streets had buildings with stores below and several floors of apartments above. A built-in market for the local shops was living right upstairs. Many people were able to do their daily shopping without even owning a car; transit was handy on these main streets; and some residents even worked in the shops, restaurants and bars right there in the neighbourhood.

Would it be possible for Canada's main streets to have the density of development that some European cities have?

Former president of the FCM Richard Gilbert pressed this idea forward. Studies were done, design competitions held and many speeches about the potential were made. To date, though, there is little to show for the words that were spoken.

I'm as guilty as the next councillor on this one. My area in Toronto includes the famous Danforth, best known for its concentration of excellent Greek cuisine. A walk up and down the Danforth shows mostly two- and three-storey buildings, with restaurants and shops on the ground floor. It's a wide street, so it could easily see two or three more storeys built on top of those stores. There's a subway underneath, so the tenants would most likely use transit, necessitating little parking requirement. Local businesses would boom. Adjacent residential streets could be left alone, or the neighbourhood could be allowed to change, to experience reinvestment and development. Most important, new affordable housing would be created. Why affordable? Because the businesses below are already successful, covering the land costs. These new apartments would be "found money" and could be rented, through development agreements with the builder and landowner, at low rent, in exchange for the right to increase the height through the redevelopment process.

Cities across Canada could accelerate urban renewal of their main streets if there were an encouraging affordable-housing construction program to work in tandem with their planning and rezoning efforts.

Infill redevelopments

Most communities have room to "remake" themselves from the bottom up. Once people put their minds to work, opportunities to creatively and effectively transform underused space into vibrant homes are more easily found than might be expected. Abandoned back-lane garages can be redeveloped. Parking lots can become housing with parking underneath. An old church can become a new church, with seniors' housing meshed neatly into the redevelopment. Local councils can encourage this sort of thing, and there are good examples in most communities. Infill projects have a downside. It's their one-of-a-kind nature. There is a lot of reinventing of wheels involved. So while the land may be less expensive, which helps to reduce costs, the time to put the project together can offset this advantage.

Special-needs integration

Imagine if all municipalities had policies ensuring that special needs and supportive housing could be located in any neighbourhood. This would prevent some communities from blocking this kind of housing, a tactic that forces other communities to absorb higher concentrations of special-needs housing. The policy of "fair share" was emphasized in Anne Golden's report, because she noticed that several areas in the city had virtually no housing or shelters for people with mental-health problems or for recovering addicts. At present, too many neighbourhoods are able to use zoning laws to prevent a reasonable share of this kind of housing and service being located in their community. If attempts were made to block people on the basis of skin colour, religion, culture or any other trait, we'd be at the Supreme Court. The same equality and human-rights issues arise in the context of supportive housing. Let's make sure our by-laws reflect this.

Innovate and experiment

Sometimes our layer-upon-layer of regulations restrict or prevent innovation and lower-cost construction methods. Take, for example, building-code requirements that preclude stacked townhouses and small apartment buildings from being built with wood, because they are taller than 3.5 storeys.

Rules requiring concrete construction for medium-sized buildings were put in place for good reasons at the time, but new approaches to building mid-sized structures with wood seem promising. The Swedish wood industry is building six-storey apartment buildings on a demonstration basis, hoping to enhance the market for its wood industries. It so happens that this kind of construction is much less expensive than concrete forming, so housing costs could be reduced using innovations like this—especially if local governments acted as catalysts for experimentation and innovation.

To permit this kind of innovation, as John Sewell points out, municipal governments need to remove or modify some of the barriers that have been created over the years.[17] He uses the example of standards for new developments, some of which he says are "gold-plated," creating extra costs of construction, thus increasing the price of the ultimate housing. One of the most devastating standards is the requirement, in suburban subdivisions, that local roads be as wide as major arterials—vast expanses of asphalt and concrete that are not needed for the volume of traffic. Further standards then say that cars cannot be parked on these wide streets. Houses are *required* to have large, paved driveways and garages for each and every car that the occupant might own.

We've had twenty years of houses with the dominant feature of the architecture being the two- and three-car garage projecting in front. Fortunately, new approaches are bringing back "the back lane," which is reducing the size of the streets and the omnipresence of the car. Careful analysis of this "new urbanism" may show us, though, that the new developments have a similar amount of pavement, just organized differently.

Really creative solutions would involve designing communities in which the automobile did not have to be dragged out for every trip to the corner store, school, church or work trip. Communities organized to maximize the number of trips that could be managed on foot, by bike or by local transit would ultimately be less expensive to live in, and the housing costs could drop because the gross amount of land required per housing unit would drop.

Generally, a shift to "performance-based" regulation would help. Rather than having by-laws and regulations that try to tell private, public and non-profit developers exactly how they must build, it would be better to tell them the goals that *must* be met, leaving it to the creativity of the building team to determine how. Sewell gives the example of the requirement that kitchens have plug outlets every three feet. Why not five feet? Why not just say that a specific number of circuits with certain ratings need to be provided to ensure fire safety and let the developer figure out the most cost-effective placement of outlets. There are hundreds of examples of this sort.

Using regulations to prevent deterioration

The flip side of the regulation role of municipalities is important, too. Local councils and their buildings departments can enforce their property-standards by-laws so that deteriorating housing can be caught and fixed before it becomes substandard. Why should Canada have so many substandard housing units when by-laws just about everywhere say that these conditions should not exist? Something is wrong with the regulatory environment, the penalties or the way in which laws are enforced. It's true, there is a delicate dance that must be performed by the building inspectors. If they are too tough on offenders, the landlord can use the building-repair orders as an excuse to evict tenants and raise rents after the renovations and repairs are complete. Or the repair work is done around, on top of and underneath the tenants, making life unbearable. Strategies like this are unfortunately found when an unscrupulous landlord is involved. The trick is to nip the repair issue in the bud, before the home has deteriorated to such an extent that major work is required.

Let's also remember our earlier discussion about how regulation of condominium conversions and demolitions—as well as luxury renovations—can help preserve perfectly good, affordable housing.

Taxation

Most tenants do not know that they are being "hosed" by the property tax system, and that this is driving up their rental payments. The inequitable property tax burden faced by renters—compared with homeowners and condos and co-ops—has been well documented, but little is ever done about it. In Ontario, it is not uncommon for two-bedroom apartments to be paying $2,000 to $3,000 in annual property taxes. This compares to large homes on large lots paying similar taxes. Sprawling suburban homes are much more expensive for the municipality to service, yet they are paying similar taxes to the apartment dweller, who usually receives fewer municipal services. Besides, we've already seen in this book that most tenants have lower incomes than homeowners. So the tenant's property taxes are more difficult to pay. That is because the property taxes form a greater percentage of the typical tenant's income than they do of a typical homeowner's income.

Generally, tenants know nothing about these injustices, because the information is not provided to them—the taxes are buried in their rent payments. Apartment rents could be reduced significantly if there were a more equal application of taxation. The effect of this skewed taxation system raises rents in the range of $50 to $150 a month. When taken in the context of average rents, correcting this problem could reduce rents by 10 to 25 percent! A significant number of tenants would no longer be in the at-risk or core-need predicament.

Standing in the way of reform of tenants' property taxes is the fact that homeowners and business owners would see a raise in their taxes, if this injustice were corrected. Every local councillor and mayor knows that homeowners and local businesses vote at municipal election time (upward of 40 percent show up at the polls), while tenants tend not to turn out (15 percent would be normal). Political rocket science suggests that the politicians will be less likely to lower taxes for the low turnout group while raising them for the high turnout group.

Modified development charges, lot levies and taxes

Local governments often charge new developments for the costs of installing various services and supports. These lot levies and development charges could be reduced or waived, to encourage affordable housing. It's true that the new costs of services would still face the municipality as a whole, but there are savings to a community that ensure that there is more affordable housing. Reduced emergency-shelter and support-service costs for the homeless and poorly housed can help to offset the value of the waived fees.[18] Several cities have decided to adjust or forgo these fees completely for affordable-housing projects. More need to consider doing so. Leaving these fees in place amounts to a financial barrier to affordability in a community—more subtle perhaps than zoning, but equally devastating and unjust.

Communities making housing happen

Here's where the 4,000 local governments in Canada fit into a national strategy. Municipalities should all take direct leadership roles in achieving the housing targets we have suggested. Municipal governments are best positioned to make affordable housing happen in their communities. Whether alone or in regional combinations, municipal governments have the advantage of being close to the people who need to be housed. Local non-profit organizations, like housing co-operatives and housing associations, can work together with municipal housing corporations to put housing on the ground faster than a large national or provincial organization.

Some large cities are already involved through housing companies, agencies and departments that they have established to create and manage affordable-housing developments. A great many more have not taken these steps—leaving the proactive housing-development function to other levels of government or to community groups. There is a real vacuum in places where the local council has not made new affordable housing a priority. And when projects come forward from community groups, they have a more difficult time negotiating their way through the approval processes. What a contrast to the situation where an active local council has embraced the housing agenda and is ambitiously pursuing new projects, bringing the community on side, engaging stakeholders and making things happen!

Where these city agencies do not exist, they have to be created. Enabling municipalities to form housing-development corporations is a key instrument in the effort. Cities, towns and rural areas can work alone or in collaborative clusters. In smaller provinces, perhaps, municipal governments could pull together at the provincial level.

Why not a Canada-wide national affordable-housing development company? The most innovative, efficient and creative housing development companies are not huge. Giant development conglomerates have tended to collapse of their own weight. We have the case of Bramalea Developments in Canada.

That's not to say that Canadians don't know how to put together effective development companies. In fact, we have a reputation for doing just that. Over the years, though, our firms' skills have tended to focus on building privately owned houses, suburban complexes or urban condos. Experts at financing, Canadian builders have branched out into other countries with their expertise. Yet they cannot house our own people! Nor do they generally seem to show much desire to do so. With few exceptions, the real-estate industry and property developers have not come forward to say, "How can we help to house those who are too poor to afford our product?" We need them now more than ever, yet there is still silence. This has to change.

It's clear, though, that private developers cannot be expected to meet the needs we've described. Urban and suburban governments alike can put together the organizational strength, the financial clout, the planning and development expertise and the sense of mission needed to do the job. It would be like waiting for Godot to bide our time for the developers to act independently and build housing affordable to the millions of Canadians living in the lowest 20 to 30 percent of the population.

Also, let's remember that whenever municipal housing companies build new communities or buildings, they are working with the developers. Architects, non-profit development experts, construction companies, building-trade unions and building-materials suppliers are all involved in the effort. In a sense, the municipal housing-development corporation is the catalyst for affordable-housing construction, nothing more. Without that catalyst, however, little will happen and local councils will be left struggling to open emergency shelters and cope with the homeless on our streets.

As Michael Dennis and Susan Fish said as far back as 1971, "While overall responsibility for program planning should be provincial, the development and administration of individual projects and the planning for program delivery in particular municipalities should be a municipal function, at least in those cities that have the necessary capability or can quickly develop it. That allocation of responsibility has been federal policy since 1949. It is the pattern in most European countries and in the U.S."[19]

If we didn't have so many city housing-development successes, we could dismiss this idea.

What resources do local government housing-development companies have? Many. They are missing a strong tax base for housing development, but they do have a very significant asset base to secure loans on. Generally, very good credit ratings and prudent fiscal management have put municipal governments in enviable positions in borrowing markets. Assembling the initial funds to finance projects has usually been the key challenge. When federal housing grants and loan and mortgage programs were in place from the 1970s to the early 1990s, local housing-development companies were in their heyday, building tens of thousands of units every year, along with their partners in the non-profit and co-operative development world. That is why local development companies need financing partners at the federal level, with assistance and participation of the provinces where they wish to be players.

Land as a lever

I'm always surprised at the amount of land Canadian cities own. What is even more surprising is how much of this land is unused, just lying around waiting for an opportunity. Some of this inventory is land once bought or expropriated for projects that never became more than a gleam in a local council's eye, or land that fell into the hands of the property-tax collection department, because the owner walked, leaving an unhealthy, unpaid balance. Other property becomes "surplus to the needs of the municipality" because of changed programs, consolidations, amalgamations and reorganizations. And swapping one piece of city land for a privately owned piece somewhere else might be possible, too.

All this land gives local communities an opportunity to shape the evolution of their city. Hong Kong is famous for its conscious accumulation of property on the outskirts of the city so that it can design the way in which the buzzing metropolis can grow. Rather than being subject to the dictates of the property speculators (which in Canada have produced costly sprawl) Hong Kong is able to manage densities—and affordability as well.

Some Canadian cities have used publicly owned land as a tool to build marvelous affordable-housing neighbourhoods and projects. The problem they most often face today is the complete absence of assistance from federal and provincial governments, which would allow them to build affordable homes on the land they own. So all Canadian cities should have a strong mandate provided by their councils to utilize land for new housing that will meet the needs of the lowest-income households. Some have Housing First policies in place on paper, but their real-estate departments do not ensure that the "lofty" desires of the politicians are put into practice. Far too often, bureaucrats run the show. It took the United Way of Greater Toronto and a fierce *Toronto Star* editorial[20] to point out the actions of bureaucrats who had plunked a For Sale sign unceremoniously on a piece of city land attached to a wonderful new project for low-income singles. City staff had helpfully removed the sign for the ribbon-cutting ceremony for the new homes, only to allow the eager real-estate agent (acting for the city) to hammer it back up the next day, hoping that no one would notice that the sale would violate the city's own policy—to put all suitable sites aside for more housing. Arm-wrestling between a real-estate division eager to meet its targets for city revenue and councillors trying to meet their public commitments eventually saw the councillors win—at least for the time being.

Then there's the hope to be found in urban "brownfield" sites. Once used by heavy industries in the central portions of cities and along railway lines, thousands of acres of now silent territory called brownfields are deserted and desolate. Urban sorespots, they usually contain toxic cocktails in their soils. But as the National Round Table on the Environment and the Economy has pointed out,[21] the opportunity cost of leaving these sites fallow is substantial. Cleaning the lands and allowing housing—combined with other employment-related uses—could meet many goals simultaneously: removing toxics from the water table, providing housing and job opportunities, revitalizing derelict areas, substituting inner-city density for urban sprawl, not to mention generating property tax revenue.

Ironically, many brownfield properties in Canadian cities today are well known to the homeless because they live there in makeshift tents and struggling encampments.

Cities like Vancouver have been proactive in their use of their own brownfield lands. Plans for the False Creek Redevelopment include a provision that sufficient land will be reserved so that a minimum of 20 percent of the housing, to be built in the area, will serve the needs of low-income households. As approved by Vancouver Council in March 2000, the principles of development are also the most advanced from an environmental and urban-planning point of view to be found anywhere in Canada.[22]

With land so fundamental to affordable housing solutions, municipalities require a comprehensive policy to ensure that sufficient property is available to help solutions to happen.

Pro-active city champions and structures

All these ideas for solutions sound interesting, but without people introducing motions on council floors to achieve them, they'll remain ideas on paper rather than become housing in communities. Political and bureaucratic champions have to lead the way, supported by structures of decision making designed to produce affordable-housing results.

Comedian George Burns once said that it was "too bad that all the people who know how to run the country are busy driving taxicabs and cutting hair."[23] Every cabby I ask has the solution to the housing crisis:

"Why don't they just roll up their sleeves and get some housing built?!" Answering the cabby's question is painfully easy in most Canadian communities today: no one is charged with the responsibility.

After years of drought in the fields of new low-income housing, many communities now have nobody on the payroll with housing construction in their job description. The result? No senior staff are being asked by the mayor or council, "How many folks in need of housing did we house this year?" It's hard to find a housing champion on the senior staff team of the many municipalities in Canada today. No chief administrative officers in cities I know have housing production in their job-evaluation process. Council bureaucracies, which used to be capable of producing thousands of non-profit affordable units a year across Canada, have atrophied from disuse and, in most cases, have been amputated.

Parallel vacuums of political leadership on these issues existed throughout the early and mid-1990s on too many Canadian municipal councils. Why? The large private-development lobbies and the most significant rental-housing property owners and their associations had successfully mounted and maintained propaganda campaigns against the extensive Canadian social-housing programs throughout the 1980s.[24] As the crescendo of views against housing policies (that interfered in any way with free markets) swelled, politicians began to back away. Attacks on politicians living in co-ops—with the allegation that they were taking housing from those in need—had a bruising impact on the reputation of social housing.

When my wife, who was then a school trustee, and I were vilified for living in Hazelburn Co-op by some council colleagues who opposed social housing in general, the story hit Toronto's front pages, the provincial legislature and even Canada's House of Commons. Headlines did not initially explain that many people live in co-ops and pay market rents, creating mixed-income communities. It's true that the controversy eventually allowed stories to be printed that explained how mixed-income social housing worked—and how important it was for the economics and social success of the modern forms of public housing. Still, misrepresentations and nasty media spins had begun to solidify in the public's mind. Meanwhile, private-sector lobbyists fanned the flames in the back rooms and generated a mood that led to the withdrawal of federal financial support and an attempt by the feds to download social-housing to the provinces. This was accomplished in most provinces, although a spirited campaign by the Ontario co-op sector, supported by Liberal MPs from Ontario, prevented the anti-social-housing thugs in the Mike Harris government from sinking their meathooks into the tens of thousands of federal co-op units in that province.

After all this brouhaha, many local politicians became gun-shy, and they backed off their previous support for new affordable housing. But that cool climate heated when homelessness began to rise in the late 1990s—a product of the sustained absence of new housing supply coming on board that was affordable by those without means. Because of this lacuna, without councillors or mayors spending time and effort to bring the problem and some solutions forward, Canada's municipal bureaucracies inevitably turned to other priorities.

Champions on councils will be needed to re-establish the urgent priority of affordable housing. Mayors interested in seeing solutions move forward should appoint a small team of representative councillors and give them the mandate to deliver new housing. Councils should hold this group accountable for achieving some agreed-on targets. The councillors would then work with the many bureaucracies involved to get things moving. Councils should also mandate their designated housing hitters to remain accountable to the community groups working on the homelessness and housing issues in their cities and towns. This team would also draw on community partners—workers in front-line homeless services and low-income housing sectors—to help raise public awareness and to suggest creative strategies and solutions. Calgary Council has set the pace with its spring 2000 establishment of just such a political quarterback committee. Regina was not far behind. Where these special council political structures do not exist, community advocacy groups should insist that they be created as soon as possible. Otherwise, people working on housing issues across Canada are going to continue to experience that wonderful feeling of banging their collective heads against city-hall walls.

Creating and Protecting Affordable Housing

A healthy housing sector in any country today would have four key components:

- Rental housing
- Ownership housing

- Social housing with a mix to include low-income households
- Support for people who need special assistance to live independently

All these parts should be linked so that people can move through their phases of housing needs smoothly, over the years, as circumstances change. We would all agree that no Canadian should have to worry about whether adequate housing will be available. So how can we create the healthy housing system that would provide the security that all Canadians have a right to?

To answer this question, the FCM's National Housing Policy Options Team joined with the Canadian Housing and Renewal Association to convene a round table of Canada's top housing experts in the spring of 2000. Emerging from this session were some key principles:[25]

- Recognize that housing is a fundamental right and that all governments are morally obligated to ensure their citizens have access to safe, sound and affordable housing
- Allow for the development, where feasible, of collaborative intergovernmental mechanisms to ensure equivalent and equitable levels of housing assistance across all provinces and territories
- Recognize that sound, safe, affordable housing is a critical foundation for individual and community health and well-being, particularly for children
- [Ensure that affordable housing is] financially sustainable with finite levels of government financial contribution
- Optimize the use of existing assets, including the stock of social housing developed over the past forty years
- Recognize and rebuild the non-profit and community-based delivery infrastructure, which was created in Canada over the past four decades
- Leverage the participation and involvement of the private sector
- Emphasize the development of responsive local initiatives—initiatives designed and delivered locally, building on local resources and partnerships but supported with flexible funding from federal and provincial governments
- Recognize local conditions and encourage local creativity and resourcefulness

- Where possible, assist, facilitate, support and encourage recipients to graduate from reliance on assistance[26]

Our work at the FCM is leading us to propose the following framework for the development of a National Affordable Housing Strategy, to make sufficient new and existing housing affordable to achieve the goals we have set for Canada:

1. Flexible Capital Grant Program for Housing—a program of locally designed and administered initiatives supported by a federal or joint federal/provincial capital fund
2. A Private Rental Program—to encourage private rental production
3. Creation of Investment Pools of Money for Affordable Housing—to attract new funding for the development, acquisition or rehabilitation of affordable housing
4. Provincially Administered Income Supplement Programs—to help tenants who are unable to afford market rents; this program would complement capital grants, to ensure that new housing would reach those most in need[27]

With 45,000 to 50,000 new rental households coming on board each year in Canada for the next decade—and about half of these being unable to afford market rents—something has to be done to ensure an adequate supply of rental housing affordable to this large, less-wealthy group. For this new rental-housing demand, subsidies can bridge the gap between the costs of producing a new unit of rental housing and the lower level of market rents in the community. Until this gap is bridged, low-rental housing is unlikely to be built.

Evidence aplenty exists for this proposition across Canada. In a typical large urban centre, $1,000 a month may be required to pay for all of the financing and costs of building a new rental unit. However, the lower end of the rental market typically stands $300 a month below this threshold in most markets—Ontario, Alberta and British Columbia being the most extreme cases. Bridging this gap with a capital grant in exchange for ensuring that the landlord keeps rents in the affordable range can be the most powerful and effective tool for the creation of low-end rental housing. And one-time capital contributions to housing projects are a cost-effective way of bridging this gap.[28] This investment in the equity of new homes is less complicated, less costly, quicker to impact affordable supply and more flexible than Canada's previous efforts to write down mortgage interest rates in an effort to make housing affordable. Long-term commitments to cover interest costs made these earlier programs cast long financial shadows on governments' books, locking them into obligations for thirty years or more. One-time capital grants, while more expensive than mortgage write-downs in the first instance, have an immediate positive economic "hit" on governments' books through new construction, GST and PST payments, income tax paid by all those involved in the housing industry and reduced social-assistance program costs resulting from the expanded affordable housing supply.

An arm's-length foundation should be created to run this program. With the best housing minds Canada can find sitting on its board, this foundation would be provided with resources from the federal government, supplemented by provincial support where possible. Programs such as the Residential Rehabilitation Assistance Program could also be turned over to the foundation, to bring the rehabilitation of existing housing into a co-ordinated program with the construction of new affordable rental housing. The foundation would distribute funds to municipalities across Canada. Municipal governments are the ideal partners for this role, because local city and town councils are in close touch with communities and local needs. Quebec already has such a funding mechanism in place, so national funds should be added to the total funds to build more housing.

In rural areas, where municipal governments have less infrastructure to put programs together, groups of municipalities (or even provincial associations of municipal governments) could be given the resources to do the job. In all these models, the key would be to have municipalities work in partnerships with the local organizations and community groups. No massive central bureaucracy is going to do the job well. But the decentralized delivery system will require that communities be given the training, monitoring and accountability tools they need to excel.

Here is how the decisions could be made for the foundation funds to municipalities:

- Clearly identified criteria (e.g., households needing assistance, housing conditions)

- Municipal agreement to some level and type of participation
- The development of a local housing strategy[29]

What kind of projects would be funded and what guidance would be given to communities to be sure that these dollars would be well spent?

- Flexibility is key, so that different cities and towns can address their own needs and priorities. Some might need additional affordable housing; others might need upgrading of existing housing. The capacity of housing builders in the community will have to be considered. What is the capacity of the not-for-profit or private-sector builders to do the job?
- Capital grants would be given for new construction for non-profits and co-operative rental housing projects in order to reduce rents.
- Capital grants for the acquisition and upgrading of existing affordable rental units could be permitted where this is cost-effective. FCM analysis shows that in some markets in Canada, this may be a very efficient use of resources in light of the rapid escalation of rents in substandard private-sector buildings.
- Rehabilitation of affordable housing could be supported by grants and forgivable loans, expanding the RRAP model.
- Foundation funds could be used to help low- and moderate-income tenants to purchase a home, thus freeing up the rental accommodation, as well as providing long-term security for families who might otherwise never get access.
- Granting initiatives would be designed to help community groups work with the people being helped by the program. These at-risk or homeless people would also have support and opportunities to earn income and, if it works out, become more self-reliant in the community.
- A portion of the funds should be earmarked for building the capacity of communities to design and implement local initiatives.[30]

Next, we need to determine the cost of this essential tool. To this end, respected housing economist Steve Pomeroy was asked by our team to evaluate scenarios. In all cases, he was asked to target 20,000 units of new affordable rental housing each year for ten years, in order to meet the objectives set by the FCM in its effort to reduce the crisis by half in a decade. (See Table 6.1) He found that there were several ways to lick the affordable-housing problem, but fundamental issues emerged. Some provinces have much higher land costs and construction costs because of their relatively hot economies. As a result, producing a new unit of affordable housing in one of these provinces can be much more expensive than in others. To illustrate: A capital grant adequate to bring down rents in a new unit (so that low-income households could live there) would require a subsidy of $131,000 in Ontario. Alberta units would need $107,119 and B.C. apartments would require $103,457 to achieve an equivalent situation for one of that province's households. On the other end of the cost spectrum would be Quebec, where the housing market and costs structure is so different that the same objective could be achieved for $48,000 a unit.[31] While this differential could cause some interprovincial consternation, shifts over time in the economies of provinces would accomplish some equalization as the years pass.

Reducing Poverty

Rising rents in combination with falling incomes for so many Canadians are driving forces behind homelessness and the affordability crisis. Figure 6.2 shows a fifteen-year trend in which those with the least have fallen the most (represented by 1, the lowest decile on the figure). Earners in the top 10 percent (represented by 10 in the figure) have been the gainers. You can almost see the cash marching from one end of the figure to the other, a legacy of the policies of the Mulroney government, accentuated by subsequent administrations.

How can we tackle rising poverty and declining standards of living for so many Canadians in the midst of business-media reports of a thriving economy? Not only millions of Canadians have experienced the loss of full-time jobs to part-time lower-paid ones. All over the world, the same trends are pervasive.[32] As wealth and its creation are transformed into speculative "paper" assets that can be traded at will in a massive gambling game—to which few have access—there are growing pressures to squeeze ever-increasing profits from the operations of all firms.[33] These must come from increased "efficiencies" in the extraction of value from the foundations of the productive process—labour, natural resources and technology. So wages and employment are forced down, creating increased profitability for

Figure 6.2: Changes in Real Annual Earnings by Decile, from 1981 to 1995

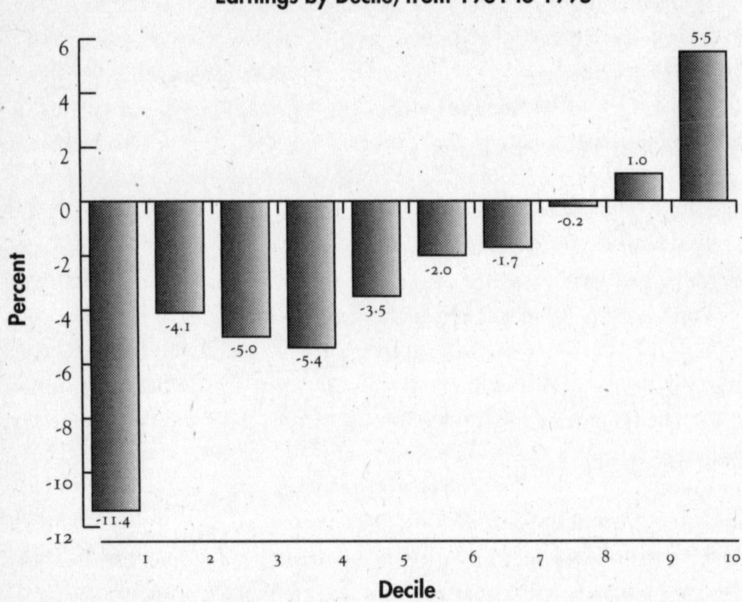

Source: Mel Hurtig, *Pay the Rent or Feed the Kids* (Toronto: McClelland & Stewart, 1999), p. 151.

shareholders—a direct shift of wealth from the low to the upper end of the economic spectrum.

Jim Stanford tells of one case, where CN Rail was privatized, leading to widespread conclusions, except among the workers, that terrific improvements had been made:

> The privatization of CN Rail in 1995 is often heralded as a fantastically successful economic initiative. To be sure, the private company has been a hit with investors, whose share values tripled in the three years after privatization. The federal government, meanwhile, earned a billion dollars towards its deficit-reduction priority (not much in the grand fiscal scheme). But in actual operational and economic terms, has the privatized company really been so successful? In 1998, the company hauled barely as much freight as it did in 1994 (before

> privatization), and it actually earned less in total revenue. Its real investment in new machinery and railway structures has declined substantially under private ownership. But the company did all this with 10,000 fewer workers—the sole reason for its transformation from "basket case" into "profit machine." Eliminating 10,000 well-paying jobs at a time of chronic unemployment and falling incomes is hardly a positive achievement in the big picture.[34]

I've since talked with some of these former railway workers, broken and struggling with their demons, in Toronto's shelters for the homeless.

National anti-poverty strategies have been constructed by many groups in Canada since Parliament adopted a resolution in 1990 to eradicate poverty by the year 2000.[35] Virtually all contain a call for a major investment in affordable housing as a foundation element. Increasing the minimum wage, restoring the cuts to social assistance programs—like unemployment insurance, disability pensions and welfare programs—and establishing a Canada-wide child-care initiative also need to be included in the strategy. Finally, new economic instruments need to be created to stem the upward flow of wealth. Investments in public ventures to lever private funds (such as those suggested by the Centre for Public Policy Alternatives) could become a centrepiece of an economy that is more balanced, just and effective at meeting Canadians' needs and hopes.[36]

A Learning Experience

Here is what happened in our efforts to change national housing policies in the past couple of years. It will show you the complexity and uncertainties of "the game."

Following years of growing community pressure for action, a possible federal awakening to the homelessness crisis took place when Toronto's Mayor Lastman invited the prime minister to join a meeting in March 1999.[37] Days before the conference began, the prime minister appointed his minister of labour, Claudette Bradshaw, to co-ordinate the federal government's response to homelessness. The gambit worked: The threat of Mel Lastman lashing out against Ottawa's inaction was sufficient. But Bradshaw was put in a tough spot—she was sent to the large gathering empty-handed. She had to address a capacity crowd in City Hall, which included homeless people, city representatives from as far afield as Calgary,

Edmonton, Vancouver and St. John's and the Ontario government delegates. All she could bring was her famous hugs and passionate stories of her efforts as a youth worker in Moncton. Her heart was in the right place, and there was a sense in the room that she should be given a chance to show what Ottawa could be persuaded to do.

Throughout the spring and summer, the FCM pressed hard, as did community groups and networks across the country. At the 1999 FCM Annual Convention in Halifax, over 1,000 mayors and municipal councillors listened to Lastman tear a strip off Ottawa for inaction. He was followed by Mayor Brian Murphy (himself a Liberal) from Moncton, Bradshaw's home constituency. Although more temperate than Mel, he made it clear that homelessness was not a problem of a few huge cities like Toronto but was spreading to cities like Moncton, which was building its first shelter. Mayor Doug Archer of Regina brought a Western perspective. My job on the panel was to present the National Housing Policy Options Team proposals, which were later adopted unanimously by the convention. Claudette Bradshaw sat in the audience and took in the gathering momentum.

The summer and fall of 1999 were filled with preparations to press the finance minister, Paul Martin, the prime minister and premiers to devise a national program. Community groups and municipalities worked in parallel to encourage the momentum. Frustration was building that Canada's homeless were about to experience yet another winter in the elements without any help from their national government. (A year had passed since the mayors had declared homelessness to be a national disaster.) The FCM sent a delegation to meet with Paul Martin in his Ottawa office. The FCM president, Marystown mayor Sam Synard, FCM's CEO James Knight, FCM environment policy wizard Louise Comeau and I put our case to Martin. He did respond well to some ideas on environmental initiatives and green infrastructure, but there was discouragingly little sign of movement on the housing issue.

What we did *not* know was that after her four-month cross-country research tour in the summer and fall of 1999, Bradshaw had broadcast to her colleagues an emotion-packed video, complete with the voices of homeless people, right in the cabinet's meeting room. With her credibility, and that of the prime minister, on the line, she pressed for a pre-Christmas announcement of $753 million in funding over three years to address homeless issues. This happened, and almost half of the money went to expanding the Residential Rehabilitation Assistance Program, some funds were earmarked for aboriginal initiatives, and the rest was reserved for community-based plans to deal with the worst consequences of homelessness. Explicitly excluded was any possibility that the funds could be used for actual housing. Bradshaw repeatedly argued that she was not, after all, the minister of housing.

While the emergency assistance was welcomed, housing critics lashed out. How could a minister working on homelessness walk away from providing affordable housing? Although she stuck to her guns, Bradshaw did arrange for a meeting with the executive of the FCM in the winter of 2000 along with her colleague, Alfonso Gagliano, who held responsibility for CMHC. He told us that he personally supported the federal government having another look at the possibility of a housing role.

A few weeks later, eleven mayors from across Canada sat in the prime minister's small, private briefing room just prior to the opening of the House of Commons, a couple of weeks before the budget for the year 2000 was announced by Paul Martin. After typical jovial pleasantries, Lastman exploded: "We're here about housing—people are dying in our streets!" Edmonton's mayor, Bill Smith, got the hint and tore into the federal government for ignoring the plight of the homeless. One mayor after another underlined the point, to which Chrétien said, "You know, we gave it [housing] over to the provinces; they wanted it, and, you know, you lose interest."[38] He did express some interest in an infrastructure program. The idea to include housing in the program was floated, but there was no apparent taking of the bait. I remember feeling quite discouraged. A few days later, Lastman took me aside and said, "You've got to get to Martin before the budget. He's the one who'll make the decision."

I called on behalf of the mayor and was put through to Martin's chief of staff. She was clear—there would not be a national housing program announcement. The Bradshaw money was all we were going to see in the budget. However, she asked, if we included affordable housing as one of the types of projects that could be funded by a new infrastructure program, would cities respond favourably? The problem I outlined to her was that municipalities were very reluctant to have to pay one-third of the costs of new affordable housing from the property tax. (An infrastructure program would be based on equal funding by the federal, provincial and municipal governments.) Thrown in with all the other pressing urban infrastructure needs, housing would likely receive only modest municipal funds. We continued to believe, I insisted, that a full-fledged housing program was essential. Still, I confided, "If housing was mentioned in the budget speech at all, this would be the first signs of a reversal of the federal exit plan."

A few days later, Martin announced a multibillion-dollar federal/provincial/municipal infrastructure program as proposed by the cities. Housing was listed as one of the permitted categories of spending. The foot had found its way into the door.

As of this writing, the projects to be funded from the infrastructure program are in the early stages of submission. It would appear that only a few cities are intending to include modest affordable-housing initiatives in their proposals.

It remains to be seen if all this effort becomes the early stages of a snowball effect. That will be up to Canadians and their continued efforts to press governments at all levels for action on housing.

The Social Union Framework

Although not signed by the Province of Quebec, the Social Union Framework Agreement (SUFA) hammered out by First Ministers in 1998 sets a new constitutional context for social programs like housing. Signed on February 4, 1999, the agreement aimed to commit the federal, provincial and territorial governments to work more co-operatively and efficiently in the funding and delivery of social programs for Canadians, while leaving existing constitutional jurisdictions and powers untouched. There was no specific mention of housing in the agreement, but implications for the intergovernmental tools at our collective disposal to tackle homelessness may flow from this new agreement.

Read one way, the framework could be seen as very restrictive and an obstacle to social-policy innovation. Another perspective suggests that the SUFA frees us from the past—the old view that only one-size-fits-all social policy is acceptable in the Canadian federation. SUFA suggests that governments must ensure that they "provide appropriate assistance to those in need."[39] It also calls for the signing governments to "ensure adequate, affordable, stable and sustainable funding for social programs."[40]

Is this new agreement good news for the housing crisis? These day it depends on whom you ask. Commenting on the problem of housing and homelessness, the senior federal bureaucrat responsible for the SUFA had this inspiring vision to offer: "You will never be able to claim success; it does not end."[41] She later added, "In the new citizen-focused agenda of the federal government, leadership is not being there sometimes."[42] I thought to myself as I listened, incredulous, that perhaps this was the peculiar logic that had propelled Ottawa to walk away from housing.

SUFA seems to remove the concept of national standards from the discussion of federal programs and social spending. This would not be good news for a national housing program. The Council of Canadians has also criticized the agreement, because it seems to limit the ability of the federal government to establish new national programs without the consent of the provinces.[43] A new national housing program could fall victim to provincial veto.

However, a closer look suggests some reason to be optimistic. Our review at the Toronto City Council noticed that the federal government would only need the consent of six provinces (which could represent as little as 15 percent of the population of Canada) to approve new social programs. Besides, their agreement is needed only if the funding is cost shared. Where the federal government "goes it alone," there is only the requirement for three months' notice to the provinces. This opens the door to federal transfers for affordable-housing projects directly to municipalities, individuals, non-profit organizations and community groups.[44] Still, as Sharon Chisholm, the executive director of the Canadian Housing and Renewal Association points out, all is not clear sailing: "The agreement, as it turns out, is more a process agreement as opposed to a revised division of powers. It is telling that already there are disagreements as to the interpretation of the agreement with provinces taking away an understanding different from the federal government."[45]

Is it worth seizing the moment and creating opportunities here? Perhaps, but I'm inclined to concur with those who suggest that the voluntary-sector non-profit groups, and (I would add) municipalities need to organize themselves to develop concrete ideas for social policy, in this case affordable housing, and submit them to the Ministerial Council of Social Policy Renewal, which has been set up to pursue the Social Union Framework Agreement. This is exactly what the National Housing Policy Options Team, the Canadian Housing Renewal Association and the developing coalition of housing groups (known as the National Homelessness and Housing Network) have been attempting to do. To make this work, the following steps have been suggested:

- The development of stronger coalitions by sub-sector (i.e., housing)
- The co-ordination of provincial and national levels within umbrella organizations
- The development of better cross-sectoral discussions within the sector
- A plan for succession of policy expertise and leadership within national and regional organizations.[46]

While some early moves in these directions are underway, there are vital steps that should be incorporated into a national campaign for affordable housing, discussed below. In summary here, creative and skilful use of the possibilities buried in SUFA may provide some opportunities to break the constitutional log-jam facing a renewed housing agenda in Canada.

A federal/provincial housing forum

As a sign of the changing times, the federal and provincial ministers responsible for housing have taken tentative steps to reactivate something called the federal/provincial housing forum. This forum had not met for a number of years. But faced with growing concern about the aimless drift in housing policy, First Ministers agreed that they would reconvene the group in the fall of 2000 in Moncton. The FCM and community groups took aim at this opportunity to call for a new national policy on housing. Working with the new president of FCM, Councillor Joanne Monahan from Kitimat, we wrote to every association of municipalities in every province and territory and secured their co-operation in pressing their provincial ministers of housing to accept an FCM intervention. We will, at the meeting, lay out our whole program to reduce the homelessness and affordable-housing crisis in Canada by half in a decade.

Perhaps some new tools will be created as a result of these meetings with housing ministers across the country. The mere fact that they are meeting suggests some interest on their part.

Apparently it's hard to get federal and provincial ministers together. Thirteen months after agreeing to meet, the gathering finally took place in Fredericton in September 2000.

Convened by Percy Mockler, New Brunswick's very well-intentioned minister responsible for housing, the ministers worked their way through a two-day agenda. On the second day, the federal liberal minister responsible for Canada Mortgage and Housing, Alfonso Gagliano, joined the group.

Our Federation of Canadian Municipalities pushed hard to join the discussions. After all, in provinces such as Ontario housing was almost exclusively a municipal responsibility, while in others, cities were witnessing growing homelessness and urging action. We wanted to discuss our national housing strategy with the ministers, to convince them to join in our call to the federal government to put its shoulder to the wheel again.

Other well-informed groups like the Canadian Housing and Renewal Association and the National Homelessness Coalition also wanted a chance to talk with the ministers. At first, all were refused outright by the bureaucrats who tightly control such meetings.

Homelessness activists, including the National Coalition and FRAPRU, constructed a makeshift—but effective—house outside the fancy hotel where the meetings were going on. The media did not have a hard time appreciating the contrast between what was going on outside and the pedantic policy meetings inside.

Then, after a last ditch effort and a promise that FCM would have a delegation sitting outside the meeting talking with the press, our municipal delegation was invited to meet with Mockler and Gagliano. It was a good meeting. There was sympathy for our efforts and interest in our ideas. In the end, though, the ministers' communiqué from the meeting did not mention a partnership with municipalities and committed only to meeting again in a few months to study a workplan that was to be developed by a team of bureaucrats. The worst news was that the Province of Ontario would plan and host the next meeting—the very province with the worst record on all aspects of affordable housing.

Still, I said to the press that we should take heart at the fact that Ministers of Housing were meeting at all. It was the first time they had talked in six years, since they collectively celebrated the funeral of Canada's affordable housing construction policies under Prime Minister Chrétien in 1994.

What individual Canadians are doing

Finally, looking still deeper into the toolbox, we find determined Canadians beavering away on the affordable-housing issue one brick, one plank and one plan at a time. With involvement ranging from the Co-operative Housing Federation of Canada to the Canadian Institute of Planners, from the Canadian Housing and Renewal Association to the Canadian Home-builders' Association and Habitat for Humanity, efforts are being made. Thousands of non-profit groups, housing co-ops, advocacy organizations, trade unions, service clubs and church-based social-justice coalitions are working valiantly to meet the obvious need. Some Canadians simply take steps on their own. Bill, living under a bridge near the Don Valley Parkway on-ramp in Toronto, told me that "a guy pulls over every morning and leaves hot food by the road. Traffic is whizzing by. He can see me. He just smiles and gets back in his car."

In some ways, there are so many motivated people in our communities now that we cannot help succeeding in the end. The trick is to create a public will and a momentum that links many communities to reinforce these efforts, to empower people who are active, to give them the financial and technical wherewithal to realize their dreams about an affordable roof over every head.

Governmental responsibility

There is a bigger question: Are nation-states in this globalized age only supposed to function in a market context? According to the dominant viewpoint, the absolute infallibility of market forces produces the best results in virtually all sectors. So are democratically chosen governments allowed to act? Or are they primarily supposed to get out of the way— "to reduce red tape and taxes"? Faced with such eventualities as homelessness, are we not driven to the conclusion that one purpose for national governments should be the crafting of "systems of survival" for their people?[47] When it comes to basic needs of people in just about any national community, the nation-state should be charged with the inherent authority and obligation to step in with corrective measures, wherever the dominant market processes are missing the boat. National politics has much to do with the allocation of collective resources of society. The question is whether they will be allocated to ensure that every child, mother and father has certain basic necessities at hand, irrespective of personal circumstances.

Once upon a time, this kind of thinking was quite common within Canadian governments and most provincial governments. And Canada was not entirely out of sync with other Western nation-states in proposing ideas and the policies to back them up. But with the rise of globalized economic thinking, any process that might distribute resources in any fashion other than the rough-and-ready mechanism of the marketplace is viewed with disdain. And along with this change, values began to change dramatically in government.

Commenting on the housing field a generation ago, one of Canada's most committed housing experts of the past fifty years, Albert Rose, caustically observed,

> The mystery is that a nation which by every physical, social and statistical measure is among the best-housed in the world cannot maintain a sufficient supply of dwellings to meet the needs of approximately one in every ten of its population, and that another three in every ten experience increasing difficulty in meeting their needs within the housing market. How can this nation convert or divert its resources, wealth and riches to the solution of a problem which rests within one of the three elements in living standards [the other two being food and clothing]?[48]

When Rose was writing (1980), the first food bank was opening in Toronto and there were few homeless citizens having to sleep outdoors. Church-basement flops had not been invented. No one had been reported freezing to death owing to a lack of residence. No First Nations teenager—stranded in big-city Canada and pregnant—had lost her life under a bridge. Yet Rose's questions are even more powerful today: "The issue becomes one of social versus individual responsibility."[49] Rose was writing at the height of the government housing program initiatives. He was able to say,

> One issue has certainly been settled during the past twenty-five years. Canadians are no longer afraid of government interference in the housing market, of vast governmental allocations of funds or of a public role in the development and allocation of housing accommodation. Subsidy is no longer a dreaded word to those who must be taxed to assist the dependent poor, the working poor and the working class.[50]

Rose was too complacent. Attitudes have swung on the social-versus-individual-responsibility pendulum to the point that, we hope, public opinion will be driven back towards the notion that our nation must act. The sheer sucking sound of the vacuum created by the Mulroney and then

Chrétien governments' withdrawal from housing issues may be bringing the policy back into view—but it's a big "may be."

I can't imagine that many Canadians who have now reviewed the evidence here would be left feeling that nothing needs to be done at the national level to address the affordable housing crisis.

Few would accept that community groups, charities and municipalities alone should (or can) be left to address the crisis. Canada stands alone among developed countries: all other OECD nations and our NATO allies have national housing strategies; we have none. I never thought I would be suggesting that we consider (let alone copy) American urban policy as embodied in the actions of the U.S. Congress. They have beaten us to the punch in many ways with their significant investment in housing for the lowest-income Americans. Perhaps their concern is more than altruistic. Healthy cities for investment are healthy cities for inhabitants; Americans have learned. Canadians have not.

In fact, Canadian governments seem to largely believe that healthy cities have little to do with their more important agendas. Happy taxpayers seem much more important, judging by the massive sums returned to the taxpayers in recent budgets. Low-income Canadians don't have enough money to pay income taxes. But low-income Canadians have increased the share of government revenues because their GST payments have risen with inflation. The same goes for provincial sales taxes, where they exist. But higher-income earners have been able to withdraw (through tax shelters and gymnastic accounting) a great deal of their financial support for the base funding of government redistributive programs, leaving these elements of the social safety programs gasping for air, if they are alive at all.

Isn't it time for a rejuvenation?

7 Canadians Can Make Housing Happen

Homelessness seems to create a slow burn among Canadians. Years ago, shoppers would have "walked on by" or scoffed at the street people who occasionally held out a hand for spare change. Now they are becoming angry at various governments' indifference to the growing destitution amid the accelerating affluence.

This is good. Complacency is collapsing and a quiet sense of activism is brewing.

It took some people dying on streets to get us there. That's not something to be proud of, but at least Eugene Upper's death and that of others like him will have significance.

Efforts started small with the community. We've seen mayors and councils of municipalities join that effort. Media outlets are raising their editorial voices and assigning reporters and photographers to portray the story and, to a lesser extent, explore solutions. Homelessness has made its way into political pronouncements by all and sundry. Every national party leader has uttered the phrase "affordable housing" with varying degrees of priority—and sincerity. A minister for homelessness was given responsibility to tackle the issue by the prime minister. Three-quarters of a billion taxpayer dollars was promised. The first of these dollars will be arriving in communities as this book is printed. On February 29, 2000, for the first time in fifteen years, the phrase *affordable housing* was uttered by a federal minister of finance in connection with a new funding program, on the floor of the House of Commons.

We've come a long way. But many worthy causes reach this point in the political process, only to fizzle and be forgotten. Homelessness fatigue. Homelessness backlash, which follows when people are tired of feeling guilty. Stigmatizing the poor and blaming the victim become the course of least resistance.

So what path must Canada take, if we are to put homelessness at the top of the political agenda?

These final pages sketch some ideas for a way forward.

We must move our national government to take the next step. We must persuade our elected representatives to go beyond the tokenism of the finance minister's suggestion (in the spring of 2000) that affordable-housing construction could be included in the modest municipal/provincial/federal infrastructure investment program that the government was announcing at the time. How can we make inaction impossible for the mandarins and politicians in Ottawa?

We have some advantages. I suspect that Canadians are very tired of one government blaming another (Canadians blame them all). Therefore, if Ottawa proposes a national housing policy along the lines recommended by the Big City Mayors, the provinces will have less room to attack. We also have new allies. Mayors across Canada are truly committed to a national housing program. These people, almost all of whom are very popular, represent huge numbers in their communities—more than the prime minister or his many local MPs from these cities.

Numerous and diverse groups have begun to address homelessness and affordable housing as a priority—from the Canadian Labour Congress and the Canadian Council of Churches to various Boards of Trade.

The continued acceleration of the misery of the homeless everywhere in Canada helps us, perversely, towards our goal. We seem to be able to count on this economy to malfunction: Even when it is succeeding wildly for the few, the incomes of one-third of our people continue to fall, and basic necessities become increasingly at risk. Homelessness results for more people each month, and more and more of these are children.

Barriers

Some serious obstacles could catch us off guard. Determined opponents might deliberately blindside us with constitutional conundrums, cloaked in mystery. These and other tactics could bog down bold efforts to build affordable housing. Ideologues, who are becoming attuned to the potential of the homelessness crisis to propel social policy, abhor this new activist direction—as do all free-market adherents. Voices opposing the "social-housing boondoggle" are dusting off their rhetoric of a decade ago, hoping that it will still waken the same sentiments of resentment against the "undeserving" poor and their "bleeding heart" allies.

Achieving a successful plan to house Canadians in a safe, affordable way will take creative and hard work. The more who join the effort, the more likely it will be to succeed.

What Can Individual Canadians Do?

For starters, we simply cannot afford to do nothing. It's too expensive. As a Toronto housing expert once put it to me, "For every dollar not spent on housing, it takes eight dollars to bring people back to housing."[1] Once people have been pushed or allowed to fall out of the world of the securely housed, the downward spiral precipitates social and personal financial costs just to cope. It then requires more financial investments and immense support to bring someone back to the point that he or she can function again in a new home.

There is a "payoff" of sorts: Someone is making money from homelessness. It's the sector of our economy that actually benefits from the artificial shortages of accommodation, because it boosts profitability. The relatively small number of large firms that direct these housing markets, by virtue of their size, are the giants that must be brought to heel somehow. This is why public policy and community-based solutions are legitimate and important in any attempt to deal with the housing challenges.

I've coined the term *Lilliputianism* from the name of a group of people in Jonathan Swift's *Gulliver's Travels*. We must be like these tiny, fictional people who tied down the giant traveller, Gulliver. He seemed far too huge to be subdued. Our giant is homelessness and affordable housing. Collective complementary action can bring about the changes we need. Consider what some Canadians are doing. My guess is that you can find, among these samples, at least one or two ways to pitch in.

Nearly everyone in Canada has seen people who are homeless, but do you know a homeless person? Why not start by joining the thousands of volunteers in many communities who help out in emergency programs and services? At least pay a visit to a shelter to experience what it's like. Then pass along your experiences to family, friends and neighbours. Tell your story. Invite others to join you next time.

Volunteers will tell you about the terrific satisfaction they receive from being involved, but they'll usually also tell you about some homeless person who completely changed their views about homelessness. For people who have lost so much of their personal identity and security by losing their home, meaningful contacts with others are important—to help re-establish their identity, self-respect and sense of capability.

Out of the cold

Many who are regular volunteers also comment that there is frustration, dissatisfaction and even anger that inevitably accompany the work. This came through loud and clear when 1,000 volunteers from Out of the Cold programs in the Toronto area responded to my invitation to meet at the Metropolitan United Church the evening before the National Symposium on Homelessness in March 1998. It was amazing to see so many volunteers working to help homeless people gathering in one place. Arriving in groups of five or ten, they represented hundreds of emergency-shelter and food programs. Everyone there seemed to feel stronger just because we were all together and recognizing our numbers—and this turnout was only a portion of the 5,000 people who help in any given year.

Each Out of the Cold group had been asked to report to the meeting on whether they thought the problem was getting worse. They all did, and they brought stories and statistics to prove it. Groups were also asked to recommend what they believed should be done. As people took their turn at the microphones in the cavernous cathedral, it was as though they were all singing in the same choir, even though most of them had never met: "Affordable housing, that's what these people need! We don't want to put more and more mats on our church basement floors; these people should have their own homes!"

I remember thinking that most of these people would never join a "demonstration." Middle-class, philanthropic (with their time and money), value-driven people were in the room, not protestors. But they had created their own demonstration right there in the pews.

A realization set in: If our voices could somehow be regularly combined, perhaps other groups of people, the media and, most important, our elected governments and their advisers and bureaucracies could be made to hear, could be made to feel obligated to respond. We had to become informed, motivated and effective "advocates"—advocates for affordable housing.

The most important gatherings are those involving the homeless themselves. Given the barriers they face daily, such empowering meetings and protests are inspiring to witness and gratifying to support. A truly democratic decision-making process would put these folks right at the centre of the table. But it rarely happens. When homeless people do find themselves invited into their government's decision-making processes, the experience is usually negative. The intimidation of the formal committee room, the bewildering complexity of the legislative process, the patronizing tones, the failure to recognize simple needs—like the provision of a transit ticket to attend the meeting, or childcare, or translation. That's why some angry homeless people protest. Unfortunately, clashes with the police are sometimes the sad result.

What are the ways we can advocate?

Here are some samples. Pick a few—or just pick one:

- Write a letter to your elected representatives directly. Handwritten notes or e-mails with a personal tone seem to be the most persuasive these days. Always send a copy of what you have written to at least one group in your community that is already advocating change. This combination of voices is important.
- Check that your municipality is an active, supporting member of the Federation of Canadian Municipalities' National Housing Policy Options Team. And then ask what your elected person is doing to achieve more affordable housing.
- Letters to your local newspaper's editor can be effective. You would be surprised how many people read them and how politicians monitor the tone and balance of opinion. Get others to write letters.
- Talk shows are everywhere. You can use their flexible formats for your "personal advocacy" moment. Pick up the phone.

The rather amazing Oprah Winfrey has put forward her resources. More important, she called on her viewers, readers and fans to join in with money and sweat to support Habitat for Humanity and build housing for low-income families to own, in every state in the U.S.A. Habitat for Humanity is also active in most parts of Canada. If you like the idea of swinging a hammer on a Saturday afternoon as your contribution to solving the housing crisis, the nails are waiting. Be sure to swing a figurative hammer at the stalled political process while you're at it.

- Corner your local elected representative at a community function. Better yet, get a few friends together and make a formal appointment to meet him or her. Prepare yourselves so that you know exactly what you are asking, by way of a commitment, from your councillor, mayor, or provincial or federal representative. By staying in touch with housing issues through advocacy groups in your community, websites, library resources and the news, you can effectively influence these people. I'm surprised by how few voters actually ever raise issues in an organized way with their chosen representatives. Highly paid lobbyists are always clamouring for meetings to push their clients' agendas. Real-estate developers, landlord organizations, lawyers—speaking on behalf of new laws to benefit their clients in the housing field—never miss an opportunity. We need more citizens to push back hard. Ask your elected representatives where they stand, ask for their policies in writing and, most important, ask exactly what they have done lately and will do soon about the homelessness crisis.
- Form a group or join an existing advocacy organization to help out. Usually, these groups are made up of dedicated volunteers, working their fingers to the bone, believing that their efforts are helping. A chronic shortage of helpers means that you will be warmly welcomed. Find a group working on these issues in your community. Many of the websites listed in the endnotes of this book can lead you there. Check your local newspaper and contact the groups you read about who are pushing governments to act.
- Perhaps most rewarding of all would be to help directly in creating affordable housing in your community. Start a neighbourhood group: "Yes, Housing in My Back Yard"—YHIMBY, the *H* would

be silent, but your group would not. Your group could look for opportunities to encourage development of housing in your community. Have your municipality—as well as the federal and provincial governments—consider surplus lands for housing. Link with other groups that could provide support.
- Form a tenants' association in your rental building, or join the one that already exists, so that you can do whatever is possible to protect the affordability of your apartment and to lobby for laws that will.
- Protect yourself and your neighbours from demolition plans, condominium conversions or unfair rent increases.

Link your efforts to the national housing initiatives being developed by the Canadian Housing and Renewal Association and the Co-operative Housing Federation of Canada.

A National Homelessness and Housing Coalition is forming now, to strengthen efforts across the country. With the Internet providing rapid access to information and each other, we can respond quickly to the shifting political winds and sands. In the past, governments have rarely demonstrated their ability or willingness to respond to crises with speed and focus. But citizen-based groups—on a wide variety of issues—have often been disorganized. Without tools to communicate quickly and determine common courses of action, citizen groups face a tough challenge. Fortunately, this is changing with "electronic citizenship."

Elections

Election campaigns are opportunities not to be missed. But the work has to be done many months beforehand to develop the political terrain for a municipal, provincial or national debate and discussion. My great grandfather was blind. But that didn't stop him from working for a coalition of people to achieve economic justice for the blind. Through their efforts, they won the first-ever monthly pension for disabled people in the 1930s. He is reputed to have said, according to family lore, "I don't care which of them becomes prime minister [referring to the Liberal candidate King and the Conservative candidate Borden], they've both told us they'll bring in economic justice for the blind, and if they don't, we'll be on the steps of Parliament Hill with our white canes—and we won't be feeling our way around either!" The pensions were implemented. His lesson? Political movements are best structured if you can convince all the players to adopt your position. In Canada, some work is underway to urge political parties to incorporate strong housing elements in their platforms. With road construction, water purification and tax-reduction agendas all competing for limited space in the election platforms and, more significant, shares of the limited funds that any government has to work with, affordable housing and homelessness have a tough challenge. Canadians can put pressure on their Members of Parliament, who then take it through policy processes. Letters to party leaders can influence decisions about party platforms. Most essential, though, is public opinion, which is forever being tested to determine "what Canadians want," or "are Canadians buying the line we are feeding them?" In this context of the poll-and-policy nexus, Canadians need to lend the weight of their citizenry to the objective—to raise homelessness and housing issues so that they show up regularly and forcefully, no matter what the poll or party. Canadians need to make it unacceptable for any government in this country to have anything less than a fully developed plan to house all Canadians decently, and to end the disgrace of homelessness.

When the proclamation "I am Canadian!" follows with the statement "I am well housed in my community!"—and when these two statements are true for every Canadian—our job will have been done. Then, perhaps, Eugene Upper, and the many other homeless lives we have lost, can rest in peace.

Appendices

Table 1: Vacancy Rate, Privately Initiated Apartment Structures of Three Units or More, St. John's CMA, 1989–98

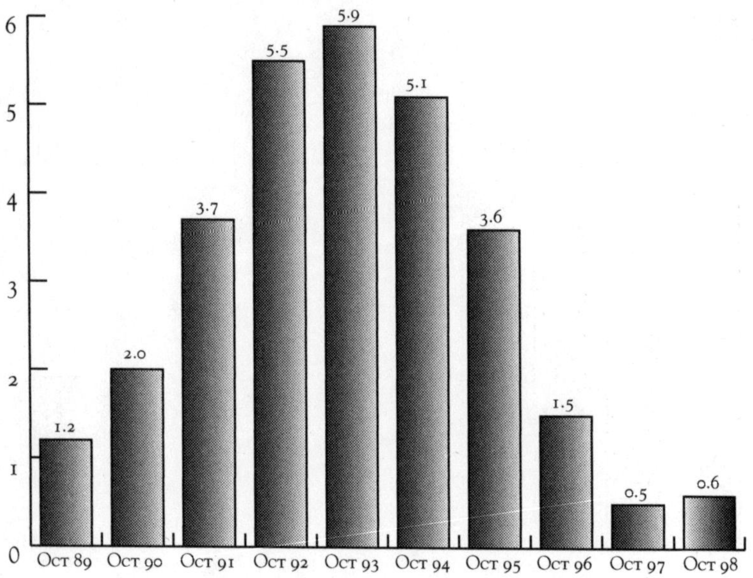

Source: *FCM National Housing Policy Options Paper, Municipal Profiles.*

Table 2: Vacancy Rate, Privately Initiated Apartment Structures of Three Units or More, Toronto CMA, 1989–98

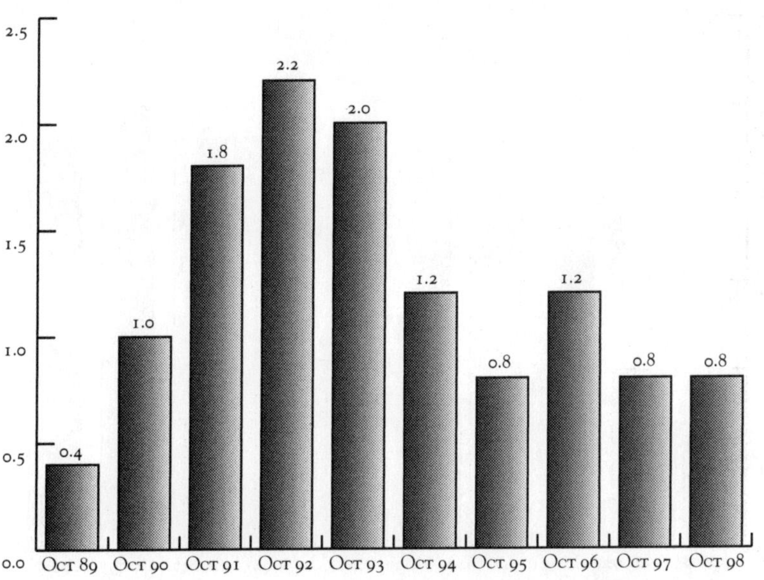

Source: *FCM National Housing Options Paper, Municipal Profiles.*

Table 3: Vacancy Rate, Privately Initiated Apartment Structures of Three Units or More, Calgary CMA, 1989–98

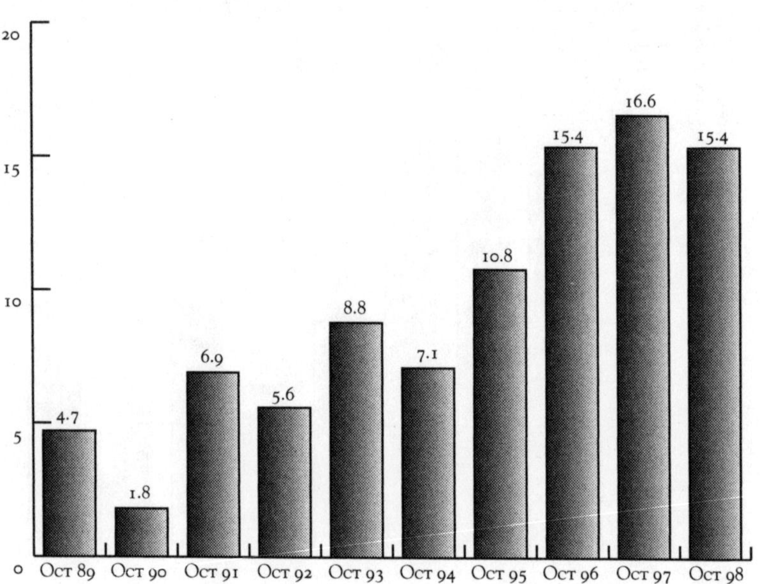

Source: *FCM National Housing Policy Options Paper, Municipal Profiles.*

Percentile Family Incomes (Total Income from All Sources), Percent Change, Selected Regional Municipalities and Municipalities, Current Dollar Value

	10%-ile	20%-ile	25%-ile	30%-ile	40%-ile	50%-ile	60%-ile	70%-ile	75%-ile	80%-ile	90%-ile
Halifax	-11.1	-7.0	-5.9	-3.5	-0.8	1.3	2.2	3.2	3.7	4.8	6.3
Ottawa	-21.0	-14.5	-10.3	-7.4	-3.4	-1.4	0.1	1.6	2.3	3.2	5.4
Toronto	-23.6	-12.6	-9.6	-6.8	-3.9	-1.5	0.9	2.6	3.4	4.1	6.1
York	-30.6	-13.1	-9.2	-6.8	-2.7	—	2.3	3.7	4.5	5.2	7.0
Peel	-29.4	-13.6	-8.7	-6.6	-3.0	-0.8	1.4	2.9	3.6	4.5	6.3
Hamilton	-12.9	-2.9	-1.1	—	2.3	4.0	5.4	6.5	7.1	7.6	8.5
Waterloo	-9.7	0.4	1.6	3.2	5.5	6.3	7.2	8.2	8.4	8.9	9.7
London	-18.1	-7.6	-5.4	-2.8	—	1.7	2.8	3.8	4.5	4.9	6.1
Windsor	-10.1	3.2	5.6	7.5	9.9	12.1	13	13.8	14.2	15.0	16.1
Winnipeg	-8.7	-0.8	—	1.0	1.6	2.9	3.5	4.1	4.6	5.2	6.6
Regina	-3.9	0.4	0.3	1.8	3.5	4.1	5.5	6.0	6.4	6.9	8.2
Saskatoon	-5.1	—	0.8	2.0	3.5	4.5	6.0	7.1	7.8	8.3	9.5
Calgary	-10.7	-1.2	-0.3	0.6	2.4	3.4	4.6	6.0	6.8	7.8	10.2
Edmonton	-16.9	-3.7	-4.0	-3.8	-2.7	-1.1	-0.2	0.8	1.3	1.7	2.8
Burnaby	-33.6	-16.8	-15.9	-13.3	-9.3	-6.3	-3.1	—	1.5	2.4	4.6
Vancouver	-15.3	-4.9	-6.6	-6	-3.1	-1.2	1	2.8	3.8	4.7	5.6
Canada	-10.7	-1.8	-1.6	-0.3	1.7	3	4.5	5.4	5.9	6.3	7.5
Numerical Average	-16.3	-5.9	-4.3	-2.6	-0.01	1.8	3.3	4.6	5.2	6.0	7.4
Population Weighted Average*	-18.8	-8.0	-5.8	-3.9	-1.3	0.7	2.4	3.7	4.4	5.2	6.8

Source: FCM, *The Quality of Life Reporting System* (Ottawa, May 1999).

Notes: 1992 Dollar value expresses the gain or loss in real purchasing power between 1992 and 1996, by including the decrease resulting from inflation.

The inflation adjustment comes from StatsCan CPI figures.

Percentage of Tenant Income Spent on Rent, 1991 and 1996, Canada and the Provinces and Territories

	Paying 30% or More of Income on Rent				*Paying 50% or More of Income on Rent*			
	1991		1996		1991		1996	
	#	%	#	%	#	%	#	%
Canada	1,273,175	34.8	1,670,770	43.2	583,710	16.0	833,555	21.6
Newfoundland	12,555	33.9	18,285	43.3	6,215	16.8	9,430	22.3
PEI	4,200	36.3	5,605	42.2	1,835	15.9	2,325	17.5
Nova Scotia	34,330	36.8	47,030	47.3	16,620	17.8	23,310	23.5
New Brunswick	23,770	36.7	29,360	42.1	10,290	15.9	13,575	19.5
Quebec	404,035	35.1	518,705	42.6	194,220	16.9	273,825	22.5
Ontario	432,915	33.3	615,985	44.5	194,920	15.0	300,645	21.7
Manitoba	46,250	35.8	52,445	40.6	20,165	15.6	23,485	18.2
Saskatchewan	32,675	32.5	38,820	36.7	14,950	14.8	18,980	18
Alberta	106,210	33.3	115,275	37.7	46,570	14.6	51,240	16.7
British Columbia	174,075	39.7	226,665	46.9	77,115	17.6	115,525	23.9
Yukon Territory	745	19.2	1,125	28.1	255	6.6	560	14
NWT	1,365	12.5	1,465	12.8	540	4.9	650	5.7

Source: FCM, *National Housing Policy Options Paper: A Call for Action* (Ottawa, June 1999), p. 14.

Housing Built in Canada by Market Segment, 1989–98

	Rental	Share %	Homeownership	Share %	Condominium	Share %	Co-op	Share %	Total	Share %
1989	37,279	20.1	107,661	58.0	36,834	19.8	3,839	2.1	185,613	100
1990	35,389	20.2	100,964	57.7	36,418	20.8	2,308	1.3	175,079	100
1991	30,172	22.3	74,548	55.2	27,885	20.6	2,554	1.9	135,159	100
1992	30,497	20.8	85,747	58.6	25,193	17.2	4,837	3.3	146,274	100
1993	22,073	16.6	80,025	60.3	26,879	20.2	3,772	2.8	132,749	100
1994	18,137	13.5	82,726	61.7	31,295	23.3	1,918	1.4	134,076	100
1995	10,488	10.6	60,257	60.8	27,409	27.7	935	0.9	99,089	100
1996	8,222	8.6	65,189	67.9	22,160	23.1	409	0.4	95,980	100
1997	7,542	6.4	83,687	71.0	26,056	22.1	536	0.5	117,821	100
1998	7,287	6.4	81,053	71.4	25,118	22.1	71	0.1	113,529	100
Average per year 1989–1993	31,082	20.1	89,789	57.9	30,642	19.8	3,462	2.2	154,975	100
Average per year 1994–1998	10,335	9.2	74,582	66.5	26,408	23.6	774	0.7	112,099	100
Decrease from 89–93 to 94–98	66.7%		16.9%		13.8%		77.6%		27.7%	

Source: FCM, *National Housing Policy Options Paper: A Call for Action* (Ottawa, June 1999), p. 73. Created for FCM by Lapointe Consulting, using CMHC data.

Social Housing Units Built in Canada, 1989–98

	Social Housing Completions	As a % of Total Completions	Total Completions
1989	9,628	4.4	217,371
1990	9,135	4.4	206,163
1991	9,273	5.8	160,014
1992	19,621	11.3	173,245
1993	15,718	9.7	161,794
1994	9,886	6.1	162,085
1995	5,271	4.4	119,501
1996	3,659	3.1	117,834
1997	1,997	1.4	143,386
1998	1,439	1.1	133,941
Average per year 1989–93	12,675	6.9	183,717
Average per year 1994–98	4,450	3.3	135,349
Decrease from 89-93 to 94–98	64.9%		26.3%

Source: FCM, *National Housing Policy Options Paper: A Call for Action* (Ottawa, June 1999), p. 74. Created for FCM by Lapointe Consulting, using CMHC data.

Notes

Introduction

1. Jennifer Caldwell's body was found on 7 March 2000. Between the writing of the book and its publication, many more homeless people may have died. Current information is listed on the website <http://www.geocities.com/CapitolHill/Lobby/2744/>, which lists homeless deaths by name and date.
2. Jane Jacobs, *The Death and Life of Great American Cities* (New York: Random House, Modern Library, 1993), p. xviii. This book was originally published in 1961.

1: Beginning the Debate

1. James Lorimer, *Working People* (Toronto: James Lewis and Samuel, 1971).
2. Paul Martin and Joe Fontana, *Finding Room: Housing Solutions for the*

Future, Report of the National Liberal Caucus Task Force on Housing (Ottawa: National Liberal Party, 1990).

3. Anne Golden et al., *Taking Responsibility for Homelessness: An Action Plan for Toronto*, A Report of the Mayor's Homelessness Action Task Force (City of Toronto, 1999), p. v.
4. We should remember not just that ten people died in the Rupert Hotel fire, but rather that the lives of ten individuals were lost. They were Donna Marie Cann, Vincent Joseph Clarke, Stanley Blake Dancy, David Didow, Edward Finnigan, John Thomas Flint, Dedomir Sakotic, Ralph Oral Stone, Vernon Stone and Victor Paul White.

2: Defining Homelessness

1. Lower Income Urban Singles Task Group, *Nowhere to Live: A Call to Action* (Victoria, B.C.: Provincial Department of Social Development and Economic Security, 1995), p. 20.
2. Ibid., p. 21.
3. George Fallis and Alex Murray, eds., *Housing the Homeless and Poor* (Toronto: University of Toronto Press, 1990), p. 3.
4. Mark Liddiard, "Homelessness: The Media, Public Attitudes and Policy Making," in Susan Hutson and David Clapham, eds., *Homelessness: Public Policies and Private Troubles* (New York: Cassell, 1990), p. 83.
5. David Olive, "Unsheltered Lives," *Toronto Life* 22, no. 18 (November 1988), p. 95.
6. David Clapham, "Conclusions," in Susan Hutson and David Clapham, p. 232.
7. William Ryan, *Blaming the Victim* (New York: Vintage, 1976).
8. *The Street Speaks* (Calgary: 1995), p. 28. Available online at <http://www.gov.calgary.ab.ca/81/housing/ssspeaks.htm>.
9. Anne Golden et al., p. iii.
10. *The Toronto Report Card on Homelessness 2000* (City of Toronto, 2000), p. 2.
11. Kaye Stearman, *Homelessness* (Austin, TX: Raintree Steck-Vaughn, 1999), p. 5.
12. The Linda Houston Memorial Fund's website is <http://www.streethaven.com/spring98/page4.htm>.

13. Joseph H. Springer, James H. Mars and Melissa Dennison, "A profile of the Toronto homeless population," in Anne Golden et al., Background Papers, vol. II, p. 2.
14. Philip W. Brickner and Brian G. Scanlan, "Health Care for Homeless Persons: Creation and Implementation of a Program," in Philip W. Brickner et al., *Under the Safety Net: The Health and Social Welfare of the Homeless in the United States*, (New York, NY: W. W. Norton & Co., 1990), pp. 4–6, 8.
15. Joseph H. Springer et al.
16. Philip W. Brickner and Brian G. Scanlan, pp. 4–6, 8.
17. Joseph H. Springer et al.
18. Anne Golden et al., "Letter of Transmittal."
19. *Report on Homelessness in Niagara* (Fonthill, ON: Niagara District Health Council, 1997), pp. i, ii.
20. Ibid.
21. J. Arboleda-Flòrez and H. L. Holley, *Calgary Homelessness Study, Final Report* (Calgary, 1997), p. vi.
22. Ibid.
23. Ibid., p. 4
24. Ibid.
25. Karen Halling Burch, *1998 London Homelessness Survey: A Snapshot of Homeless People* (London Social Planning Council, 1998), p. 3.
26. Ibid., p. 19.
27. H. Peter Oberlander and Arthur L. Fallick, *Shelter or Homes? A Contribution to the Search for Solutions to Homelessness in Canada* (British Columbia: Centre for Human Settlements, University of British Columbia, 1987), p. 5.
28. Quoted in ibid., p. i.
29. Jerome Tognoli, "Residential Environments," in D. Stokols and I. Altman, eds., *Handbook of Environmental Psychology* (New York: Wiley Interscience, 1987), pp. 657–65.
30. George Fallis and Alex Murray, pp. 16, 17.

3: Counting the Homeless

1. Jennifer Quinn, "Burned Relics Outline Plight of Homeless," *The Toronto Star*, 27 March 2000.
2. Homeless Initiative Ad Hoc Steering Committee, *Community Action Plan* (City of Calgary, 1998). The 3,800 persons were identified over four months in 1997.
3. Irene Ying-Ling Wong, "Patterns of Homelessness: A Review of Longitudinal Studies" in Dennis P. Culhane and Steven P. Hornburg, eds., *Understanding Homelessness: New Policy and Research Perspectives* (Washington, DC: Fannie Mae Foundation, 1997), p. 159.
4. Anne Golden et al., pp. 26–27.
5. Michelle Landsberg, *This Is New York, Honey! A Homage to Manhattan with Love and Rage* (Toronto: McClelland & Stewart, 1989).
6. Homeless Initiative Ad Hoc Steering Committee, p. 21. As far as I know, Calgary is the only city to permit this practice.
7. John Sewell, *Houses and Homes: Housing for Canadians* (Toronto: James Lorimer & Company, 1994).
8. Ibid., p. 211.
9. Commissioner of Social and Community Services, *Report to Council* (City of Toronto, June 1997).
10. Mel Hurtig, *Pay the Rent or Feed the Kids: The Tragedy and Disgrace of Poverty in Canada* (Toronto: McClelland & Stewart, 1999).
11. Libby Davies, House of Commons Report, summer 1999.
12. A provocative discussion of the definition of poverty can be found at the website of Child and Family Canada, <http://collections.ic.gc.ca/child/docs/poverty.htm>.
13. John Stackhouse, "I'm Tired of Being a Slave to the Church Floor," *The Globe and Mail*, 21 December 1999.

4: A Cross-Canada Survey

1. NHPOT, *National Housing Policy Options Paper: A Call for Action* (Ottawa: FCM, June 1999), p. 25.
2. NHPOT, *National Housing Policy Options Paper, Municipal Profiles* (Ottawa: FCM, June 1999), p. 32.

3. Ibid.
4. Ibid.
5. Communication with the author, December 1999.
6. City of Toronto and the FCM, *National Symposium on Homelessness and Housing*, symposium binder (Toronto: FCM, 1999), p. 119.
7. Ibid.
8. Ibid., p. 114.
9. Ibid., pp. 1–2.
10. Ibid., p. 115.
11. CMHC, "Rental Market Report: Montreal CMA," 1999.
12. City of Toronto and the FCM, materials submitted by the City of Montreal.
13. Ibid.
14. More popularly known by its French acronym FRAPRU (Front d'action populaire en réaménagement urbain).
15. Arnold Bennett, ed., *Shelter, Housing and Homes: A Social Right* (Montreal: Black Rose Books, 1997), p. 98. The definition of homelessness used was established by the Comité des sans-abris de la Ville de Montréal in 1987.
16. City of Toronto and the FCM, materials submitted by the City of Montreal.
17. NHPOT, p. 23.
18. Ibid.
19. Ibid., p. 67.
20. Ibid., p. 69.
21. Arnold Bennett, p. 115.
22. Ibid.
23. *Montreal et le défi de l'intégration–Un nouveau program pour revitaliser les quartiers "sensible" de Montréal* (City of Montreal, 30 April 1999).
24. NHPOT, *Municipal Profiles*, p. 18.
25. Ibid.
26. Ibid., p. 69.
27. See Gerald Friesen, *The West* (Toronto: Penguin/McGill Institute, Toronto, 1999) for an account of Western Canada's historic grievances about Toronto.
28. Ontario Non-Profit Housing Association and Co-operative Housing Federation of Canada, *Where's Home? A Picture of Housing Needs in*

Ontario (Toronto: Ontario Non-Profit Housing Association, 1999), p. 6.

29. Ibid.
30. Ibid., pp. 7–9. See also Appendix D.
31. Ibid.
32. Author's calculation: 500,000 homeless person-nights logged in eight cities. This figure should be augmented by 30 percent to include those homeless people in these eight cities who were not logged because they were in shelters, church basements, couch surfing or in other situations that were not counted. This brings the total for eight cities to 650,000. The eight cities represent approximately half of the population of Ontario. If we conservatively assume homelessness "rates" in the balance of the province equal to half of the rates found in the eight large communities, a further 325,500 homeless person-nights should be added. This produces a credible approximation of 975,000 homeless person-nights in 1998 in Ontario. An assumed 20 percent increase in homelessness in the period 1998 to 2000 is based on accounts provided to the author from front-line homeless workers in Ontario cities. This would bring the total estimated nights of homelessness to 1.2 million for the year 2000. Ontario's eight million citizens passed a cumulative total of 2,920,000,000 nights (rounded to three billion). This produces a housed to homeless ratio of 1:2433.
33. Anne Golden et al., p. 26.
34. Ibid., pp. 11, 49, 72–73, 76–77.
35. Ibid., p. 11. Based on data from the Ontario Association of Food Banks.
36. Typically, according to housing economists, a higher percentage of rental accommodation turns over annually, therefore the 10 percent estimate is very conservative. The author is indebted to Professor John Bossons of University of Toronto for examining and verifying the assumptions in the analysis.
37. Ontario Non-Profit Housing Association and the Co-operative Housing Federation of Canada, *Where's Home? A Picture of Housing Needs in Ontario* (Toronto: Ontario Non-Profit Housing Association, 1999), p. 34.

38. See pro forma calculations in such studies as Anne Golden et al. and the Commissioner of Social and Community Services, *Report to Council* (City of Toronto, June 1997).
39. "Background to Homelessness Issues in Waterloo Region," 18 and 19 February 2000. Submitted as a background document to the Big City Mayors' caucus of the FCM, p. 1.
40. Ontario Non-Profit Housing Association and Co-operative Housing Federation of Canada, p. 60.
41. Ibid.
42. City of Toronto and the FCM, materials submitted by Kitchener-Waterloo Region staff.
43. NHPOT, *Municipal Profiles*, p. 10.
44. Karen Halling Burch, *1998 London Homelessness Survey: A Snapshot of Homeless People* (London Social Planning Council, 1998).
45. Ibid., p. 13.
46. Margaret Philp, "Homeless without Health Cards Likely to Go without Care," *The Globe and Mail*, 2 March 2000.
47. Jane Sims, "Aid for Poor OK'd," *The London Free Press*, 14 October 1999.
48. Karen Halling Burch, p. 19.
49. NHPOT, *Municipal Profiles*, p. 12.
50. City of Toronto and the FCM, materials submitted by City of London, p. 117.
51. Ibid.
52. Memorandum to Mississauga Mayor Hazel McCallion from Keith Ward, Peel Region. Tabled at the Big City Mayors' caucus, April 2000.
53. NHPOT, *Municipal Profiles*, p. 13.
54. City of Toronto and the FCM, materials submitted by Region of Peel.
55. Ibid.
56. Ontario Non-Profit Housing Association and Co-operative Housing Federation of Canada, pp. 74–75.
57. NHPOT, *Municipal Profiles*, p. 15.
58. Ibid.
59. Jennifer Wells, "Her Town, Her Rules," *Toronto Life* 34, no. 8 (May 2000) pp. 82–88.

60. Ontario Non-Profit Housing Association and Co-operative Housing Federation of Canada, p. 78.
61. Memo to the Big City Mayors' caucus and the NHPOT, from the Commissioner of Social Services, City of Windsor, 14 April 2000.
62. NHPOT, *Municipal Profiles*, p. 64.
63. Ibid., pp. 64–65.
64. NHPOT, *Municipal Profiles*, p. 19.
65. The FCM Quality of Life Reporting System, *Quality of Life in Canadian Communities* (Ottawa: FCM, May 1999), p. 24.
66. Ontario Non-Profit Housing Association and Co-operative Housing Federation of Canada, pp. 70–71.
67. NHPOT, *Municipal Profiles*, p. 20.
68. Ontario Non-Profit Housing Association and Co-operative Housing Federation of Canada, pp. 70–71.
69. Ibid.
70. I want to acknowledge photographer Jodi Cobb's metaphors, drawn from Eve Sinaiko, ed., *The Way Home: Ending Homelessness in America* (Washington, DC: Corcoran Gallery of Art, 1999), p. 23.
71. Anne Golden et al., p. 27.
72. *The Toronto Report Card on Homelessness 2000*.
73. NHPOT, *Municipal Profiles*, p. 49.
74. Ibid., p. 50.
75. Ibid., p. 39.
76. Ibid.
77. City of Winnipeg, *Report to Citizens*, Spring 2000, available online at <http://www.city.winnipeg.mb.ca/interhom/news/1999/dec21%5F99.htm>.
78. City of Regina, *Update on Homelessness*, memorandum to the FCM Big City Mayors' caucus, April 2000, p. 2.
79. Ibid., p. 1.
80. Ibid., p. 1.
81. NHPOT and the City of Regina, p. 1.
82. City of Regina, p. 2.
83. Saskatoon Real Estate Board; see <http://www.sreda.com/housing.htm>.
84. Ibid.
85. NHPOT, *Municipal Profiles*, p. 29.
86. Ibid., p. 30.

87. Ibid.
88. Ibid., p. 28.
89. Ibid.
90. "Frozen Bodies Bring to Life Fears of Police Cruelty," *The Toronto Star*, 4 March 2000, p. H-1.
91. Ibid.
92. Information on this program can be found at <http://dlcwest.com/~sim/library/shipsmap.htm>.
93. Ad Hoc Steering Committee, *Homelessness Initiative, Consultation Summary*, c/o Alderman Bob Hawkesworth, City of Calgary, May 1997, unpaginated. Quotations drawn from interviews of homeless people in Calgary in 1997 as reported on various pages of this document.
94. Ibid.
95. City of Calgary, memo to FCM Big City Mayors' caucus meeting, Vancouver, April 2000. *Update on Homelessness in Calgary*.
96. Ibid.
97. Ibid. Calgary staff reported this as follows: "The best estimate we could come up with is the Calgary drop-in centre's unofficial count of ten in the last year."
98. NHPOT, *Municipal Profiles*, p. 2.
99. Ibid., p. 1.
100. Ibid.
101. Ibid., p. 2.
102. Ibid., p. 1.
103. Ibid., p. 3.
104. *Calgary Street Survival Guide 1998: Information That Can Help You* (City of Calgary, 1998).
105. See <http://www.gov.calgary.ab.ca/81/housing/cplanint.htm> for more information.
106. *Community Action Plan, Housing Supply* (City of Calgary, Homeless Initiative Ad Hoc Steering Committee). Available online at <http://www.gov.calgary.ab.ca/81/housing/plansupp.htm>.
107. *Housing Our Homeless: A Stakeholder Consultation Assessing Shelter Needs in Calgary* (Calgary Homeless Foundation, 23 March 2000), p. 33.
108. Ibid., pp. 9, 13, 30.

109. Edmonton Task Force on Homelessness, *Homelessness in Edmonton: A Call to Action* (City of Edmonton, 1999).
110. Ibid., p. 48.
111. These households fall below the low-income cut-off as defined by Statistics Canada. For a detailed definition of the low-income cut-off, see the Statistics Canada website at <http://www.statcan.ca>.
112. NHPOT, *Municipal Profiles*, pp. 4–6. Year 1999 rents and year 2000 increase forecasts from City of Edmonton, Memorandum to FCM Big City Mayors' caucus, April 2000, Vancouver, p. 6.
113. Regional Municipality of Wood Buffalo, *Update on Homelessness and Affordable Housing*, memorandum to the Big City Mayors' caucus in April 2000.
114. Linda Mix, for the Housing Homeless Network of B.C. in an unpublished letter to the Federation of Canadian Municipalities, Big City Mayors' Caucus, 26 April 2000.
115. British Columbia, Lower Income Singles Group, *Nowhere to Live: A Call to Action*, Vancouver, 1995, p. 5.
116. Ibid., p. 19.
117. Ibid.
118. NHPOT, *Municipal Profiles*, p. 34.
119. British Columbia, Board of Commissioners of B.C. Housing, *Homelessness—A Call for Action*, June 1999, p 3.
120. City of Vancouver, Mayor's Office, Letter to FCM/NHPOT and presented to the Big City Mayors' Caucus, Vancouver, 29 April 2000.
121. NHPOT, *Municipal Profiles*, p. 34.
122. British Columbia, Board of Commissioners of B.C. Housing, p. 2.
123. FCM, Quality of Life Reporting System, "Quality of Life in Canadian Communities," May 1999, p. 47.
124. NHPOT, *Municipal Profiles*, p. 35.
125. Ibid., p. 35.
126. Downtown Eastside Residents Association, "Community Housing Plan," Vancouver, no date.
127. Ibid.
128. Ibid., p. 3.
129. Penn Thrasher, *And Miles to Go—Housing and Lower Income Urban Singles in Victoria*, Victoria Cool Aid Society and Victoria Street Community Association, Victoria, 1997, p 2.

130. Ibid., pp. 15–16.
131. Province of British Columbia, *Toward More Inclusive Neighbourhoods*, Housing Ministry of British Columbia, February 1996, available by mail order through B.C. Housing Ministry, 1019 Wharf Street, Victoria, B.C. v8v 1x4.
132. Obonsawin–Irwin Consulting Inc., "A Planning Framework for Addressing Aboriginal Homelessness in the City of Toronto," for the Mayor's Homelessness Action Task Force, 30 November 1998.
133. Data from City of Calgary website: <http://www.gov.calgary.ab.ca/81/research/hless98tb.htm#table4> and <http://www.gov.calgary.ab.ca/81/research/dethnic.htm>.
134. Edmonton Homelessness count committee on City website and Edmonton socioeconomic outlook also on website: <http://www.gov.edmonton.ab.ca/>.

5: The National Picture

1. NHPOT, *Municipal Profiles*. Full data and charts can be found on the FCM website at <http://www.fcm.ca>.
2. NHPOT, *Toward a National Housing Strategy*, pp. 17, 18. The Calgary data were updated with a further memo from Calgary staff in April 2000.
3. NHPOT, *Toward a National Housing Strategy*, p. 12.
4. Ibid., p. 12.
5. John Sewell, *Houses and Homes: Housing for Canadians* (Toronto: James Lorimer & Company, 1994).
6. John R. Miron, ed., *House, Home, and Community: Progress in Housing Canadians, 1945–1986* (Montreal and Kingston, McGill-Queen's University Press, 1993), p. 12.
7. Ibid.
8. Lynn Hannley, "Substandard Housing," in John R. Miron, p. 204.
9. Ibid., p. 205.
10. NHPOT, *Toward a National Strategy*, p. 18.
11. Ibid., p. 5.
12. Ibid.

13. A good review of provincial housing policies in the 1990s is found in Tom Carter, *Current Practices for Procuring Affordable Housing: The Canadian Context*, Housing Policy Debate 8, no. 3, pp. 593–630.
14. For more information on Quebec housing programs: <http://www.shq.gouv.qc.ca/indexeng.html>.
15. For more information about B.C. housing programs: <http://www.bchousing.org/>.
16. For information, visit the CMHC website at <http://www.cmhc-schl.gc.ca/cmhc.html>.
17. Personal conversation with the mayor of Winnipeg, Glen Murray.
18. NHPOT, *A Call for Action*, p. 19.
19. NHPOT, *Municipal Profiles*, p. 60.
20. NHPOT, *A Call for Action*, p. 73.
21. This is a partial list because it includes only fourteen cities.

6: The Way Forward

1. The Canadian National Housing Act can be found online at <http://www.cmhc-schl.gc.ca/cmhc.html>.
2. See <http://www.fcm.ca> and select "Affordability and Choice Today (A-C-T) program" on the "Select a Program/Service" pull-down menu.
3. Michael Dennis and Susan Fish, *Programs in Search of a Policy* (Toronto: Hakkert, 1974).
4. John Sewell, p. 231.
5. NHPOT, *National Housing Policy Options Paper: A Call for Action*, p. 54.
6. Roger Lewis, *The Long-Term Housing Outlook: Household Growth in Canada and the Provinces*, 1991–2016, (Ottawa: CMHC, 1997).
7. David K. Foot, *Boom, Bust, and Echo* (Toronto: Macfarlane, Walter and Ross, 1997).
8. NHPOT, *National Housing Policing Options Paper: A Call for Action*, p. 54. Details of these estimates are contained in the FCM/NHPOT documents at <http://www.fcm.ca>.
9. Ibid., pp. 19–20, 61–65.
10. Ibid., p. 20.
11. Ibid., p. 54.

12. Ibid., p. 55.
13. See Appendix C for more information.
14. NHPOT, *Toward a National Housing Policy*, p. 56.
15. Anne Golden et al., *Taking Responsibility for Homelessness: An Action Plan for Toronto,* A Report of the Mayor's Homelessness Action Task Force (City of Toronto, 1999).
16. See <http://www.indigenous.bc.ca/v3/VoL3Ch4s1tos3.asp>.
17. John Sewell, p. 226.
18. Ibid., p. 228.
19. Michael Dennis and Susan Fish, p. 219.
20. Editorial, *The Toronto Star*, 15 July 2000.
21. National Round Table on the Environment and the Economy, *The Financial Services Sector and Brownfield Redevelopment* (Ottawa: 1997).
22. See Vancouver City website: <http://www.city.vancouver.bc.ca/commsvcs/planning/SEFCpolicy.htm#table_of_contents>.
23. Armand Eisen, *Politics: An irreverent look at the mighty and misguided* (Kansas City: Andrews and McKeel, 1996), p. 144.
24. The effort began as early as 1975 with organizations like the Fraser Institute in their publications such as F. A. Hayek, et al., *Rent Control: A Popular Paradox* (Vancouver: The Fraser Institute, 1975); and Walter Block and Edgar Olsen, eds., *Rent Control: Myths and Realities* (Vancouver: The Fraser Institute, 1981).
25. The following observations and summaries are those of the author, who chairs the FCM's National Housing Policy Options Team. None of these observations are meant to indicate that everyone involved in the workshop would be in agreement with any particular point.
26. NHPOT, *A Call for Action*, (Ottawa: FCM, 1999), p. 6.
27. Ibid.
28. NHPOT, *Municipal Profiles* (Ottawa: FCM, 1999) p. 36. See also <http://www.fcm.ca>.
29. NHPOT, *A Call for Action*, p. 8.
30. Ibid.
31. Steve Pomeroy, "Costing Analysis of the FCM National Housing Policy Options" (Ottawa: FCM, 3 October 1999), p. ii.
32. See such books as James Laxer, *The Undeclared War: Class Conflict in the Age of Cyber Capitalism* (Toronto: Viking, 1998); Jim Stanford,

The Paper Boom (Toronto: Lorimer, 1999); the many studies by the Canadian Centre for Public Policy Alternatives: <http://www.policy alternatives.ca>.

33. Jim Stanford, *The Paper Boom* (Toronto: Lorimer, 1999), p. 385.
34. Jim Stanford, p. 392.
35. See the variety of sites indexed at <http://www.povnet.web.net/welf links.html>.
36. Jim Stanford, pp. 399–406.
37. City of Toronto and the FCM, *National Symposium on Homelessness and Housing* (Toronto: FCM, 1999).
38. Author's notes from the meeting.
39. Government of Canada, Social Union Framework Agreement. See Government of Canada website: <http://socialunion.gc.ca/news/020499_e.html>.
40. Ibid.
41. Ruth Dantzer, assistant secretary to Cabinet for social development, Government of Canada, speaking to a conference organized by the Canadian Housing Renewal Association entitled "Toward an Affordable Housing Policy for Canada," 23 March 2000.
42. Ibid.
43. Council of Canadians, *Power Game: Five Problems with the Current Social Union Talks* (Ottawa, Council of Canadians, 1999), p. 8. See also the Council of Canadians website for details of its campaign concerning the Social Union at <http://www.canadians.org>.
44. A. Noel, *Will the Social Union Divide Canadians?* (1999) available online at <http://hssfc.ca/PolicyIssues/Breakfasts/NoelEng.html>.
45. Sharon Chisholm, "No Place to Stay: Social Policy Reform in Canada and Its Impact on Affordable Housing," *Canadian Housing*, no. 2, p. 14.
46. S. Phillips, "Of Windows and Doorjams: Making the Social Union Frame Work," discussion paper prepared for the National Voluntary Organizations (NVO), 1999.
47. Jane Jacobs, *Systems of Survival: A Dialogue on the Moral Foundations of Commerce and Politics* (Toronto: Random House, 1994).
48. Albert Rose, *Canadian Housing Policies 1935–1980* (Toronto: Butterworths, 1980), p. 195.
49. Ibid., p. 196.

50. Ibid.

7: Canadians Can Make Housing Happen

1. Author's conversation with housing activists, winter 1998.

Index

A

D

E

F

G

H

L

M

N

P

Q

R

S

T

U

V

W

Y

Z